# PRAYING

# GENESIS

# BOOKS BY ELMER TOWNS

*Praying the Scriptures Series*

*Praying the Psalms • Released 2004*

*Praying the Proverbs, Ecclesiastes, and Song of Solomon*

*Released 2005*

*Praying the Book of Job • Released 2006*

*Praying the Book of Revelation • Released 2007*

*Praying the Gospels • Released 2007*

*Praying the Acts of the Apostles and the General Epistles*

*Released 2008*

*Praying Paul's Letters • Released 2008*

*Praying the New Testament • Released 2008*

*Praying Genesis • Released 2008*

**AVAILABLE FROM DESTINY IMAGE PUBLISHERS**

# PRAYING

# GENESIS

Elmer L. Towns

DESTINY IMAGE® PUBLISHERS, INC.

P.O. Box 310, Shippensburg, PA 17257-0310

*"Speaking to the Purposes of God for this Generation and for the Generations to Come."*

This book and all other Destiny Image, Revival Press, Mercy Place, Fresh Bread, Destiny Image Fiction, and Treasure House books are available at Christian bookstores and distributors worldwide.

For a U.S. bookstore nearest you, **call 1-800-722-6774.**

For more information on foreign distributors, **call 717-532-3040.**

Reach us on the Internet: **www.destinyimage.com.**

ISBN 10: 0-7684-2722-3

ISBN 13: 978-0-7684-2722-6

For Worldwide Distribution, Printed in the U.S.A.

1 2 3 4 5 6 7 8 9 10 11 / 12 11 10 09 08

# ACKNOWLEDGMENT

All noted times of stories throughout *Praying Genesis* are taken from The Companion Bible, notes and appendixes by E.W. Bullinger, "50 Chronological Charts and Tables" (Grand Rapids, MI: Kregel Publications, 1999), Appendix 50, 40-72.

# TABLE OF CONTENTS

# FOREWORD

His bones creaked and his forehead still perspired from chasing sheep all day. *They are so stubborn and dumb, just like me,* old Moses thought to himself. Moses remembered he was a prince in Pharaoh's palace but a selfish act exiled him to the Sinai Desert. He was no longer the son of Hatseput; he was a common shepherd.

Moses struggled to make a fire, the desert sun had blistered his arms, but the approaching cold night breezes would chill his weary body. The smoke ascended straight toward Heaven because there was no breeze. Then Moses' prayers followed the small spire of smoke into Heaven. "Lord, I pray, use me again"—he once felt powerful in Pharaoh's palace but now Moses felt the opposite feeling of uselessness in the Sinai wilderness. "I'm sorry for killing a man—an Egyptian—forgive me and use me properly to help my people, the Jews."

"SHALOM..." a voice disrupted the silence of the desert. Moses thought no one was within miles of his campfire. The voice he heard was a Hebrew voice and he was shocked because there were no Hebrews in the Sinai Desert.

"SHALOM," Moses yelled back in Hebrew. Since visitors fear death for walking into a campsite unannounced, people treat the intruders as attackers. The voice in the wilderness had seen the smoke and followed its beacon until he saw the red glow of the small fire.

The voice belonged to an escaped Hebrew slave from Egypt—the old man staggered into the camp, leaning on a beautiful walking stick.

Moses shared his meager meal then they shared names trying to determine if they had any common relatives in Egypt.

As the black cold fingers of night crept into the campsite, the two men huddled close to the fire for warmth. The escaped slave clutched his walking stick protectively to his chest as if he were afraid of losing it.

Moses asked, "What's special about that shepherd's rod?"

"It's not just a shepherd's rod." The old man glanced into the darkness; he didn't want anyone to hear what he was going to tell Moses. "It's the rod of God," was all the old man said.

"The rod of God?" Moses repeated the phrase as a question. "Tell me why you call it the rod of God."

The old man held the walking stick close to the fire for Moses to see all the fine carvings. His old boney finger pointed to the signet carved at the top, "That stands for Abraham."

There was a long silence around the fire. The breeze now pushed the smoke toward the horizon. Moses broke the mood asking, "Was this actually Abraham's walking stick that he brought from beyond the Euphrates River?"

"I don't know," was all the old man said. Then he pointed to the next signet, "That stands for Isaac, son of Abraham." Moses held the stick to the light and read the third signet with a name—Jacob. Moses wondered if this were actually Abraham's walking stick or if someone else carved the lineage because they respected the history of the Jewish people.

Jacob's twin brother—Esau—was also carved there, but out of the lineage on the back of the rod. Moses examined the rod closer; there were 12 signets under Jacob. Moses said under his breath, *The twelve sons of Israel.*

Moses was trained in the universities of Egypt. Of course he spoke and wrote Egyptian, and he also studied Ugaritic, Akkadian, and Chaldean. But the Hebrew language was his favorite pursuit.[1]

A Phoenician had taught Moses their alphabet.[2] They did something other civilizations had not done. They created letters to match the sounds of a word—they invented phonics—and with that knowledge, Moses had begun writing Hebrew words.

When Moses saw the signets of the patriarchs on the rod, it was another piece in his heritage puzzled. As he went to sleep that night, Moses determined to learn everything he could from the old man. Then he prayed as sleep closed another day, *"Lord, I want to learn everything I can about my people—the Hebrews—so I'll know You better...."*

In the following days as Moses watched his sheep, the old man told Moses of other walking sticks. Each pioneer of a new tribe carved his mark or signet on his walking stick, then passed it on to his son, who then added his signet.

The old man told how children memorized the names of their aunts and uncles, then their cousins. Fathers made sons repeat their genealogy perfectly. Since family was important, names were important.

Moses told the old man, "We must find all these walking sticks and write down the genealogies—like the Egyptian pharaohs wrote their history— the history of our fathers is the history of Jehovah worship. The names of those who followed the Lord God is more important than the people who worship Re—the sun god—followers.

Moses determined in his mind he would find as many walking sticks as possible. He also determined he would find out as much as possible about the history of God's people—the Hebrews—and he would write down an accurate record of how God had led his people. One more thing, Moses determined he would write everything in the Hebrew grammar that he was creating.

What Moses didn't know was that the Spirit of God would come upon his writing, just as 1,500 years later Jesus would say that Moses wrote the first five books of the Bible.[3] Moses didn't know the word *inspiration* but he would write by the inspiration of the Holy Spirit so that what he wrote was exactly what God wanted said.

You, the reader, know the rest of the story well. The old man died, as it is appointed unto all men once to die (Heb. 9:27). The old man bequeathed the walking stick to Moses but he never told Moses where he got it. Whether it was the actual walking stick that Abraham carried when he came from Mesopotamia was not known. Nevertheless, Moses received it as the rod of God.

Whether that rod had an anointed past is not known, but we do know it was a rod that parted the Red Sea when Moses waved it in faith to God. It was a rod that Moses struck the rock at Horeb, and water gushed out. It was a rod that Moses held over the battle between Israel and the Amalekites where God gave the victory. It became the rod of God.

The story of the old man and the history of the rod is conjectured from the way patriarchs kept their genealogy.[4] It's highly likely God's people kept their family history on walking sticks. But somehow Moses learned the many genealogies he wrote in Genesis and the other books of the Pentateuch.

Many of the events that Moses wrote came by way of divine revelation— God telling Moses things unknown to humans.

The word *Genesis* means "beginnings" and as you pray through Genesis you will connect with the beginning of all things important.

As you pray through the first book of Scripture, you will read to know God's Word. Then your prayers will stir your heart, that is if you're really *Praying Genesis* to God. And you'll face a choice of living for God today, like those in the beginning made that choice, as did Adam, Noah, Abraham, Isaac, Jacob, and Joseph. But sadly, many in Genesis choose against God. As *Praying Genesis* brings you to that life-changing decision, choose God and live.

As you pray through Genesis, you see the beginning of many forces that contribute life about you today. Obviously the first was the beginning of creation itself, then the first man, the first son, the first family, and many other firsts.

We see here the beginning of the Jewish race, also the beginning of prayer and the beginning of sacrifice for sin and the first promise of a coming Deliverer for the human race, Jesus the Messiah.

I *translated* the Book of Genesis "idea for idea" so the Bible would become real to your life. Then I *transliterated* it into prayers so you could ask God to apply His truth to your life.

As you read how God began everything, why don't you make a new beginning in your relationship with God? May this manuscript help you to know and love God in a new and better way.

Enjoy reading the most foundational book ever written. If it were not for Genesis, there would be no rest of the story. May you touch God as you pray Genesis, but more importantly, may God use the story of Genesis— The Beginnings—to touch you, so you will begin to serve Him in a renewed way.

Sincerely yours in Christ,
Elmer Towns
Written at my home
at the foot of the Blue Ridge Mountains

# Genesis 1:1-31

# GOD CREATES THE HEAVENS, EARTH, AND MAN

Lord, in the beginning You created the heavens and earth,
But You had not yet formed
The earth into its final form,
It was void.

Everything was dark upon the face of the deep,
And You—Spirit of God—hovered over the waters.

Then You said, "Let light appear" and light shone;
You saw that light was good,
So You divided light from darkness

You called light day, and the darkness You called night,
So the evening and the morning were the first day.

*Lord, thank You for giving spiritual light to see You more clearly.*
*Help me live by the light You give.*

You said, "Let there be atmosphere around the earth";
You divided the waters under the atmosphere
From the waters above the atmosphere.

You called the atmosphere sky,
And it contained the air that gives life to all;
So then evening and morning were the second day.

You said, "Let the waters under the atmosphere
      Be gathered together in one place
      And let dry ground appear."

You called the dry land earth, and You called the waters seas

      And you said, "This is good."

You said, "Let the earth bring forth grass
      And plants and trees with fruit to give life,
      With each having seed bearing fruit to reproduce itself."

So the earth brought forth grass and plants
      And trees with seed bearing fruit to give life,
      With each having seed-bearing fruit to reproduce itself.

And You said, "This is good";
      So the evening and the morning were the third day.

You said, "Let there be lights in the sky
      To divide the day from the night,
      And let them give light to the earth,
      And let them reflect seasons, days and years."

You made two great lights, the larger to light the day
      And the lesser to light the night,
      And You also made the stars;
      So the evening and morning were the fourth day.

You said, "Let the waters swarm with living creatures,
      And let birds fly in the open sky."

And all kinds of creatures appeared in the waters
      And all kinds of birds flew in the sky
      And You saw that it was good.

You said, "Be fruitful and multiply, and fill the waters
    With living creatures and the sky with birds," and it was so;
    Then the evening and the morning were the fifth day.

You said, "Let the earth bring forth wild beasts,
    Crawling things and livestock."

So You created livestock, crawling things, and beasts of the field,
    And You said, "This is good."

*Lord, thank You for creating a good world*
    *In which I live and see You.*
*Help me use the world You've provided*
    *To glorify You and further Your Kingdom.*

Then You said, "Let Us make humans in Our image,
    And in the likeness of Ourselves."

And You said, "Let them rule over the fish of the sea,
    The birds of the air, the animals of the earth
    And everything that crawls over the earth."

So You created humans in Your image, in Your image You created them,
    Male and female You created them.

You blessed the human and said, "Be fruitful, and multiply
    And fill the earth and make it obey you;
    Rule over the fish of the sea, the birds of the air,
    And everything that crawls on the earth."

Then You said, "Have dominion over the whole earth;
    I am giving to you food from every plant and tree that
    Has life in its seed-bearing fruit."

"And I am giving it as food to every animal on the earth,
    Bird in the sky and every thing that creeps on the earth."

And You saw that everything You had made was good
    So the evening and the morning were the sixth day.

    *Lord, thank You for life and opportunity*
        *To live for You in the good world You've created.*

        Amen.

# Genesis 2:1-25

## FIRST DAYS IN THE GARDEN OF EDEN

Lord, in six days You finished creating everything
     On earth and in the heavens along with everything in them;
     Then You rested from Your work on the seventh day.

Lord, You blessed the seventh day, and made it holy,
     Separating it from the other days of the week,
     Making it a symbolic day of rest for all;
This is the end of the history of the heavens and earth.

You had not yet caused it to rain, but
You watered the earth with a mist
     And a heavy atmospheric cloud that covered the earth
     And there were no weeds or wild bushes.

You, Lord God, formed the first man from clay
     Then the most auspicious miracle thus far was a picture of
     You bending over the clay body to breathe into his nostrils;
     Then man became a living soul.

You, Lord God, planted the Garden of Eden
     East of the Euphrates River.

You, Lord God, planted every tree with good fruit in the garden;
     Also, You planted in the garden the tree of life
     And the tree of knowledge of good and evil.

A river watered the garden, and from it flowed four streams;
     The first was Pison that flowed through the land of Havilah,
     There's gold there with onyx stone and sweet-smelling resin;

The second river is Gihon that flows through Kush,
The third river is the Tigris River flowing to Ashus,
The fourth river is the Euphrates.

You, Lord God, put the man—Adam—in the garden
    To cultivate and care for it.

You, Lord God, gave Adam this positive command,
    "You may eat of the fruit of every tree in the garden."

You also, Lord God, gave him a negative warning,
    "Don't eat of the fruit of the tree of knowledge of
    Good and evil because you'll begin dying and ultimately die,
    the day you eat of it."

Lord God, You gave Adam a task. You brought to him
    every bird, animal, and livestock to see what he would call them.
    What he called them was its name.

When all the animals passed before Adam in pairs,
    Then You declared Adam didn't have a suitable companion.

Lord God, You said, "It isn't good for Adam to live alone;
    I will make a companion for him."

Then You, Lord God, put Adam into a deep sleep;
    While he was sleeping, You took one of his ribs
    And closed up the side of the man.

You made the rib into a woman
    And You brought her to the man who said,

"This is bone of my bone, and flesh of my flesh;"
    Adam called her woman because she was taken out of man.

Therefore, a man must leave his father and mother
    And cleave to his wife for they shall be one flesh;
    Adam and Eve were both naked and were not ashamed.

# Genesis 3:1-24

## THE FIRST SIN

The serpent was more crafty and deceptive than any of the animals
or crawling things that You, the Lord God, had made.

The serpent said to the woman, "Did God actually say you must not eat of
any tree in the garden?"

The woman answered, "We may eat from any fruit off any trees of the
garden, but we can't eat the fruit of the tree in the middle of the
garden, neither can we touch it, because we shall begin to die and
end up dead."

The serpent said, "That is not true that you will die, God told you not to eat
it because He knows that when you eat it, your eyes will be opened
and you will be like God, knowing good and evil."

When the woman saw the fruit would make her happy, and that it looked
attractive, and that she could become wise, so she took some
and ate it.

Eve gave to her husband Adam and he ate it; both their eyes were opened
and they realized they were naked. So they made clothes out of
fig leaves.

*Lord, I'm as weak as Adam and Eve so I can't judge them;*
*Forgive me of my sin, just as You forgave them.*

Lord, then they heard Your voice as You walked in the garden in the cool of
the evening. So Adam and Eve hid themselves from Your presence
among the bushes in the garden.

Lord, You called out to them, "Where are you?" Adam answered,
"I heard Your voice and I was afraid because I was naked so I
hid myself."

Lord, You answered, "Who told you that you were naked? Have you eaten
the fruit of the tree that I commanded you not to eat?"

Adam blamed You, God, "The woman You brought to me, gave me the fruit
and I ate it."

Lord, You said to the woman, "What have you done?" The woman
answered, "The serpent tricked me to do it."

Lord God, You said to the serpent, "Because you have successfully
tempted them, you are cursed more than the animals and livestock,
you will crawl on the ground among the dust. I will put hatred
between your seed and the seed of the woman. You will bruise His
heel, but He shall bruise your head."

*Lord, thank You for this first promise of Jesus, the Savior, Because
You said "He would crush satan's head."*

*Lord, this is also the first promise of the virgin birth
Because a woman has an egg, not a seed;
So the seed of the woman points to a supernatural Birth.*

Lord God, You said to the woman, "I will greatly increase your conception
and you will have pain in childbirth, therefore, you will desire your
husband who will rule you."

Lord God, You said to Adam, "Because you listened to your wife and
disobeyed My command not to eat of the tree, I will curse the earth.
The ground will grow thorns and weeds that will make it hard
to grow  food. You will work the ground by the sweat of your brow
until you return to the ground from which you were taken; dust
you are, and you will return to dust."

Lord, the man called his wife Eve because she
    Became the mother of all living.

Then Lord God, You made clothes of skin
    For Adam and Eve to wear.

Lord, You covered their nakedness—a symbol of their sin,
    With the skins of an animal taken by blood

To remind me that my sins were also covered by blood,
    The blood of Christ who died for me.

Lord God, You talked among Yourself, saying, "The humans have
    become like one of Us to know good and evil.
    Let's not allow him to eat of
    the tree of life so they will live forever."

So, Lord God, You sent him from the Garden of Eden to grow
    his food elsewhere. You placed an angelic cherub to
    guard the tree of life, one who had a flaming sword who
    could also see in every direction.

*Lord, I'm so glad You did let mankind return to the garden,*
    *Help me always go forward after failure,*
    *Just as Adam and Eve had to go face*
    *The world they created.*

        Amen.

## Background Story of
## The Temptation and Fall of the First Family

### Genesis 2:1-3:24

Place: Garden of Eden ✍ Time: A few days after Creation

The woman gazed deeply into the pool of water, then wiggled her nose. The reflection in the water wiggled its nose back at her. She laughed; it laughed back at her.

Then standing, the woman studied the reflection of her slender olive body in the still water. Reaching out, she picked a beautiful scarlet orchid, with a crème-colored throat. Curious about its deep red leaves and fragrant aroma, she smelled its fragrance, then stuck it in her hair, smiling again at what she saw mirrored in the water. Finally, she splashed her hands into the pool; the image disappeared under the ripples. She wandered off from the man—Adam—just to smell another orchid, then to follow a splashing creek to find a playful waterfall, and to cuddle a playful animal.

*I'll never remember all I see,* she thought. *I'll never be able to smell every flower and touch every animal.* The Garden of Eden was beautiful but without any comparisons, she would not fully appreciate its beauty until she was driven from its gates, never to return. However, this day there was no thought of loss or hurt.

"Adam..." she called innocently to show him the cuddly rabbits she found under a bush. He was not there.

*I'm so happy,* she thought. Life was wonderful, but she wouldn't fully understand her contentment until she experienced pain and dread—negative emotions that would come from her choice.

Eve waded across a clear stream, never fearing she could drown; then she climbed some rocks to view a waterfall from the top, never sensing the threat of falling. She had no thought of dangerous animals, no anxiety of poisonous plants and no physical discomfort or ache.

Her path led Eve to the center of the garden, but she didn't know it was the center; nor did she know she was near the tree of knowledge of good and evil. In all the places Adam showed her, he had not brought her here, even though he had warned her about the tree. Adam told Eve,

"The instant you eat the fruit of this tree, you will start to die until you are dead."

*The tree must be ugly!* Eve thought when Adam told her to stay away from it. *The fruit must taste terrible,* she concluded. Eve was not prepared for what she saw.

*"Magnificent..."* Eve whispered her response to the stunningly beautiful tree in the center of the garden. Its blossoms were more beautiful than the orchid she recently placed in her hair. She couldn't look away from its alluring branches; its yellow and orange fruit. She found herself wanting to touch it...to eat it...to smell it. She was confused by her feelings; she didn't understand her doubts.

Eve walked completely around the tree, viewing it from every direction, but carefully keeping her distance. However, the seductive fruit was too compelling to put from her mind, *What does it taste like?...How does it feel?...Does it have an aroma?*

Eve cautiously tiptoed to the tree, for the first time she wanted to hide her actions. A sense of excitement swept through her breast, her hands tingled to touch it, yet she sensed another feeling—a sense of dread. She wanted to run away because she knew intuitively she shouldn't eat the fruit; yet she hesitated. Her passion burned unlike anything she previously felt. Freedom to do the forbidden was a tantalizing prospect. A voice startled Eve,

"Come closer!"

Eve jumped back, she had never heard any other voice in the garden but Adam's voice and God's voice. This sound was exciting...fearful...and calming at the same time. The command frightened her, yet at the same time its melodious tone pulled her toward the tree.

Eve didn't see who was talking to her. She looked under the tree and behind branches, creeping closer to the tree all the time, until she was close enough to touch the fruit. Then she heard it again,

"What are you looking for?"

This time she saw it, the voice was coming from the most beautiful creature she had seen. There coiled about the branches of a limb was a serpent, its dark green colors blended with ruddy brown scales. Eve could barely see the serpent among tea green leaves of the tree. Beautiful speckles of yellow and red extended from the serpent's head to its tail. Beauty that is lovely to tantalize us, may also be beauty that destroys us.

Eve had never felt this strong compulsive urge to enjoy the beauty of an animal, she wanted to reach out to stroke the serpent's wet skin; but she resisted her urges.

"What did God tell you about this tree?" the voice continued to ask, but Eve was still too stunned to respond. She was intrigued because the serpent's mouth didn't move when it talked; as the mouth of Adam when he talked with her. Then Eve answered the snake,

"God told us not to eat the fruit...not to taste the fruit...we are never to touch the fruit." Eve remembered Adam's warning about the tree, yet she couldn't run away from the enticing fruit that also terrorized her at the same time.

"We might die if we touch it."

Eve's emotions confused her thinking. God said nothing about touching it—God said, "Don't eat it." Being unsure, Eve added the little bit about touching it.

The serpent slithered up the branch to be at eye level with Eve. Sliding its weight effortlessly through the tree, its movement was beautiful to behold. Then the serpent suggested,

"You won't die...there's no such thing as death."

Eve reached for the fruit to softly stroke its silky texture. With her slight touch, the fruit fell into her hand. She tenderly fingered it, turning the fruit 360 degrees in her hand.

"See..." the serpent reasoned with her, "I told you its touch wouldn't hurt you."

Eve didn't look at the speaking serpent; she couldn't take her eyes off the fruit. Her eyes glazed. She held the fruit in her hand, but it held Eve in a vice grip that was almost inescapable. The serpent coaxed Eve,

"When you eat this fruit, your eyes will be opened...you'll be as smart as God...you'll know good and evil."

Eve wanted to be as wise as God; she wanted to know everything, then she'd be perfectly satisfied. He bent her arm to lift the fruit, just as she ate other fruit—but she didn't bite it. Instead she put it to her nose to enjoy its aroma. She closed her eyes to dream thoughts...pink thoughts...yellow thoughts...orange thoughts. Just holding the fruit was the most tantalizing experience in her short life.

*How can this thing be wrong?* she thought.

The serpent said nothing, he knew Eve was under his influence. It would only be a matter of a few seconds until she would be under his domination.

*If I want something,* Eve thought, *I should have it.*

With that decision, Eve bit into the fruit and instantly what the serpent promised came true—her eyes were opened. She experienced the dark side of disobedience. Eve realized her act was not just eating forbidden fruit, she had done the one thing God told her not to do—she had disobeyed God. She felt evil.

Eve went running through the garden, looking for Adam, finding him back at the place where they slept. She told him about the tree in the center of the garden...about the beautiful serpent...about holding the fruit...and how she became as wise as God. Eve told Adam she knew something he had never experienced. She knew both good and evil. Eve gave him the fruit to hold and smell. Adam experienced the same temptation as Eve. Then, Adam ate the fruit.

"Look at you," Adam pointed to her nakedness. An erotic impulse seized him, a sensation hitherto unfelt. Eve felt the same sensation, so they wove together fig leaves to cover the parts of their body that aroused the other. Then they felt better. No sooner than they finished covering their nakedness, that they heard the Lord walking in the garden. They hid among the foliage of two trees. God's voice rang out,

*"ADAM…WHERE ARE YOU?"*

It was not an angry voice, it was a searching voice. God was not asking a question to find out where they were hiding, God knew where they were because He knew everything. God asked a question to make them think about what they had done. When Adam realized it was hopeless to hide from God, he answered,

"We hide ourselves in the bushes because we were naked."

Adam had always run to worship God, but this time he held back because of shame and regret. God knew what they did because He knew everything. As God always does, He reaches out to remove any barrier that comes between Him and His people. The Lord asked,

"Have you eaten the fruit I told you not to eat?"

Adam blamed his actions on Eve, "The woman gave the fruit to me." But avoiding responsibility has never satisfied the human heart, so Adam blamed God, "You gave me the woman."

Adam was first created and the woman was made from him—Adam was responsible, and Adam was strong—yet in weakness Adam groveled in self-doubt. God asked Eve,

"What did you do?"

Eve blamed the serpent, "The serpent lied to me, he made me touch it…then I smelled it…then I tasted it."

God talked to the serpent because of its part in the temptation, God told the snake,

*"You will be cursed more than all the animals I have created, all snakes will crawl on their belly from now on. People will be afraid of snakes and will try to kill snakes, but I'll give you poison in your mouth to defend yourself."*

God knew that lucifer, His enemy the devil, had used the snake to tempt Eve. God knew that satan would eternally try to destroy His plan with people, so God looked down the annals of history to the Cross, and predicted the destruction of His enemy,

*"A seed will be born to the woman. My enemy will strike the male child on the heel temporarily impairing Him, but the Deliverer will crush the head of the serpent, finally destroying it."*

Adam and Eve listened to God administer justice, shivering in guilt. Previously they had not felt regret, but the severity of God's manner chilled any joy they had in Paradise. Then it was their turn to be judged. God said to Eve,

"Because you disobeyed Me, you will have life-threatening pain when giving birth to children."

Eve inwardly rationalized she would not have sex. But she didn't realize God knew her thoughts. God said to Eve,

"You will love your husband with such great desire, that you will get pregnant with many babies."

Adam was next in line for judgment. God told him, "Because you didn't listen to Me, I will curse the ground with thorns that will hurt you, weeds will choke out the food you want to grow, and some plants will poison you."

Adam's eyes dropped, reflecting the sorrow he would experience because of coming hard times. God added to Adam's judgment,

"You'll work hard...your body will ache...the ground will stubbornly give you its fruit...you'll have to use all your ingenuity to stay alive. You will work hard, sweating to barely get enough to eat."

Adam and Even would find that their sin produced germs, bacteria, disease, and toxic poisons to make their bodies sick.

Animals that were once gentle will snarl...bite...claw. Some animals will become predators, preying on smaller animals. A seemingly beautiful cat will feed on mice, and a tiger will feast on antelopes. A beautiful passive world will become vicious. God warned,

"You will have many fears, not knowing harm from safety."

God explained to Adam and Eve that their spiritual life was reflective of the blood flowing in their veins. "But I'll not shed your blood to punish your disobedience." To give them a picture of forgiveness, God brought clothes to them, not fragile leaves, but leather clothes. The blood of an animal was spilled to teach them that the life of another could substitute for their disobedience. Another would die to cover their sin. The skin of an animal covered their nakedness.

"You can't stay in Paradise," God told them.

He pointed the path out of Eden and placed an angel there to keep them from returning. They would not be able to return to Paradise. They faced a world of danger and uncertainty. Questions plagued them,

Where would they live? What would they do? Why were they created? Would the human race survive?

## My Time to Pray

- Lord, Eve didn't have to sin, she didn't have a sinful nature, but I have one and I'm prone to disobey. Give me power over my sinful nature.

- Lord, You sacrificed the blood of a lamb to cover the sin of Adam and Eve, cover my sin by the blood of *the* Lamb—Jesus Christ.

- Lord, I worship You for giving me physical life, similar to the physical life You created in Adam. I worship You for giving me spiritual life, just as You forgave Adam's sin and prepared him for eternity.

- Lord, I'm sorry for Adam's sin, for he gave us pain, sickness, misery, and death. What Adam experienced, I also suffer. Thank You for redeeming Adam with blood from a lamb, and thank You for redeeming me with blood from *the* Lamb.

- Lord, I will spend time with You each day, just as Adam and Eve met You in the cool of the day.

- Lord, when sin has ruined my life—as it did Adam and Eve—give me another chance to serve You, as You gave Adam and Eve.

# Genesis 4:1-26

# Beginning Life Outside Eden

Adam had sex with his wife Eve; she conceived and gave birth to a son and
called him Cain, which means *acquired* then she said, "I have
acquired a man from the Lord."

Eve also gave birth to Abel who loved to keep sheep, while Cain worked the
earth.

Both sons brought a sacrifice to You; Cain brought an offering to You from
the soil, Abel brought an offering to You from his sheep.

Lord, You accepted Abel's offering, but you didn't accept Cain's, and his
face showed his anger.

You asked Cain, "Why are you angry? You don't have to worry if you do
what is right. A sin offering is crouching at the door of opportunity.
You can do the right thing if you want to."

The brothers argued when they were in the field.
Then Cain killed his brother Abel.

Lord, then You asked Cain, "Where is your brother Abel?" Cain answered,
"I don't know, am I my brother's keeper?"

Lord You asked, "What have you done, your brother's blood crieth to Me
from the ground."

Lord, You cursed Cain saying, "Your brother's blood has cried to Me from
the ground, so it (the ground) will no longer give you a good
harvest.
You will be a fugitive wandering from place to place."

Cain answered, "My sin is my punishment. You are sending me away from
Your presence and my homeland. I will be a fugitive and
whoever finds me will kill me."

Lord, You told Cain, I am putting a mark on you to warn people that
anyone
killing you will receive sevenfold punishment."

*Lord, I don't understand how "bad" children come from
"Good" parents,
But the example of Cain helps me accept this as a fact.*

Cain left Your presence and lived in Nod, a land east of Eden that meant
*wandering*. Cain had sex with his wife and she gave birth to a son
named Hanokh. Then Cain built a city and named it
Hanokh. Then the following children were born in order: Irad,
Mehujael, Methushael, and Lamech.

Lamech married two wives, Adah and Zillah. Adah bore a son Jabal; Zillah
gave birth to Tubal-Cain—who forged metal tools and living in tents
became a cattle rancher.

Lamech said to his wives—Adah and Zillah—"I killed a man for attacking
me."

Adam again had sex with his wife Eve and she gave birth to a boy and
called him Seth which meant "appointed." Eve told everyone,
"God has given me another seed to take the place of Abel." Seth
had a son named Enosh, then people called on the name of the
Lord.

Amen.

## Background Story of
## Beginning Life Outside Eden

### Genesis 4:1-26

Place: Outside Eden ᴄ Time: After the Fall

Adam and Eve walked north along the broad Euphrates River; not looking back, the Garden of Eden behind them. God put an angel to guard the entrance to the garden, they couldn't return. They explored the new world that their disobedience had created. Thick foliage on the riverbank entangled their feet...walking was difficult...Adam perspired in the heat. In high grass, Adam almost stepped on an unseen serpent, but it slithered away for fear of being trampled; then a few feet away it coiled, its mouth revealed fangs dripping with poison.

"Oh...!" Eve whimpered, a thorn from a low-hanging branch scratched her shoulder. Adam quickly wiped away the small drops of blood. They looked with concern at one another; this was their first experience with human blood. The curse meant pain.

The growl of a tiger running down a frightened antelope terrified them; in a cloud of dust the tiger caught the smaller animal, killing it.

The approaching night frightened them. They previously embraced darkness for rest and comforting sleep, now they were fearful of what they couldn't see. It was too dangerous to stay in an open field. They couldn't sleep in the high grass because of mosquitoes and poisonous serpents. They were fearful of falling if they slept in a tree. They chose a cave where Adam built a fire to protect its entrance.

That night Adam slept with his wife, they had sex and she conceived. Because God had given them perfect knowledge, they understood the gift of a child. Relying on that knowledge, he heated ore found in nearby rocks to prepare tools. Then Adam built a home for protection from the elements.

Nine months later, it was time for the birth of their first child. Eve was afraid of the unknown. She remembered the warning the Lord gave her about pain in childbirth. Her emotions ran the gamut from fear to excitement. The fear of coming labor pains were offset by the joy of anticipating a new baby. She found herself dreaming of what the child would be like...what he would do...where he would live...what kind of life would they have outside the Garden of Eden?

"Wa-a-a-a..." the new baby sucked in its first breath of air and cried. Adam carefully washed the baby, after performing the delivery of his first son. Although Adam and Eve had never experienced birth, they inherently knew what to do because of the pattern after which they were created. The baby was cleaned, prepared, and the first time it hungered, was fed at the breast of Eve. Adam and Eve fulfilled God's prediction that they would be one in marriage, and become one in a son.

Eve named her first boy Cain which means acquired. Eve remembered God's promise that her Seed would bruise the head of the one who destroyed their life. Not having the audible voice of God to give her directions, Eve thought Cain was the promised Seed who would destroy the evil one. Looking into the face of her baby, she didn't know quite what to expect. Would this son deliver her from the pain of childbirth? Would this son deliver the earth from thorns. Would the foot of Cain crush the head of the serpent?

As the years went by, Eve noticed wrinkles in her face, sagging muscles and the telltale evidence of creeping age appeared in her body, the same was happening to Adam. Would this son deliver her from aging?

"The grass dies each year, animals die, will I die?" Eve had to ask herself. As she looked into the face of Cain, she wanted to know if her baby would save her from death. How would he do it? When would he do it?

They were surprised that young Cain could not talk, walk, nor was he as agile as a full-grown man. Then they realized their son would follow the growth patterns of animal offspring. All young born to a woman, as well as those born to animals, had to learn to move, walk, and over a period of time to imitate the sounds of their parents.

Adam had sex with his wife again, and nine months later delivered a second son. They called his name Abel. Adam and Eve praised God for His goodness to them. They called their second son Abel, a name that meant *exaltation*.

"Tomorrow is the seventh day our day of rest," Adam said to his wife. "We must worship God as we did in the garden and perhaps the Lord will meet us in fellowship." They remembered God walking with them in the cool of the evening. But the seventh day was special for worship and fellowship. Now they could not return to the garden. Adam and Eve could no longer fellowship daily with the actual voice of God, but they could hear God in their conscience, God spoke to them through their inward mind.

"Let us go to the gate of the garden," Adam told his wife Eve, "let us offer an animal for our sins...just as God shed blood to cover our first sin, let's sacrifice a lamb for our forgiveness."

They got as close to the garden as they dare. They came to its entrance, remembering God had sent them away, so they dared not enter. Adam piled stone upon stone, building an altar to God. He knew certain things, "blood for blood" was required. Adam knew that the blood of the animal could be shed instead of his blood.

But what would Adam do with the animal after it was killed? Adam knew that fire purged and cleansed, so he stacked dry wood upon the altar, wood that would burn fiercely to consume the animal that was sacrificed. Adam and Eve knelt on the ground, bowing their heads to pray,

"Lord, we have sinned..." In an earnest request they asked, "Lord, forgive us of our sins...We shed this blood asking You to cover our sins..."

"Swoosh!" Fire fell from Heaven. God accepted their sacrifice by sending fire to consume the lamb and the wood. Then Adam laughed, he knew God was pleased. They worshiped God and inwardly felt clean from evil. They laughed together and enjoyed the presence of God. In a cruel world, the joy of knowing God was better than any other pleasure.

Adam and Eve were amazed at the differences in their two sons. Because both boys were born from the same mother and father; they expected the boys would look the same, act the same and want the same things; but their differences appeared almost immediately. Cain's hair was dark, but Abel had golden yellow hair. Cain cried constantly, was high-strung and strong-willed. Abel slept calmly, he was an easy baby to raise.

Cain's black hair fluttered in the wind, his growing muscular physique enabled him to work hard in his garden. Cain studied carefully the differences between the fruit in his garden and what conditions produced the most fruit. He found that digging the ground around the roots produced more fruit...larger fruit...and sweeter fruit.

*I can make a difference in my garden,* Cain concluded.

Cain constantly planted different kinds of beans, wanting the best in his garden. He dug thorns from the garden, planting different kinds of potatoes, peanuts, radishes and turnips; all that grew in the soil. Cain found that some food tasted better boiled in water, others tasted better when cooked in a clay oven and others were sizzled over an open flame.

"Taste the sweetness of the potato," he held out a steaming orange root from the ground, he called it a *sweet potato.*

Cain cooked with flavors, mixing in green peppers, red peppers, and black peppers, always looking for different taste sensations.

Cain loved food...loved learning about it...loved working in the garden...loved cooking it. Food was the love of his life.

Because of his deep love of the things he grew in his garden, Cain decided to sacrifice his food to God instead of bringing a blood sacrifice that he had seen his father Adam bring to God. Cain decided,

*I will offer food to God.* It was a natural conclusion. *I will give God my food on the next day of rest.*

But his brother Abel was different. Abel was a sensitive young man with deep feelings for his animals that he was raising. A collie dog had helped him herd sheep, so Abel would sit with his collie dog to watch the sun go down, stroking the dog's golden fur. Abel trained the dog to help him in his work. Sheep fascinated Abel, he learned how to take care of sheep, and he learned that a certain diet helped them grow healthier and stronger. When an animal was cut by the thickets or jagged rocks, Abel learned to wash its wound and on occasions he could sew a wound back together so it might heal.

Abel tended the cows that gave them milk, and the chickens that gave them eggs. He loved the animals, learned what made them grow, and spent his time taking care of them.

Saturday morning Cain and Abel made the long trek to the entrance to the Garden of Eden to worship God. They went to the pile of stones their parents had used to sacrifice to God. There was plenty of dry timber and bushes for fire.

Cain, the older brother went first. Instead of offering the blood sacrifice as he had done on other occasions, Cain opened his basket of vegetables; corn, beans, squash, the food that he enjoyed most. Meticulously, Cain arranged the wood on the altar, putting the dry tinder in place, then began arranging the vegetables and fruit in their place. As Cain finished, his young brother Abel interrupted,

"That's not the right sacrifice...our parents taught us to offer a blood sacrifice to God."

Cain shrugged off the suggestions of his brother, he continued to prepare the food in its place. He knelt before God, lifted his hands to God in prayer saying,

"Lord, God...I give You the best that my hands can produce...I give You what I enjoy most!"

There was no fire, the vegetables lay on the wood in the warm sun, but no fire from God, no response from Heaven.

Cain, prayed again, waiting for God to respond from Heaven, but nothing happened. God didn't respond, even though Cain followed the prescribed prayer, God didn't answer. Shortly, Cain arose from his knees, looked defiantly into Heaven, and then clenched his fist in anger, asking God, "Why?"

Abel had brought a lamb to sacrifice. He placed the small animal upon the wood on the rocks. Stepping back from the altar, Abel bowed his head to confess his sins before God. First he heard it, saw it, and then felt it.

"Swoosh...!" Fire from God fell from Heaven to consume the sacrifice; real flames consumed the lamb and wood. Abel heard the crackle of the flames, he felt the radiant heat on his face, and he saw the smoke ascending up into Heaven. With gratitude he nodded knowing that God had accepted his sacrifice. Then Abel heard the rage of his brother Cain,

"Why not me?" Cain's face turned red. Blood vessels popped out on his forehead and his fists clenched in rage. He kept repeating,

"Why not accept me, Lord...what's wrong with me?"

That evening Cain returned to his home, standing in the door of his home he surveyed his well-manicured gardens. Cain thought, "My garden is the best I can do...why is it not good enough for God?" The evening meal was simple, cooked beans from his vines; and roots dug from the ground...washed...and steamed. Fresh fruit was placed on the table, bananas, berries and an apple. As Cain prepared to eat his evening meal...grown in his garden...cooked by his hands...God came to his house to speak to him with an audible voice,

"Why are you angry?"

Cain knew it was the voice of God, his father Adam told him about hearing the voice of God walking in the garden during the cool of the day. His father had fellowshipped with God but Cain didn't want to worship God. He angrily told God,

"I am not mad..."

But God who knows the hearts of all men, knew that Cain was angry. So God said,

"I can see anger in your face..." God asked, "Why is your countenance fallen?"

Cain felt that he had a right to be angry. He was mad because his vegetable sacrifice hadn't been accepted. Cain didn't have any sheep, and he didn't want to get one from his brother Abel. Cain was mad because he had given God the best that he had, but God didn't accept it. God told him,

"If you bring the right offering to Me, I will accept it from you."

Cain had brought the wrong offering, Cain had not dealt with his sin. Only blood was God's picture of forgiveness—life for life, and death for death. God said to him,

"If you are sincere in wanting to sacrifice to Me, then I will provide one for you."

Cain heard the cry of a young lamb at the door of his house. It was right outside the door. Then God told him,

"There is a sin offering at your door, this lamb is for your sacrifice."

God was giving to Cain a young lamb, he could sacrifice. Then God explained,

"If you offer a blood sacrifice to Me, it will be well with your soul."

Cain ran out of the house, his anger had gotten the best of him. Running past the lamb at the door, Cain ignored the gift God had provided. He carefully straddled the rows of corn that he had planted, so not to trample on his young plants. There was not a sign of a weed or thorns any place. When he came to Abel's property, Cain used his walking stick to climb the fence, and wade through the sheep as he might wade through water in a stream. He had to talk to Abel that evening.

Yelling to his younger brother to come out of the house, Cain pointed with the walking cane,

"Let's go into the field...I need to talk with you."

As they walked through the field, Cain was still angry...angry that his sacrifice was rejected...angry with God...angry with Abel. His brother Abel asked,

"Why are you mad at me?" Abel explained that when their parents had sinned, God gave them a pattern of dealing with sin. God spilled the first blood for their sin, then brought the leather clothes to Adam and Eve. Abel told Cain his brother,

"You must sacrifice God's way…"

Hearing that, Cain viciously slammed the walking stick against Abel's head.

"Stop!" Abel raised his hands to defend himself.

But Cain's anger was violent. The sight of his brother's blood pouring from his mouth and eye was addictive. Cain struck Abel again…and again…and again.

Only the limp body of Abel seemed to quench Cain's anger, only with blood flowing from Abel's mouth, puddling on the ground, did Cain get control of himself. Looking both ways, Cain realized no one saw him. The shovel he used to till his ground was in the cornfield. He quickly dug a hole in the ground to bury the lifeless corpse of his brother from sight.

When Cain returned to his house, he had to step around the small lamb still crouched at his door. Even the presence of the sin offering didn't move him to seek God's way of forgiveness. He slammed the door. He wanted to block the murder out of his mind but there is no way to block God out of our lives. The audible voice of God spoke,

"Cain, where is your brother?" Cain knew the voice was God's. He naively thought God didn't know what he had done. He answered,

"Am I thy brother's keeper?"

The first child born on this earth became a murderer, an indication of how deeply sin penetrated the human race. The first child was born with great anticipation, but he was not the Deliverer that Eve anticipated. God had promised the Seed of the woman would destroy sin. Neither Cain nor Abel was that Deliverer. The hope of paradise was wrapped up in the future.

## My Time to Pray

- Lord, I have the challenges of the future, just as Cain and Abel had new challenges; may I make the most of every opportunity today to serve You.

- Lord, the greatest experience in life is to experience Your presence. I will meet with You today, just as the first parents met with You.

- Lord, every new child is a challenge for love, prayers, and nurture. Help me successfully meet the challenges of the young in my life.

- Lord, death was a new experience for the first inhabitants of the earth. I realize the Bible teaches, "It is appointed unto men, once to die." I will make the most of life while I have breath, then I'll look forward to living with You in Heaven.

# Genesis 5:1-32

# FROM ADAM TO NOAH

This is the legacy of Adam. Lord, You made him in Your image, and created him in your likeness; You blessed him and called him Adam.

Adam lived 130 years and bore Seth, a son in his image and likeness. And Adam bore several daughters and died when he was 930 years old.

Seth lived 105 years and bore Enosh. And Seth bore sons and daughters and died when he was 912 years old.

Enosh lived 90 years and bore Cainan. Then he bore sons and daughters, and Enosh died when he was 905 years old.

Cainan lived 70 years and bore Mahalaleel and Cainan bore sons and daughters and died when he was 910 years old.

Mahaleleel lived 65 years and bore Jared and Mahalaleel bore sons and daughters and died when he was 895 years old.

Jared lived 162 years and bore Enoch and Jared bore sons and daughters, and he died when he was 962 years old.

Enoch lived 65 years and bore Methuselah and Enoch walked with God 365 years after he gave birth to Methusaleh. He was no longer here because God took him.

Methuselah lived 187 years and bore Lamech. Methuselah bore sons and daughters and died when he was 969 years old.

Lamech lived 182 years and bore Noah, and he said "This child will help us in our labor of hard work to get a harvest from the ground

God has cursed. Lamech bore sons and daughters and died when he was 777 years old. When Noah was 500 years old, he bore three sons, Ham, Shem, and Jepheth.

*Lord, thank You for the longevity of life before the Flood,*
*Today, I won't live as long as they;*
*Help me to use every day for Your glory.*

Amen.

## Background Story of
## Re-telling the Creation Story

### Genesis 5:1-32

Place: Inside Adam's home ⌒ Time: Approximately 300 years after the Fall

Adam and Eve sat with some of their great grandchildren on the front porch of their home that overlooked a small valley facing west. Adam enjoyed telling the little ones stories as they watched the orange sunset over the green hills.

"Listen to the evening songs of crickets," Grandpa Adam put his hand to his ear to hear owls...nightingale...and the moan of their cattle.

"Tell us again the story..." the children asked their grandpa. Eve nodded approval, reminding Adam that all their children had been taught the story of Creation on this porch. It was the story that taught them how God created everything, it was the story that gave them a godly heritage.

"I'll get the book," Adam went into the house to find the scroll kept safely in a wooden box. Returning to the porch, Adam showed the children the title, *The Book of the Generations of Adam and Eve.*

As Adam unrolled the scroll to the beginning, the grandchildren saw the list of names—hundreds of names—section after section. Adam had written the names of his offspring into his book, at least all the names he could trace. The family was so widespread; Adam didn't even know where they all lived.

"Show me my name..." a great granddaughter asked.

"There," Adam unrolled the scroll to the proper section, then pointed to her name. "Your name comes after your father and mother."

"How many names are in this book?"

Adam threw his head back to laugh. He had never been asked that question. Looking at Eve, he asked,

"How many children...and grandchildren...and great grandchildren... and beyond that? There must be thousands."

Adam held up his fingers—one finger for each family—then he said there were ten children in each family, and he tried to explain to young minds how the numbers corresponded with each new generation. The children did not follow Grandpa, they just trusted his word, "There were thousands of people and dozens of cities."

"Grandpa..." she asked again, "do you know them all?"

Adam and Eve couldn't answer her question. Sure, they had tried to keep up with everyone, but when Cain rebelled against God, he moved away. They lost touch with Cain's family, because Cain refused to worship God. Their rebellion against God had breached the family.

Adam used her question as a teachable moment. "Because we worship the Lord, Cain's family ran away from God and ran away from us." Adam slowly shook his head negatively to tell the children he didn't know how many children were in Cain's line. Then he lifted his head, smiling to say,

"I must tell you the story before it gets dark," Adam found the place in his book that told about the beginning. "Gather around my chair," Grandpa commanded, "and listen with your eyes. It is not enough to hear with your ears. When you listen with your eyes, your heart will remember."

Adam began the story, just like he told all the other children and grand-children.

"In the beginning God created the heavens and the earth, the earth was a gigantic mud ball." Adam explained the Lord created this world of dirt, so God began with a large mud ball." Adam pointed a great grandson to a mud puddle near the porch, telling him to make a mud ball. The boy patted a large dirt sphere with both hands, then held the mud ball up for all to see.

"The earth looked like that, but was much larger; the world didn't have any life," Adam explained. "The mud and water were all mixed up." On the first day of Creation God said, "Let there be light," Adam told his grandson to hold the mud ball up so the rays of the setting sun could shine on it. The children watched the orange light reflect on half the mud ball. Adam reminded them God created light to warm their bodies and grow them food. Then Adam read from his book how the first day ended,

"The evening and the morning were the first day."

"What happened on the second day?" a quiet great granddaughter asked. Adam took the mud ball and told the children to watch. Then with both hands, Adam pressed hard and water was squeezed from the mud. Grandpa explained,

"God squeezed the earth." Adam laughed to explain that God separated the water from the dry land. God made oceans—Adam knew about oceans even though he had never seen one because God created him with perfect knowledge. When Adam squeezed the mud ball, he made a big dry spot on the mud ball. He explained that God separated dry land from the water. Then with a small twig, Adam drew a long line on the dry spot down one side of the ball. He explained,

"That's the Euphrates River," the children smiled, they had seen the broad Euphrates River. "God didn't use a stick, He used his big finger to dig the Euphrates River." Next to it, Adams drew another line, calling it the Tigris River. The children also knew about that river. Then Adam looked into his book and read, "The evening and the morning ended the second day."

Adam got up and walked to the edge of the porch, motioning for the children to follow him. He wanted to show them something. The instructive grandpa pointed to the leaves of a vine growing on the house. Then he pointed to grass—then bushes—then trees. Adam explained what happened on the third day.

"God made green growing things on the third day." Adam pulled some leaves off a vine and handed them to the little girl. "Vegetation grew out of the ground—just like we grow food out of the ground—God made green things appear on the third day." The children picked some grapes from the vine, popping them into their mouths, one by one. Adam picked a cluster of grapes for Eve and almost forgot the story until the little girl asked,

"What happened next?"

"Look at the sun quickly," Adam pointed to the orange wafer disappearing behind the hills. "God made the sun on the fourth day. God shaped a round ball of burning fire and hurled it up into the sky to warm our bodies and grow our food."

"Good night sun," the shy great granddaughter waved to the sun as it disappeared from sight.

"You'll see the moon in a little while," Adam told the children that on the fourth day, God created the sun...moon...and stars.

"Why did God create stars?" an inquisitive great grandson asked.

"Stars give us light on dark nights."

"Why are there so many stars?"

"Because God likes stars."

Again Adam unrolled the scroll to read how that day ended, "And the evening and the morning were the fourth day."

"Who-o-o-o-o," an owl broke the silence. That signal reminded Adam what happened on the fifth day. He returned to his chair, the children gathered around him, their eyes fixed on him as he continued telling the story. "On the fifth day God created birds. Let's see if we can locate the old owl—it's a night bird." There was still a little red glow over the mountain from the setting sun. They couldn't see the sun, but they could see the red reflection off a hawk high in the sky. The children remained on the porch, but searched the trees to locate the owl. Then they heard it again, "Who-o-o-o."

"There it is...I see the owl in that oak tree."

There were two kinds of birds that Adam wanted the children to see. First, he pointed to the owl in the dark tree; next he pointed to the hawk high in the sky where the red sun still shown. Adam wanted the children to see traces of the sun on the wings of the circling hawk.

"The hawk is a day bird," Grandpa Adam told the children, "just like the owl is a night bird."

"And don't forget to tell them about the fish," Eve interrupted Adam's story to tell them fish were created on the fifth day. Then Adam looked in his book and read again, "The evening and the morning were the fifth day."

"Let's find something that was created on the sixth day," Adam stood on the edge of the porch to look out over the fields. Then they all saw them at the same time. Two deer came out in the field below the house. "Sh-h-h-h!" Adam put his finger to his lips. "Let's watch them." He whispered to the children that God made deer and all animals on the sixth day.

"Did God make these deer?" the great granddaughter asked.

"No." Adam replied. "These deer are young—look how small they are—they are too young to have been originally created hundreds of years ago, these deer were born recently."

"Tell us how God created you," a boy asked. The children's father had heard the story on the front porch, and wanted his children to learn the same truths from Adam. This was the part of the story they all liked best. All the children of each family and each generation wanted to hear how God created Adam.

"I was not born like you or your parents." Adam smiled at the thought of his creation. He loved to tell the story how God created him on the sixth day. He began,

"Everything that God created is good," God said after making each thing, "It was good." Adam explained that God decided to create a man that was similar to God. "I was made in the image of God," Adam explained. "Because God has a mind, I think. Because God has feelings, I enjoy things like a sunset. Because God can make decisions, I was created with the power of choice. I choose to have a good life, and so can you—you must choose to obey God." Adam wanted all his children to obey God, as he had done since leaving the garden. Then Adam smiled and said,

"God made a clay man out of mud and laid him out flat on the ground." Adam explained the clay man was about as tall as he was and as big as he was. One child asked,

"Who was the clay man?"

"It was me." Adam loved when the children asked that question. "I was just a clay man."

"What happened...how'd you get skin?"

Adam puckered his lips to blow out some breath. "See that," he asked. "That's how God put life into me and I turned to flesh. God blew His breath into my nose...into the nostrils of the clay man, and I lived...my flesh lived...and I breathed...and I became a human soul."

"What happened then?"

"I got up and walked around." Adam tried to describe to the children the beauty of the garden in Paradise, but words failed him. He explained,

"No ants in my food...no dangerous snakes...my clothes didn't get dirty with sweat..."

"Ugh!" the granddaughter turned up her nose.

"What was the first thing you did?"

"First I had to name all the animals." Adam tried to explain to his great grandchildren that in the beginning he had a perfect mind, so he knew the correct name for each and could remember each one. Adam sighed at the thought of a perfect mind; now that he was getting older, he has a hard time remembering some things and other things he forgot.

"Then I got lonely..." Adam came back to his story. He explained that when he named the animals, there were two of every kind of animal—male and female—but he didn't have a companion. "There was no female for me."

"Is this the part about Grandma?"

Adam reached over to squeeze Eve's hand, then he went over to sit next to her. He told the children,

"God put me to sleep...then took your grandmother Eve out of my side. God took one of my ribs to create her." Smiling, he pointed to his side. "When I woke up, my side was closed up—perfect—and your grandmother was sleeping right next to me. I gave her the name Eve—Mother of Living Things—because every human being came from Eve, she's the mother—and grandmother—of all people."

"Just as we had children, you will marry and have children," Adam explained to his great grandchildren. Opening the scroll, Adam showed them that there were two lists of children. He pointed to a list of Cain, Enoch, Irad, Methusael, Lamech, Jubal, and Tubal-Cain.

"We don't know these people," a great grandchild asked who they were.

Adam explained the children of Cain refused to worship God. They refused to offer a lamb as a sacrifice for their sin. "They don't live around here." Even the children could sense their great grandfather was uncomfortable talking about these people. Adam went on to explain,

"The sins of a father influence the children and their grandchildren," Adam explained to the impressionable eyes listening to his story that Cain's rebellion against God rubbed off on his children and grandchildren. Cain and his children left to build communities upstream on the

Euphrates River, their towns were lawless with all types of wickedness. Adam explained,

"Your heart will deceive you—telling you to be lazy—you must work hard to have a good life."

Adam paused for a few seconds. Every eye was on Adam, they were listening with their eyes. Adam spoke, "You must choose to follow God and worship God." The wise old grandfather asked the children,

"Will you choose to do right?"

"Yes," the children nodded.

"Will you bring a sacrifice in worship to the Lord?"

"Yes."

## My Time to Pray

- Lord, thank You for leaving us a logical story of how You created the heavens and the earth. I believe this story.

- Lord, thank You for the influence of parents on their children. Help me guide my children and grandchildren to worship and serve You.

- Lord, thank You for parents who loved me, may I properly love my children and grandchildren.

# Genesis 6:1-22

# WICKEDNESS DEMANDED THE FLOOD

People began to multiply upon the earth and the sons of God were enticed by the daughters of men and they took them—some violently—for their wives.

Lord, You were not pleased with what You saw, and You said, "My Spirit will not always strive to bring people to Myself." Therefore, the life-span of man will be 120 years.

Lord, You saw the growth of oppressive evil on the earth and that people imagined every evil thing on earth to do.

Lord, You were grieved that You created people, so You said, "I will wipe out every human on this earth; not only people, but animals, creeping things and birds, for I regret creating them."

Lord, Noah found grace in Your eyes because he wholeheartedly did the right things and walked daily with You.

The earth was filled with violence and lawlessness because of evil giants and You determined to rid the earth of them forever.

Lord, You said to Noah, "I will bring an end to all living things because humans have corrupted their way of living on the earth."

Lord, You commanded, "Make an ark (the word ark means "box") of gopher wood with rooms and paint it with tar both inside and outside so it'll be waterproof. Make it 450 feet long, 75 feet wide, and 45 feet high—three stories. Build a roof, and below it around the top edges make an 18-inch opening. Then build a door into its side."

Lord, You said, "I, Myself, will make a flood of water to destroy everything on earth that has breath. But I will establish a covenant with you—Noah—and with your sons, your wife, and your son's wives, that you will live."

Lord, You said, "Bring into the ark two of every living thing—male and female—to keep them alive. From every bird, from every animal and from every crawling thing, they will come to you so they may be kept alive. Also, gather the food that is needed for your family and then put it in the ark."

*Lord, Noah did everything that You command him;*
*May I be as obedient to You as was Noah.*

Amen.

## Background Story of
## Wickedness Demanded the Flood

### Genesis 6:1-22

Place: Euphrates Valley ∂ Time: Pre-Flood

For Adam and the offspring of Seth, this was the best of times because they were carving homes out of a hostile environment. "We can work ourselves back to Paradise," they wanted to return to Eden. While work was hard and tedious, life was good for Adam and the line of Seth because they were happy and fulfilled. They conscientiously followed God, and worshiped Him with a sacrifice. They expected the birth of the Deliverer momentarily who would eliminate death and physical misery.

For Cain and his offspring this was the worst of times because they hated hard work, they distrusted one another and they cursed God for their misery. They clustered behind city walls to protect their possessions from those who would steal from them. They slept behind boarded up windows and doors because of physical fear. Ruled by their lust and physical pleasures, they had no other purpose in life than to survive. Pleasure was their goal.

The great, great, great, great grandson of Adam—seven generations from Adam—ruled a city by his viciousness. Each day Lamech slept off a hangover from the previous night's drunkenness, then stumbled to the city gate where he made decisions for the city. Because Lamech was muscular and meaner than everyone else, the city residents did what he demanded. On a particular day, Lamech was judging the complaint of one man against another,

"This man stole six of my cattle," an angry little resident demanded justice from Lamech. "The stolen animals have my markings, just like the rest of my herd." It was obvious the short man couldn't defend himself against the large hulk of a violent man who denied stealing the cattle,

"I didn't steal," the filthy defendant laughed. "He bet me he could drink the most jugs of wine before passing out; he lost." The gathering crowd laughed at the little man. The little man protested saying,

"The wager was for only one cow…the rest are mine!"

"STOP!" Lamech's mean-spirited grizzly appearance hushed the crowd. He pointed to the little man saying, "If the wager were for one animal— you keep one animal—give one animal to the winning drinker—I'll keep the rest." Lamech bellowed through his red swollen eyes, then the crowd laughed with him; the little man couldn't appeal, it was a done deal.

Another smaller man wanted justice from Lamech, he appealed to reason, "That man who stole cattle is dangerous, he came to my house and forced my wife to have sex."

The crowd moaned, this was a serious accusation because the man's honor was at stake. "What are you going to do about rape?" the little man asked for help. Silent eyes turned to see what Lamech would do.

"Is that true?" he asked the large filthy accused man, "Did you have sex with another man's wife?"

"She wanted it..."

The crowd yelled and laughed, making fun of the embarrassing scene. Finally, Lamech lifted his hands for silence. Looking at the small offended man who brought the charge, Lamech chuckled a low, mean-spirited laugh, then said,

"Go force sex on his wife, an eye for an eye."

The crowd howled with delight, not because Lamech's decision was correct, but the fleshly crowd was driven by fleshly pleasure. They imagined a bloody brawl of two men fighting over their respective honor. Then Lamech's eyes twinkled,

"I think we should all force sex on his wife."

The crowd howled to a higher pitch of laughter, no one knew if Lamech meant what he said. But it put a thought in Lamech's head, why could he not satisfy himself with more than one woman. He thought about it all day, then that night he told Adah his wife,

"I'm going to marry a second wife...someone to help you with the work around the house."

"NO!" the shocked Adah responded. "No one has two wives...that's not the way it's done."

"Sure it is," Lamech's corrupted reasoning came out. "I have one bull for all my cows..."

"We're not animals," Adah shot back at her husband. But she didn't win the argument. Because Lamech's domineering size and dominant spirit, he brought another woman—Zillah—into the home as a second wife.

Morality continued spiraling downward in the cities of Cain. Once they threw off God's restraints, physical pleasure became the motivating lust of life. Brute strength was the only way a man could protect his family and possessions. When rape was not punished, and wife-swapping was accepted, the next step was man satisfying his sexual pleasure with men. One evening as Lamech sat down with his two wives around the fire to eat, he announced almost casually,

"I killed a young man today."

The wives were shocked. Murder was unknown, except everyone knew the story of Cain killing his brother Abel. Everyone heard that God put a mark on Cain—some actually saw the mark—a physical mark that warned people God would punish any one who killed Cain. While many hated one another and there was much violence, no one in six generations had ever murdered another. But killing another man was easy for Lamech because there was no fear of God in his heart.

"I killed a man who attacked me," Lamech explained. "When the man tried to beat me with a stick, I took the club from his hands and beat him to death."

The silent mood around the fire was sobering. Lamech had murdered a man. Both Adah and Zillah knew their husband was a vicious man—he had beaten both of them many times. Both knew he took what he wanted—but now what would happen? The wives were thinking thoughts they couldn't share. *Will he beat me to death? Will he murder again. Will God take his life?*

The next day a stranger in white apparel walked through the gates of Lamech's city and climbed some steps to preach to them. Enoch's clean white tunic was a stark contrast to the filthy clothes of the people. The residents had heard how some in the Euphrates Valley grew cotton and wove it into soft-touching clothes, now they saw the fabric for the first time. The stranger had recently washed; his skin was clean, his eyes were clear and his spirit was soft. Everyone knew the stranger was from the God-fearing line of Seth, not the lineage of Cain.

"What's he doing here?" one of Lamech's wives asked. "The sons of Seth have nothing to do with us!"

Enoch was the approximate age of Lamech, both were seven generations from Adam. Enoch was a preacher of righteousness, calling people to repent of their sins and turn to God. Enoch had gone from one city of Cain to another with the same message,

"Repent of your sins, turn to God...."

The market located at the city gate was crowded; it's where women came early each morning to get eggs, vegetables, and milk. The men gathered to entertain themselves and begin drinking themselves drunk. Enoch knew when he preached at the city gate, his message would be passed to everyone in the city.

"Quit rebelling against God," Enoch lifted a booming voice over the conversations in the marketplace. He stood high on some stairs to see all, and be seen of them.

"The Lord is coming to punish those who refuse to worship Him. He will have 10,000 angels who will judge sin."

A few cat-calls were yelled at Enoch as he spoke to the crowd. Some listened quietly for they knew in their conscience the man dressed in white was right. Enoch continued his sermon,

*"The wrath of God is now revealed from Heaven against all acts of ungodliness and unrighteousness, because when you know what is right, you do what is wrong."*

*"We don't know God,"* Lamech yelled out what others were thinking. *"We haven't seen God...we haven't heard God...where is God?"*

*Enoch continued his sermon, "You know in your heart that God exists, because you see the reflection of God in nature about you. The invisible things of God are clearly seen by His power—no one can duplicate the awesome power of the sun. No one can control night and day, nor the seasons, nor the weather. You can clearly see God's power, so you are without excuse."* [5]

*"I haven't seen God,"* Lamech again yelled out to the preacher, *"why does God care about what we do?"*

*"Because when you know God in your heart, you don't worship God, neither are you thankful for all His blessings in life. But you only think about*

*pleasing yourselves. You don't have the ability to think straight. You do wrong and think it is right.*

*"You have changed God's glory into idols. You worship the spirit of animals and demons. You mold clay birds, and snakes, and beasts, and place them on your god shelves; then ask these false gods to bless you.*

*"God will give you up to filthy sins because you have unclean hearts. You change the truth of God into a lie, and worship creatures more than the Creator.*

*"God will give you up because of your vile sexual sins, because women give up their natural roles and men burn in their lust one man to another, many doing that which is vulgar and nasty. Your filthy ways and miserable lives are the consequences of your wrong thinking. You say evil is good because you have rejected God. God will give you up, if you don't repent. God will come to judge you all."*

Lamech began yelling at the preacher, others joined him, ridiculing Enoch as he shouted, "You're as dirty as we are." They threw spoiled fruit at him, then began scooping up handfuls of mud to throw at him. When the women joined in the fun, they threw stones, forcing Enoch to leave. That night Zillah asked Lamech if anything Enoch said was true. Lamech was angry at her question,

"If you're going to repent," Lamech said sarcastically to his younger wife, "tear down your idol shelf...quit praying to the spirits for rain...quit praying to the bull for a son...."

Lamech explained they must appease the spirit of the sun so famine wouldn't come, and they must worship the dark spirits for protection from disease. Lamech continued to worship the gods on his idol shelf, asking for things he needed.

Several weeks after Enoch had preached in their city, Zillah told Lamech that she heard in the city market that Enoch had disappeared.

"Did someone kill him?" Lamech laughed at the thought.

"No," Zillah said. She had talked to one of the women from the line of Seth that had been kidnapped by a city resident. The young girl told the other women at the market that,

"Enoch went walking with God, and he didn't come back."

The young girls explained that Enoch went on a walk each day to worship God, just as Adam and Eve worshiped God in the garden in the cool of each day. One day while Enoch was walking with God, suddenly he was taken to live with God. *"That's a sign from God that He will judge us?"*

One man in Lamech's town prayed with all his strength to the dark spirit. The man went to the roof of his house to lay prostrate in the sun for seven days, asking the dark spirit to give him knowledge like the gods. The man wanted what the serpent offered to Eve, "You shall be as God, knowing good and evil." Because God was worshiped with a blood sacrifice, he gashed his arms and legs yelling out, "Fill me dark spirit with the knowledge of good and evil."

The man became possessed with evil as never before. During the following week, the town's inhabitants heard another voice talking from within the *possessed* man. He correctly predicted the sex of a baby before it was born, and gave black powder to the sick, making them well. He pierced the muscles of his arms with needles claiming,

"I have one needle for each dark spirit within me."

When he gave Lamech the opportunity to pull a needle from his pierced skin, the powerful Lamech couldn't pull the needle from his side. The spirit-possessed man boasted,

"I have the dark spirit's power, stronger than Enoch who claims to have God's power." Gradually, the possessed man was venerated by the town's people because of his power.

The possessed man left the town for a few days, then returned with a young girl claiming, "She's my wife." Everyone knew his wife came from the line of Seth because of her white linen clothes. Gradually, the innocence of the young girl's face became mean-spirited as her white linen clothing got dirtier and dirtier. She washed when she first came to the town, but finally surrendered to filth in which they lived. With time, her clothes stank; she became like the sons of Cain. One evening when the men of the city were quite drunk, the spirit-possessed man livened up the conversation with his boasting,

"My wife was a virgin when I seduced her to leave her family. Sex is much more exciting with the pure young things of Seth's line than it is with the filthy women around here."

What the men of the city heard, enticed their lust. With time, they began sneaking to the villages of Seth, trying to seduce their daughters with excitement and thrills. Some girls sneaked off with the men of Cain, some were kidnapped, others were raped and left with a life of regret.

The spirit-possessed man told his wife—the one who had been pure—that he would pray for her to receive the dark spirit, so she could have power over the other women of the village. The possessed man prayed that one of the dark spirits in him would enter her when they had sex. But the spirit entered the fetus of the child conceived in her. When the child was born, it was called Nephilim, which means giant. Nephilim had a spirit seven-times more evil than his father. No one could control the child as he grew into manhood. Nephilim grew head and shoulder taller than anyone else in the city and he was seven times stronger than men, and seven times more evil than those who were his forefathers.

With time, other sons of Cain became possessed with the dark spirit and their evil spirit was passed onto their sons. A race of giant Nephilims developed. In battle it was impossible for the sons of Seth to stand against the sons of Nephilim.

## My Time to Pray

- Lord, thank You for the godly example of Enoch, I will obey Your commands and seek to live a holy life.

- Lord, fill me with Your Holy Spirit and give me victory over self, lust, temptation, and sin.

- Lord, I believe there are still demonic spirits in the world, but I will not fear them because "greater is He Who is within me, than he who is in the world."

# Genesis 7:1-24

# THE FLOOD COVERS THE EARTH

Lord, You said to Noah, "You and all your family come into the ark. Do the right thing that I commanded you. Bring into the ark seven mates of the clean animals and birds and one mate of unclean animals. Seven days from now it will begin to rain. It will rain for 40 days and 40 nights and I will destroy every living things left on earth."

Lord, Noah did everything You commanded; he was 600 years old when the waters came.

On the 17th day of the second month of Noah's birthday, the fountains under the earth broke open. The earth was flooded, as it continued to rain for 40 days and nights.

The Flood began when you commanded Noah and his wife, Shem, Ham, and
Japheth and their wives, and the animals to come into the ark. And You shut the door.

As it continued to rain, the flood rose higher and the ark was lifted by the waters. The water covered all the earth and all the mountains were covered by more than 20 feet.

All living things on the earth died—all birds, animals, livestock, crawling things, and bugs—everything that breathed. This included every living human being. Only Noah and his family lived through the Flood. The waters continued to cover everything for 150 days.

*Lord, thank You for protecting Noah and his family,*
*Thank You for preserving mankind so that*
*Life eventually reached me and my family.*

Amen.

## Background Story of
## The Flood Covers the Earth

### Genesis 7:1-24

Place: Euphrates Valley ⌒ Time: Before the Flood

Noah—from the godly line of Seth—finished sweeping the sawdust from the floor, then washed his hands. He had finished building another house. Noah had built many things, mostly houses for his friends and family. After hard work, he looked forward to fellowshipping with God each evening. He went walking with God each day, just as Adam and Enoch. But this evening was different; when he heard the audible voice of God, it scared him, but it shouldn't have. Noah was talking to God in his heart. God told him,

"I have a special job for you..."

Even though Noah lived among righteous people who obeyed with their conscience, people did not hear the actual voice of God. God told him He was angry at the sin of mankind because people were addicted with drunkenness, sexual immorality, and worshiping the dark spirits of the underworld. All the sons of Cain were obsessed with worshiping false gods; they reverenced hand-made gods. Their children were born with dark spirits, becoming powerful giants who threatened the race. Because of growing rebellion, the Lord told Noah He was going to destroy people because they had entirely corrupted themselves beyond hope of correction. God had given the sons of Cain an opportunity to repent under the preaching of Enoch. Instead of listening, the race of man was hardening its heart toward God. God told Noah,

"Build a big boat."

"How big?" Noah responded.

"Make the boat 450 feet long, three stories tall, and as wide as a tree is tall."

"Why such a big boat?" Noah asked God.

God told Noah that a flood—a worldwide flood—would destroy the earth, but those who entered into the large boat would be saved. All others would be drowned. God instructed Noah to preach repentance to everyone, and invite all people into the boat to be saved. Noah was to instruct people to repent from their sins and ask forgiveness. The boat was the only way to be saved in the coming worldwide judgment.

"Where's all the water coming from?" Noah asked.

"It's going to rain!" the Lord told Noah.

"What's rain?"

"The mist that waters the earth will all eventually come down from the sky flooding the great rivers, enough water to cover everything, including the mountain tops."

The Lord explained to Noah that the fountains underground would be broken up so that water would come from within the earth. The earth would be covered with water for one year, then evaporate into the sky. After the Flood, dry land will appear; and life will continue.

"The boat must be big enough to save two animals of every kind," God told Noah. "They will repopulate the earth after the Flood."

Noah began cutting trees—tall gopher-wood trees of hard wood—trees tall enough for the side posts of the great boat. When the dimensions of the ark were sketched out on the ground and tall side posts began to rise, neighbors traveled to see the spectacle. In his preaching, Noah told everyone about the boat and invited everyone to be saved from the Flood. They came to ridicule Noah. They had never heard of rain, they had never seen a boat that large. They shouted,

"That's going to be a large house...big enough for a palace...the biggest house we've ever seen..."

"Repent...." Noah continued preaching as he continued building, telling his mockers that God was going to judge the earth with water. He pointed to the gigantic dimensions of his boat. "There is safety for you in the ark." He invited them to repent, turn to God and enter the ark. The mockers asked,

"Where will all of the water come from?"

They had seen the Euphrates River rise slightly, but nothing like Noah predicted. He told them, "God is going to rain...."

"What's rain?"

"All of the watery mist in the sky will eventually fall in judgment."

"Ha...ha...ha...ha..."

Each evening Noah stopped his work to fellowship with God. He gathered his family together to thank God for His goodness and to pray for the Lord's blessing upon his project. The three sons of Noah helped each day to build the ark. As each began to look for a wife, many women would not associate with Noah's sons because of the ridicule heaped on them about the ark. But within time, each son found a woman to marry who believed the preaching of Noah and was willing to commit herself to safety in the boat.

After Noah built the great boat, he covered it with thick black tar, making it watertight. When finished, it was a gigantic, ugly black box that was three stories tall, had windows at the top, and was 450 feet long and 45 feet wide. Then the eventful day came, and just as every generation has one opportunity, God gave this generation one more opportunity, "Repent...turn to God...seek refuge in the boat." But the people turned their back on God. They continued laughing at Noah. Finally, God said,

"Come into the boat," God invited Noah's family to safety. Then God called the animals—male and female—compelled by the authority of God, they entered the boat—two by two. Noah herded them into the pens he had prepared. The people did not come, they only mocked at a distance. They laughed at his large black box, calling it an ark, the word for box.

When God shut the door, it was too late for anyone to enter.

First scattered drops of water fell from the sky; before long, sheets of driving rain soaked the land until it could absorb no more. Rushing water filled the steams and waterfalls became torrents of hydropower. Rivers overflowed their banks, flooding fields. Then water silently invaded the cities. The walls could not withstand the water's silent advance.

Some people climbed to their rooftops to escape the watery attack. Rather than remembering the preaching of Noah and repenting of their sins— they cursed God, shaking their fists defiantly at Heaven and its watery onslaught. When houses were covered, some tried to swim to safety to surrounding peaks. Many didn't make it. Those who held onto floating debris could hold on only so long—some survived for days, others for weeks. Eventually, everyone died. The ark lifted off the ground where it was begun 124 years earlier. The flood came.

The black box groaned, creaked, and complained, but its occupants were safe. Three floors of animals—thousands of pairs—hibernating in their semi-dark hovels, slept, ate occasionally, waited for their day of deliverance. The supernatural force of the One who created them and called them into the boat, subdued them for their yearlong voyage. Within the dark cubicles, Noah and his family fed the animals, cleaned out stalls, and gathered together daily for prayers, giving thanks for the dry safety of the ark.

"We'll all die," the wife of Noah's youngest son began to sob. Her sobs could barely be heard over the sound of the driving rain. "We've been on this boat 40 days...I'm scared."

"Hush," her husband tried to console her. Noah heard her crying, but he was not critical. He understood fear, but this threat was different. No one had ever been through the terror of a flood. Noah also listened to the muted grunts of the animals that could barely be heard over the constant pounding of rain. Then he thought he heard something, Noah cocked his ear upward…smiled…and said,

"Listen," Noah smiled as he put a hand behind his ear.

"I don't hear anything," the young wife answered.

"That's right!" Then the others realized what he heard.

Silence!

The rain had stopped. The constant pounding of water on the ark was gone, along with the howling winds. The eight people looked hopefully into the eyes of one another. Then they exchanged smiles.

Noah carved the 40th notch on the doorframe to his compartment to remind him that the rain stopped on the 40th day, the number of judgment.

Slowly the hot sun and a daily, brisk wind began evaporating the flood. Gone was the mist of the pre-Flood days. The day the mountaintops began appearing, Noah cut the 150th notch on the doorframe, over five months on the boat. The passengers on the ark kept hope alive by their daily routine of cleaning out stables and feeding the animals. Many in hibernation needed little attention. Just as Noah trusted God for protection in the dark storm, now he had faith that the floodwater would recede.

## My Time to Pray

- Lord, I have received Jesus Christ as my Savior; I have entered the symbolic protection of the ark.

- Lord, I know You will eventually judge those who reject You and refuse to repent from sin. Give me a heart to pray for lost people.

- Lord, sometimes it's hard to have faith when sin seems to dominate the society where I live. Help me look beyond the temptations of this world to see the glories You promise to those who obey You.

# Genesis 8:1-22

# THE FLOOD RECEDES

Lord, because You remembered Noah and the living things in the ark,
You sent a wind that caused the waters to go down. The
fountains of the deep were stopped and the sun shone.

On the seventh day of the seventh month, the ark came to rest on Mount
Ararat. The waters kept going down until on the first day of the
tenth month, mountains were visible.

After 40 days of sitting on Ararat, Noah opened a window and sent a raven
which flew back and forth. Then Noah sent a dove to see if the
waters were gone. But the dove found no place to rest; it returned.
Noah put out his hand and brought the dove into the ark. He waited
seven days and sent the dove again. The dove returned in the
evening with a freshly plucked olive leaf. Then Noah knew the
waters were gone and the earth was blossoming again. Noah waited
another seven days and sent out the dove again, but this time it
didn't return.

On Noah's 601st birthday, he removed the roof of the ark and he saw the
surface of the earth was dry. It was the 27th day of the second
month.

Lord, You told Noah to leave the ark with his wife, his sons, and his sons'
wives. You told him to bring out every living thing—birds, animals,
and crawling things—so they could cover the face of the earth and
be fruitful and multiply. So they went out of the ark.

Lord, Noah built an altar to You and offered a burnt-offering to You of every clean bird, animal, and livestock. You smelled the aroma and were pleased.

Lord, You said, "I will never again judge the earth with water as I have done. I know the desires of people's hearts will always be evil from their youth, but I will never again destroy life from the face of the earth. As long as the earth exists, planting and harvest, summer and winter, day and night will continue to the end."

*Lord, thank You for the promise never to judge the earth again*
   *By water,*
*I know that one day fire-judgment is coming, so I'm prepared to*
   *Meet You in the air; I pray for those who aren't.*

Amen.

# Genesis 8:1–9:29

# GOD'S COVENANT WITH NOAH

Lord, You blessed Noah and commanded them, "Be fruitful and multiply and fill the earth. Wild animals, livestock, birds and fish will be afraid of you. I have given them to you to eat. Everything that has flesh will be food to you, just as I gave you green herbs in the beginning. Only don't eat the blood of any animals."

Lord, You promised to hold accountable anyone or anything that kills anyone. You will hold accountable every animal and every human that takes the life of a human. Whoever sheds human blood—kills—another human, his blood shall be shed, because he killed a human who is made in Your image.

Lord, You said again to Noah, "Go over the whole earth, be fruitful and multiply."

Lord, You made a covenant with Noah, his sons, and all generations to come, saying, "Never again will every living thing be destroyed by a flood of water. Here is the sign of the covenant between Me and you and all living creatures for generations to come. I am putting a rainbow in the clouds. Whenever I send rain clouds over the earth, and the rainbow is seen in the clouds; I will remember, and never again destroy the earth with a flood. The rainbow will be in the clouds to remind Me of My everlasting covenant with you."

*Lord, thank You for making this Covenant with us,*
*I'm always relieved when I see a rainbow.*

The sons of Noah left the ark; Shem, Ham, and Jepheth. The whole earth
was populated by them. Ham was the father of Canaan.
Noah became a farmer and planted a vineyard. He drank wine
and got drunk and lay naked in his tent. Ham saw his father was
naked, so he went to tell his two brothers. Shem and Japheth put a
cloak on their shoulders and walked in backward to cover their
father. They did not see their father naked.

When Noah awoke, he knew what his youngest grandson had done to him,
so he said, "Cursed be Canaan, he will be a servant to his brothers."
Then Noah said, "Blessed be Shem and Japheth, Canaan will be
their servant. May God enlarge the tents of Japheth, he will live in
the tents of Shem, but Canaan will be their servant."

*Lord, may I never do anything that will bring Your curse on me,*
*May I always please You.*

Amen.

## Background Story of
## God's Covenant With Noah

### Genesis 8:1-9:29

Place: Euphrates Valley ↶ Time: After the Flood

Thump!!

Everyone felt the jolt at the same time. The ark drifted into a mountain-
top. The timbers scraped in protest as the ark settled into the rocks on the
peak of Ararat, a mountain high in the headwaters of the Euphrates River,
hundreds of miles from Noah's home. That evening Noah counted the

notches. They had been in the ark seven months and seventeen days. He knew it would be a while before they could leave.

Noah sent out a series of birds to determine what was outside the ark. When a dove returned with an olive branch—a sign of peace—Noah knew life was growing outside the ark, they could plan to leave. Then the eventful day arrived, the outside door swung open, and sunshine poured into the huge, ugly, black box.

A sense of anticipation echoed through the ark, the people cheered and the animals sounded their loud approval. Some in the family just wanted to walk on dirt once again, and some with claustrophobia just wanted to get out.

Before they left, Noah counted the notches. They left the ark exactly one year after the judgment began. Noah gathered the family together. He arranged 12 stones, then piled wood on the stones, and finally offered a lamb in worship to God. The whole family waited on their knees, then they heard it,

"SWOOSH," the fire of God fell indicating His divine approval on what was accomplished.

The smoke of burning wood and roasted meat filled the nostrils of Noah as he bowed in gratitude. But God also smelled the aroma and looked into the integrity of Noah's heart. The Lord spoke audibly,

"I will not again destroy the earth with a flood." God explained, "But the generation before the Flood had become so evil that I had to destroy all flesh." Then God commanded,

"Be fruitful and multiply...both you and all the animals." Noah looked out on a clean world—it was spring—green life was everywhere. God commanded him, "Replenish the earth."

Noah felt the warm rays on his neck—something those before him had not felt—and he knew the sun was good. God tilted the earth's axis, promising "From now on there will be four seasons...springtime to plant crops...summer for growth...fall for harvest...the frigid long nights of winter to rest the earth." Noah would no longer experience the pre-Flood, year-round uniform weather.

"But Lord," Noah asked God, "What if children become evil like Cain, who killed his brother Abel?"

Before the Flood, God relied on the conscience of individuals to restrain evil, but individual conscience was not powerful enough to hold back the evil imagination of man's heart. God needed a stronger restraint to stop the spread of evil. From now on there would be a different way to deal with sin. God told Noah,

"You and your children will be responsible when someone sins." God explained, "If anyone sheds innocent blood to kill another person, you must shed that person's blood."

God gave humans the authority of capital punishment, reminding Noah that murderers were a threat to them all. When someone killed another it was a sin against God, because people were made in God's image.

"Therefore," God said, "I give you the authority to take the life of a murderer." Then God added,

"You may eat the meat of animals," God told Noah. "Before this time people were vegetarians, but life in the future was going to be more strenuous than before the Flood. You will need more protein for energy. The mist that covered the earth is gone. Hard work in the burning sun will sap your energy."

Noah listened to God tell how life would be different. Because Noah knew the hearts of people, he expected rebellion would grow in the hearts of future generations. But not Noah and his son, he expected all to serve God. But he knew in the future, some would rebel against God,

"If You will not send another flood to punish people who rebel, what will You do when people rush to sin and rebellion?"

God told Noah. "The next time I'll judge the earth with fire."

Noah bowed in deep reverence for the second chance that God was giving to the human race. Looking up he saw bright colors high in the sky, beautiful colors. Noah had never seen such a dazzling array of bright colors, as if God had painted the sky with a brush of many colors. God saw the surprise in Noah's eyes and said,

"This rainbow is a covenant I make with you and future generations." God explained that when it rains in the future, and people became afraid that He would judge their sin by water, the rainbow that accompanies a storm was a promise that God would not flood the earth again.

"Go populate the earth," God told Noah. "Subdue everything you see; make it serve you; prosper your life and be happy in obedience to Me."

Noah and his children began following the Euphrates River down toward the sea. After hundreds of miles of travel, they began to see familiar terrain. They returned to their home area.

Noah built a house for each of his sons, and with time he had to build houses for his grandsons. But in a world with only a handful of people, there was limited need for a carpenter. Noah became a farmer. He worked hard and his ground produced everything his family needed for life and happiness. Grapes were plentiful in Noah's farm. He'd eat clusters by the mouthful; he especially enjoyed the sweet smell of grape juice.

Noah never planned to get drunk, but sometimes men in their old age forget the convictions of their youth. As a preacher before the Flood, Noah condemned drunkenness. Alcohol was one of the sins that weakened the conscience of people. Drunkenness was a trap door to transgression. How could Noah forget?

A jar of grapes had been crushed for sweet wine, but the skins were not removed. No one paid any attention to the jar in the cool storage shed. The rotting skins became the yeast to steep the wine. Removing the top, the aroma of the aged wine enticed Noah. He took one irresistible sip after another and was hooked. Before Noah realized what he was doing, he swallowed all the liquid in the jar. Noah got drunk.

That experience taught Noah to ferment wine and before long, he was drunk on a regular basis. On one particular day, Noah's drunkenness separated the family forever. He was so drunk that he lay naked on the floor...not able to get up...not knowing what was happening.

Canaan, a grandson, saw his grandfather drunk in a stupor. No one knows for sure what Canaan did, but he eventually called for his father Ham. Ham, knowing something needed to be done, quickly called his brothers Shem and Japheth.

"Quick..." Shem barked an order, "get a blanket." The brothers Shem and Japheth walked backward to their father with a blanket over their shoulders, covering his nakedness. They didn't know what Canaan did to Noah, they didn't want to know.

After Noah awoke from his drunken sleep, he realized an awful sin nature existed within his chest, and within his offspring. He had been God's human instrument to save the world, but now he was guilty of the same sin that he condemned in others. The sexual sin that caused the Flood that judged the world, was now uncovered within his family. Noah knew he had to be hard on himself and his family. Noah remembered the stories how Cain passed evil onto his sons, now here was evil within his family. As Adam was the fountainhead of disobedience, so Noah too was guilty of disobedience. The rebellion of Cain was present in Noah's family, even after the sons of Cain were destroyed in the Flood. Noah announced a curse to his grandsons that shocked the family,

*"Cursed is Canaan, because Canaan has given into the weakness of his human nature...because he is not strong...he will be a servant to his brothers."*

Then turning to his sons, Noah blessed them.

*"Blessed be Shem because he followed the Lord God of Heaven. Canaan shall be his servant.*

*God shall enlarge Japheth, but he shall live in the tents of Shem."*

Ham was given no blessing by Noah, nor was he cursed. God had commanded Noah and his sons to replenish the earth, but they remained near the Euphrates River; it had flowed through the Garden of Eden, it separated east and west, it was home.

Shem had five children, Japheth had seven. Ham had four. The memorable grandson Canaan was born to Ham. Everyone remembered it was Canaan

84

who sinned when Noah was drunk and lay naked on the floor. Ham's second son was Nimrod, a murderer like Cain, and the architect of Babel.

## My Time to Pray

- Lord, it's difficult to realize that Noah who preached against drunkenness, later got drunk. Keep me pure in my inward and outward life. Keep me from being a hypocrite.

- Lord, help me go through difficulties, as Noah went through difficulties, and give me a "trusting" spirit when I go through problems and trials.

- Lord, thank You for rainbows that promise You will never judge the earth again by water.

# Genesis 10

# THE DESCENDANTS OF NOAH'S SONS

There are 70 names[6] mentioned in this chapter who were
  Born to the sons of Noah[7], Shem, Ham, and Japheth.

## The Legacy of Noah's Three Sons

The sons of Japheth were Gomer[8], Magog[9], Madai[10],
  Javan[11], Tubal[12], Meshech[13], and Tiras[14].

The sons of Ham were Cush[15], Mizraim[16], Put[17],
  And Canaan[18].

The sons of Shem were Elam[19], Asshur, Arphaxad[20], Lud, and Aram.

Lord, You commanded these to go into all the world,
  And repopulate the entire world.

May I help fulfill the Great Commission
  To take the message of eternal life to all the world.

## The Legacy of the Rest of the 70

Gomer, son of Japheth, gave birth to Ashkenaz, Riphath,
  And Togarmah.

Javan had sons Elishah, Tarshish, Kittim, and Dodanim.

Cush the son of Ham, gave birth to Seba, Havilah, Sabtah,
Sabtechah, and Raamah who had two sons, Sheba and Dedan.

Cush also gave birth to Nimrod, a fierce leader and hunter. He began the
city of Babel, plus Erech, Accad, and Calneh, in the land of Iraq.

Asshur left this land to build the city of Ninevah in northern Iraq; plus two
other cities.

Mizraim had six sons: the Ludites, the Anamites, the Lehabites, the
Naphtuhites, the Pathrusites, the Casluhites (from whom the
Philistines came) and the Caphtorites.

Canaan gave birth to eleven sons: Sidon his firstborn, Heth, the Jebusites
(who built Jerusalem), the Amorites, the Girgashites, the Hivites,
the Arkites, the Sinites, the Arvadites, the Zemarites, and the
Hamathites. The boundary of Canaan's sons was from the Gaza
strip as one enters Egypt to Sider in Lebanon.

The sons of Shem also multiplied and they went east. They were: Elam,
Asshur, Arphaxad, Lud, and Aram. The sons of Aram were: Uz, Hul,
Gether, and Meshech. And Arphaxad fathered Salah, and Salah
fathered Eber, and Eber fathered Peleg (meaning divisions, because
the nations were scattered during his lifetime). His brother was
Joktan. Joktan fathered Almodad, Sheleph, Hazarmaveth, Jerah,
Hadoram, Uzal, Diklah, Obal, Abimael, Sheba, Ophir, Havilah, and
Jobab.

These nations were like islands of the sea, divided from one another.
Because they were not Jews, they were called Gentiles (Goyim, i.e.,
foreigners), every nation was divided from one another by their
tongues, families and ethnic divisions. They were divided because
of the following incidences in the Tower of Babel reflecting their
attitude toward God.

Amen.

# Genesis 11:1-9

## BUILDING A PYRAMID

Everyone spoke the same language, using the same words.
> After the Flood, people traveled from the east, down the Euphrates until they came to Shinar near where the original Garden of Eden was located.

They planned to build a city with a pyramid toward Heaven that was dedicated to worship. They wanted to build a reputation for themselves so they wouldn't be scattered over all the earth. They built brick kilns to bake bricks. They used clay and tar for mortar.

Lord, You came down to see the city and pyramid they were building. You talked among Yourselves saying, "The people have one purpose and have a single language, let's go see what they are doing."
You determined nothing will be impossible to them. You changed everyone's language and social orientation so they wouldn't understand what each other was saying. That way, You stopped construction on the pyramid.

Lord, You scattered everyone over the face of the earth, just as You originally planned for them to go.

Lord, they stopped building the pyramid. The unfinished project is called Babel—confusion—because it was there You confused their language and by this means, You scattered them over the face of the earth.

*Lord, help me obey Your commandment to do my part in going in to*
*All the world to preach the Gospel to every person.*

*Lord, may I never worship anything in Your place,*
*And may a building never become more important than You.*

Amen.

## Background Story of
## Building a Pyramid

### Genesis 11:1-9

Place: Babylon on the Banks of the Euphrates River
After the Flood ⌒ Time: Two Generations

The desert stretched flat and barren in every direction, hot, lifeless. With no mountains in sight, the flat tabletop terrain stretched as far as the eye could see. People stared at the horizon, trying to see tomorrow coming before it got there. The Euphrates River was a long green snake in the vast brown desert, the riverbank was lush and green, and for 200 miles it wriggled through the dry desert toward the sea. God had judged the land where the verdant Garden of Eden was created; the area was no longer well watered. Now the harsh desert punished its travelers, as God had punished the Garden for the sin committed therein.

Men had built a beautiful city on the edge of the Euphrates. Royal palm trees lined its streets, and canals took clear blue water to the homes and gardens. Ham's grandson, Nimrod, stood on the platform next to the city gate to rally support for his cause. The angry crowd was in a mood to listen. The summer's burning sun was more fierce than usual. Nimrod yelled out over the waiting faces,

"The sun hates us," he passionately preached. "The sun is a god, who punishes us with blistering rays."

"YESSS!" the crowd chanted in response.

"We have sacrificed to the sun," Nimrod passionately pleaded, "but the sun has not heard our prayers."

"YESSS!"

"We must find a new god to replace the sun." Nimrod challenged the hearers. "The moon is good to us...the moonlight is gentle...the moon guides us in darkness...."

"YESSS!"

"Let's make the most beautiful temple that man has ever constructed...let's make a temple to the moon."

Ham's grandson unfolded a beautiful vision of a pyramid built higher than any manmade structure in history, more elaborate than any in history, more beautiful than any in history. He described an altar to the moon on a platform at the top of the pyramid. Nimrod had departed drastically from the faith of his grandfather, Noah. He announced enthusiastically to the crowd,

"Our pyramid will be our launching pad to Heaven." Smiling in self-assurance, he added, "We have studied the dark nights and the bright stars where the gods live." He described tunnels in the pyramids that would align with Orion and other heavenly bodies. These tunnels will be chutes to launch a soul to God after death.

"From the top of our pyramid we can see the future coming over the horizon. We'll be like God, we'll see all."

Some of the people remembered the stories from Noah's ark landing on a mountain so high that it was covered with clouds, a mountain so high that snow crowned its peak year around. In the flat desert there were no mountains. Nimrod described building a mountain so high that they could reach to Heaven. The clouds would cover it. A voice of a pessimist rang out from the crowd,

"There are no stones to build the pyramid..." the doubter knew a pyramid could not be built of sand.

"Where will we get stone to build the pyramid?"

"We'll bake stone!" The visionary Nimrod yelled his answer. He explained that they had baked small bricks for their houses. Now they could bake large bricks for a large pyramid. He explained,

"There is tar in the ground." Everyone knew about the black, sticky substance flowing out of the ground. "Let's make bricks and use tar to glue them in place."

Over the years the building project proceeded feverishly. Religious devotion drives men to fanaticism, both psychologically and physically. Large brick kilns were constructed where brick could be baked, and large rollers were used to move them into place. Slowly, stone upon stone, the pyramid began to take shape. Each inhabitant put faith in the stones, that as they reached toward Heaven, their prayers would be answered and the moon god would be satisfied with their worship.

The city organized itself into one massive work party, each person working with fanatical zeal, deeply sacrificing for the worship of the moon. Day by day, stone by stone, the pyramid stretched higher toward Heaven. Each time a new level of stone was added, members of the city would stand on tiptoes, peering out toward the horizon, looking for tomorrow; but the only tomorrow they saw was revealed by the dawning of a new day's sun. At the end of a long hot workday, two men stood watching the sun disappear over the desert horizon. One said to the other,

"Soon we shall see tomorrow…" he paused to comment. "Soon we shall see tomorrow as clearly as we see the sun setting on this passing day."

"Tomorrow we shall see as God sees…"

"Tomorrow we shall be like God…"

The Lord God in Heaven heard the two men's conversation, because He hears everything that people say. God was grieved; these men were saying what everyone else was thinking. People had become more concerned about the moon than the Creator who had created the moon. Like the ancestors in the Garden of Eden, they wanted to become like God. The persons of the godhead talked among themselves and said,

"Let us go down and see what human creatures are trying to do."

God visited the tower. God heard the idolatrous desires of people. God knew that man worshiped himself because the idols of men were expressions of themselves. Then God said,

"Let Us confound the language of people," God observed. "When people cannot talk with one another, they won't be able to finish this idolatrous pyramid."

The race had disobeyed God, rather than scattering throughout the earth to repopulate it as God had commanded, they congregated around their self-grandizing worship. Rather than replenishing the earth for the glory of God, they built a tower to glorify their self-accomplishment.

The two men stood watching the sun descend over the western horizon, not knowing that God had visited their pyramid and reprogrammed their thinking. They didn't know that it was no longer possible to communicate with one another. The first man said, "Red rays of the sun call us to worship the evening moon."

The next man completely misunderstood the gobbledygook he heard from the first. He demanded,

"Speak clearly!"

Gobbledygook was answered with gobbledygook, and everyone heard gobbledygook from everyone else. When people were unwilling to do what God had commanded, they surrendered their beliefs about God, feeding on the desires of their mind. When people refuse to willingly obey God to repopulate the earth, God has a way of motivating people to ignorance. What people would not do willingly, they went into all the earth after God changed their languages.

The pyramid was never finished, so the inhabitants called it babel, which meant "confusion."

Slowly, each family unit began their tedious journey away from the pyramid; a centrifugal force urged them to flee Babel. They were afraid to stay there not knowing what frightened them about the place. Each family wanted to get as far away from Babel as possible.

As predicted by God through Noah, Ham and his children began gravitating toward Africa. Slowly Ham and his descendants assimilated physical characteristics from the African continent of the sun, each generation passing on their differences to the next, each generation solidifying the traits received from their forefathers. As their skin became darker, their spirits became softer toward one another.

Japheth and his family journeyed northeastward, the harsh terrain making them self-reliant and demanding.

Shem drifted west toward Europe, the farther north they drifted, the more pale their physical characteristics because of the long winters.

## My Time to Pray

- Lord, I can't speak every language, I can only speak the language of my birth. Help me use my words to glorify You and tell others about Your grace.

- Lord, people are spread all over the world and they speak many languages and dialects. Help me do all I can do to get the Gospel to them so they can believe in Jesus Christ.

- Lord, it's so easy for people to believe in every type of "god" but You. Help me tell everyone the truth that You are the Creator and Sustainer of the universe. Help me tell everyone You want to be their Savior.

# Genesis 11:10-32

## THE LEGACY OF SHEM

Shem, son of Noah, had a great legacy.

Arphaxad was his first born, whose son was Salah. Salah's son was Eber
and his son was Peleg. Peleg's son was Reu and his son was Serug
who had many sons and daughters. Serug's son was Nahor, whose
son was Terah.

The beginning of faith came from Terah who had three sons:
Abram, Nahor and Haran. They lived in Ur of the Chaldees. The
second son Nahor died. Abraham's wife was Sarai, and Nahor's
wife was Milcah. The line of Abraham almost stopped because
Sarai was barren and couldn't have children.

Lord, You called Abram to serve You in the land of Canaan so Terah
took his son Abram and Sarai and his grandson Lot and they left
Ur of the Chaldees to head to Canaan. But they only went to
Haran (means halfway). It was there Terah died.

*Lord, may I never give up when I'm half way*
*To the place You called me to go.*

Amen.

## Background Story of
## From Babel to a New Land

### Genesis 11:10-32

Place: From Ur to the Promised Land ↝ Time: 1964 B.C.

The young boy clenched his father's hand tightly as they climbed the steep steps up the pyramid, pausing to worship the moon on each step. The little boy's white linen tunic was specially sewn for this occasion; his pure robe was to be worn when worshiping the sun god. His father, Terah, gazed up to the top pinnacle in anticipation; the grey-bearded old man was an idol maker who helped carve the solid gold idol to the moon at the pyramid.

This was not the Tower of Babel, this was the city of Ur. Even though a different city, the pyramid was similar. Pyramid building was not an outward occupation of man, pyramids came from the inner recesses of his heart that refused to have the Lord rule over it.

The young boy, Abram, was not mesmerized by the golden idol, he glanced back down at the beautiful city of Ur surrounding the pyramid. Royal palms lined the brick-paved street; canals of crystal water kept the gardens green. The little boy knew that Adonai, the God of Heaven, created the trees, and water, and sand, and even the sun.

The little boy looked up, smiling at his father. As the youngest of three boys, his father created his name *Ab*, which means "father" and *ram*, which means "he loves." Abram was a little boy who dearly loved his father, because his father loved him. The father, Terah, pointed to the top,

"One day you'll make an idol even greater than mine." Abram didn't correct his father, but in his heart he believed differently. Abram believed the stories that God created Adam; he believed everyone came from the first parents. Abram believed Noah saved the world during a great flood. In his heart, his little-boy faith believed the Lord was the Creator who created the moon.

As Abram grew into manhood, none of his father's practices changed his mind, he believed God's power was greater than the sun, moon, and stars.

Abram stopped climbing the ziggurat to worship the moon god when he became a man. Because he loved his father, Abram didn't rebuke his father's moon worship.

When Abram was 50 years old, the Lord God of glory appeared to him in dazzling glory—Abram saw God and heard God. The Lord spoke in an audible voice, saying:

"Get out of this country because it's addictive idol worship...leave your family because they will corrupt your faith...go to a land where you can worship Me with no interference...the Deliverer will come through you."

God chose Abram to be the channel to bless the world, to save the world, and to bring glory to Himself. God wanted the world to be obey Him, but the Tower of Babel demonstrated that rebellious people make their own gods, after their image. Yet Abram had questions that were as important as breath, food, and life itself.

*"Can I leave Ur, the city of my birth...?"*

Abram was ready to leave the evil influences of Ur. From every place in the city, he could see the gigantic pyramid to the moon god. Leaving would be easy—idolatry, sexual sins, immorality, drunkenness. *"It will be difficult to leave my people, my father, my family."*

Abram rationalized that he couldn't leave his father, but he could leave his relatives, the larger extended family. He told Terah his father that he had heard the voice of God telling him to leave Ur. Terah's immediate question,

"Where should we go?"

Abram's only answer, "We will go to a land where God leads."

Terah agreed to go with his son.

On the appointed day, Abram had everything ready to go. They had packed their belongings, sold their property, and said goodbye to friends and relatives. Finally, they were ready to go, Abram, Sarai his wife, Lot his nephew (Abram had legal responsibility for the young man when Lot's father died), and Terah.

"Let's go," Abram pulled the camel into a walk and the caravan left Ur of the Chaldees.

Traveling up the Euphrates River was easy. Going from village to village was an educational experience, because they went from civilization to civilization. Each place spoke a different language, people dressed differently, and did things differently. The larger villages had a pyramid. It seemed each city had a different god and a different way of sacrificing.

When Abram got to Haran, a sprawling city that was halfway between the civilization of Babylon and the Mediterranean Sea, they stopped. The name *Haran* meant halfway, and when camel caravans reached Haran, they were halfway to their commercial destination. Abram was only halfway to his spiritual destination, the land God promised to show him.

God pointed Abram south through the desert toward Damascus and toward Egypt. God pointed Abram across the parched sandy desert; a dangerous trip. Some caravans didn't make it across the desert because they ran out of water. Others caravans were vandalized by robbers who left their victim's bodies to rot in the desert. Abram was ready to launch out across the desert in obedience to God; but Terah the aged father refused,

"No! I won't go into that desert."

"But we must follow the Lord," Abram reasoned with his father.

But Terah was stubborn, the desert terrified his advanced age, he was 175 years old; too ancient to fight the desert and thieves and the unknown. But Abram suspected his father Terah had another reason. Terah was fascinated with the large pyramid in Haran dedicated to worship the moon god. The ziggurat was a temptation to anyone who was mystified by the moon; for the pyramid in Haran was taller, larger, and more exquisite than the one they left in Ur. Abram wanted to obey God, but he couldn't leave Terah. He didn't know what to do, but finally decided, "I won't go without my father."

And for the next 25 years Abram remained only halfway toward God's destination. Why do some refuse to follow God? Many reasons, but God gives many a second chance. The sovereignty of God allowed the death of Terah to finally separate Abram from his past. Just as death must visit all, when Terah was 200 years of age he died in Haran and Abram buried him there. Abram wondered,

"Will the voice of God speak to me again?"

## My Time to Pray

- Lord, thank You for calling me to follow You, similar to the way You called Abraham.

- Lord, Your call to Abraham changed the course of human history. Your call to me just changed my life. May I be as faithful to my call as was Abraham, and may I influence those around me.

- Lord, Your call to Abraham influenced his family; may I likewise influence my family.

# Genesis 12:1-9

# THE ABRAHAMIC COVENANT

Lord, You previously said to Abram, "Leave your country and
relatives and father's household. Go to a land that I will show you.
When you obey Me, I will make the following covenant with you.

- "I will make you a great nation.

- I will prosper you.

- I will make your name famous.

- You will influence all other nations.

- I will prosper those who prosper you.

- I will curse them who curse you.

- Through you will come the Deliverer who will
  bless all families of the earth."

Lord, Abram obeyed as You commanded him. He was 75 years old when he
left Haran. Abram took his wife, Sarai, his possessions, his nephew,
Lot, and his possessions, as well as the servants they had acquired
and left for Canaan. Eventually, they arrived in Canaan.

Abraham walked through the land, passing through
Sichem and came to the place called the oak of Moreh.
The Canaanites still controlled the land.

Lord, because Abraham sacrificed, You appeared to him and
added an eighth promise to the covenant.

- "I will give you and your children this land
  as your territorial legacy."

Amen.

## Background Story of
## The Abrahamic Covenant

### Genesis 12:1-9

Place: Entering the Holy Land ∼ Time: 1934 B.C.

Just as God was merciful in the death of Terah, so God graciously spoke to Abram, "Get thee out of this land…leave it for good." God promised to show Abram a land. God gave him the same command that He gave 25 years earlier, leaving the people of Mesopotamia, leave his family, and to go to the Promised Land. God gave Abram a promise.

*"I will make you into a great nation and I will bless you; I will make your name great, and you will be a blessing. I will bless those who bless you, and whoever curses you I will curse; and all peoples on earth will be blessed through you"* (Genesis 12:2-3).

After making the desert trek, Abram and his family approached Damascus from the east. His caravan went directly through the city on the street called Straight. He remained long enough in Damascus to acquire one servant, Eliezer, a servant his age.

Arriving in the Promised Land, Abram realized it was truly a perfect paradise, a perfect place for his family. But the Canaanites lived there. They were descendants of Canaan, the grandson of Noah. The Canaanites were not God-worshipers as Noah, but rather they were sexually-driven, brutal men who loved drunkenness, thievery, and were known for lying.

The wickedness in the villages of the new land was just as evil as Abram left in Mesopotamia. Their sin disgusted Abram as did their sacrifice to profane idols. Abram couldn't live in their cities.

"We will live in tents," he announced to his nomadic family. We will separate ourselves to live in the hill country.

God had promised Abraham would be a great nation and that he would influence other nations. If that be so, Abraham decided to do something other chieftains of tribes did. He decided to carve his signet on the top of his tall walking stick. He thought, "If I'm to start a nation, my name should be first—at the top—of my walking stick."

Abraham dreamed of one day carving the name of his son underneath his signet. Then perhaps he would carve the signet of his grandson next. The walking stick would be passed down from father to son, a symbol of power and prestige, but more than worldly authority, the walking stick symbolized spiritual leadership.

As Abraham carved his signet, he knew he must be godly and always act in a righteous way with others. At the time, Abraham didn't realize he would one day lie, but his spiritual heritage—carved in his walking stick— would convict his conscience and Abraham would come back each time to the altar where he would spill an animal's blood that was symbolic of another dying in his place so he could live before God.

## My Time to Pray

- Lord, Abraham forsook the pleasures of city life to live separate from the world. Help me separate myself from sin, even when I have to live in a city.

- Lord, I believe Your promises to me of salvation, just as Abraham believed he would become the father of the Hebrew nation.

- Lord, Abraham didn't come to Canaan the first time You called him. Thank You for giving him a second call 25 years later. Have the same patience with me when I don't answer every time You call me.

# Genesis 12:10–13:3

# ABRAM'S SOJOURN IN EGYPT

There was a famine in the land, so Abram kept moving south, passing east of Bethel. He kept traveling toward the Negev, the desert.

As Abram approached Egypt, he became afraid. He told Sarai, "Men consider you good looking. When the Egyptians see you, they will think you are my wife and kill me, so they can take you. Tell them you are my sister, and things will go well for you. They won't kill me."

When Abram entered Egypt, the sons of Pharaoh saw Sarai was beautiful, so they told Pharaoh. Sarai was taken to Pharaoh's house. Then Pharaoh gave Abram sheep, cattle, donkeys, slaves, and camels.

But You, Lord, inflicted plagues on Pharaoh and his household because of Sarai. In Your own way, You told Pharaoh why he was being judged.

Pharaoh called Abram and rebuked him, "What have you done to me? Why didn't you tell me she was your wife? Why did you tell me she was your sister? Here is your wife."

Pharaoh immediately sent Abram out of the country with all his family and goods and everything they had.

Abram left Egypt with his wife, his possessions and Lot with him. They went back into the south Negev desert. Abram had become very wealthy with an abundance of herds, gold, silver, and tents.

Lord, Abram returned to Bethel where he previously pitched his tent
before going to Egypt to the place where he built an altar. There
Abram called on Your name.

*Lord, I'm embarrassed because Your servant, Abram, lied.*
*May I always tell the truth, even when it's hard.*

Amen.

## Background Story of
## Abram's Sojourn in Egypt

### Genesis 12:10-13:3

Place: Egypt ↶ Time: 1914 B.C.

The lush green of Abram's new paradise turned brown and died in the
winter, but the green leaves did not return the next spring. The rain
didn't fall for over a year, the hills were parched brick-hard; a drought set
in and everything died. They couldn't grow food, wildlife died. Even the
dew vanished that nourished the few remaining leaves on the trees.
Famine came to the Promise Land.

"We have to do something," Sarai told Abram.

The naked limbs of the trees no longer protected their large Bedouin tent
from the sun; the searing heat sapped their energy.

"God has led us here, now He's forsaken us." Sarai continued her complaints, "Egypt is always green." Abram's eyes twinkled. He heard stories
about the Nile River of Egypt that kept the land green and fruitful. Abram
knew that the people worshiped the Nile; the river was their god. They
also worshiped the sun, so he said, "If we go to Egypt, we don't have to
worship their gods, but we can eat their food."

It was night when they arrived in Beer-sheba, the last oasis in the Promise Land before they launched out across the Negev toward Egypt. Sitting around the pool of water with other travelers, Abram heard stories from travelers returning from Egypt,

"Pharaoh has many wives…"

The traveler looked at Sarai remarking,

"Pharaoh will take her into his harem as a wife…" then pointing to Abram said, "and kill you." The traveler continued, "The Pharaoh likes olive-skinned women from Mesopotamia, they're much more dainty than the dark-skinned women of Egypt. Pharaoh likes shy eyes…a pointed nose…and delicate fingers…Pharaoh will like Sarai."

Sarai thought that she was too old to be attractive to a man. Then she realized she wore a veil, *"It hides my wrinkles, Pharaoh won't know my age."*

Later that night as the couple prepared for sleep, Abram said to Sarai,

"If Pharaoh thought you were my sister, he wouldn't kill me."

Sarai didn't answer immediately, she knew that the statement was not a lie, but it was not the whole truth. Sarai and Abram had the same father, but a different mother; she was his half sister. Abram continued,

"When we get to the custom's house at the border, if you tell them you're my sister, they won't kill me."

Sarai nodded.

The road was dusty, stifling; nothing was growing in the desert. And then suddenly right in front of them was the custom's house, they had not seen it on the road. They couldn't turn back and they didn't have time to check their stories with each other. The custom's agent began asking questions,

"Who is she?"

"She is my sister."

Abram didn't mean to tell a lie, but in his heart he knew that he had deceived the custom's agent, even thought Sarai was his half sister. He felt guilty; his eyes did not meet the eyes of his wife.

Nothing happened at the custom's house, and for two weeks Abram and Sarai forgot about their deception. Then suddenly Egyptian soldiers swooped in to take Sarai with them. The soldiers had their orders. Sarai was taken to Pharaoh. As they left the house, a quartermaster showed up from Pharaoh to announce,

"Pharaoh wishes to reward you and your family for the gift of your sister."

The quartermaster brought cattle, sheep, cows, donkeys, even men and women servants for Abram. Then he counted out silver pieces to Lot whose outstretched hand was first,

"One hundred...two hundred...three hundred...," he counted much higher.

Sarai was placed in Pharaoh's palace, the household dwelling for his harem. He did not immediately take her as one of his wives, but rather she was quarantined for purification; to determine if she was with child or had disease. She was robed in the most exquisite clothes she had ever worn, and was daily washed in a marble tub, then showered with lovely perfume. But Sarai couldn't get over the thought,

*I'll never see Abram again...I'll be one of Pharaoh's wives.*

It wasn't until Sarai was taken from him, that Abram understood the extent of his deception. God had promised to bless the world through his seed, and now his wife would be polluted through Pharaoh and the Egyptians. Abram wondered,

*Can the Savior of the world come through me?*

In the providence of God, no human can thwart God's will. God sent a plague to Pharaoh's palace, none of his wives got pregnant. Then in the deep blackest of night, God told Pharaoh that he was being judged because of Abram's wife. Early the following morning Abram was dragged into Pharaoh's court, the king was boiling with rage,

*"What have you done to me!"* Pharaoh yelled his anger at Abram.

He then asked,

*"Why didn't you tell me she was your wife?"*

Abram tried to explain that he was afraid in the custom's house...that the new land intimidated him...that the misunderstanding just happened; but Pharaoh would have none of his explanations. The king pointed to the door and yelled,

"GO!"

Then turning to the captain of his guard, Pharaoh commanded that Abram and his family be accompanied immediately out of Egypt by an armed guard.

Abram and Sarai looked across the room at each other, for the first time in several days they exchanged glances. Their eyes were heavy with guilt. Abram was glad to get out of Egypt alive; but much to his surprise, the soldiers gathered up all his livestock, servants, and Lot; then accompanied them on a forced march to the border.

Abram and Sarai said little to each other as they traveled the caravan route north toward the Promise Land. Abram walked like a man possessed, pressing each day to walk just a little farther than his physical stamina would allow. He was heading for Bethel, the place known as "the House of God." When they arrived, the stones that Abram used to construct an altar were still intact. Before unpacking, before setting up his large Bedouin tent, before eating a meal, Abram selected a lamb to sacrifice to God. He pleaded to God for the forgiveness of his sins. There Abram and Sarai called on the name of the Lord, bowing before the Lord they prayed,

"Forgive us...restore us...receive us."

On the other side of a clump of trees, Lot's servants were erecting their master's Bedouin tent. As they staked out the pegs, one of Abram's servants looked questioningly at the dimensions thinking it was too big. When they unfolded the tent over the ground, Abram's servant asked,

"Where did you get such a large tent?"

"From Egypt."

As soon as Lot's tent was erected, he pulled down its flaps and disappeared behind its cover. Taking several money sacks from the baggage, he began counting his money that he had gotten from Egypt.

"One hundred...two hundred...three hundred..."

*"Come pray with us..."* Abram yelled to his nephew.

"SOON," Lot yelled back, he didn't want Uncle Abram knowing that money was more important to him than anything else.

## My Time to Pray

- Lord, Abraham lied about his wife, Sarai, because he couldn't trust You to take care of him, even when You promised to make him the father of many nations. May I always look to Your promises and trust You with all things.

- Lord, it's strange to me that You blessed Abraham even though he sinned and You used the circumstances of his lie to bless him financially. Lord, I will be pure and honest and I want You to bless me.

- Lord, Abraham's sin negatively influenced his nephew, Lot. Keep me from sin so I won't hurt friends and family.

# Genesis 13:5-18

## ABRAM AND LOT SEPARATING

Lot also had herds and tents in addition to what Abraham had, so
that the place was too small to support both Abram and
Lot to live together. The herdsmen of Lot and Abram
quarreled and the unsaved Canaanites and Perizzites saw it.

Abram said to his nephew Lot, "We should not be quarreling
since we are related. Is not the whole land before us?
Separate yourself from me. If you go to the left, I will go to
the right, or if you go to the right, I will go to the left."

Lot lifted up his eyes to see the well-watered Jordan Valley before
You destroyed Sodom and Gomorrah; it was like Your
Garden, or like the Nile River valley in Egypt. Then Lot
chose the well-watered Jordan Valley and moved there and
separated himself from Abram.

Abram lived in the hill country of Canaan and Lot lived among the
cities of the plain and pitched his tent toward Sodom. And
the men of Sodom were evil, sinning greatly against You, Lord God.

*Lord, it's so easy to get selfish and greedy,*
  *That lust influences my decisions;*
  *May I be delivered from wrongly grasping after riches.*

Lord, You said to Abram after Lot left, "Lift up your eyes to see the
place I will give you—northward, southward, eastward, and
westward—all the land you see I will give you and your
descendents forever. I will make your descendents as

numerous as the grains of dust of the earth, you will have
more descendents than can be counted."

Lord, You told Abram, "Get up and walk through the land from
one end to the other, for I will give it all to you."

Lord, then Abram moved his tent to Hebron, and lived in
the high plain of Mamre. There he built an altar to You.

*Lord, You had an earthly inheritance for Abram,*
*I know mine is spiritual in Heaven;*
*Thank You for present blessings and a future inheritance.*

Amen.

## Background Story of
## Abram and Lot Separating

### Genesis 13:5-18

Place: Bethel  *↶*  Time: 1912 B.C.

When they returned from Egypt, the flocks were herded together. The shepherds knew their sheep, knowing which belonged to Abram and which belonged to Lot. But on a certain day, the servants of Lot separated their flocks to a different hillside. They wanted to choose where their sheep grazed; they wanted to move higher where the grass was greener. But as they separated their sheep, a squabble broke out,

"That's Abram's sheep..." an older shepherd of Abram demanded.

"No...I helped give it birth," Lot's servant answered. "He would have died without me...it's mine."

112

From that day forward the servants of Lot withdrew in small ways from Abram's camp. They sat by themselves around the fire, they didn't offer help in drawing water, and jealousy grew into bitterness like weeds slowly choking a garden.

Lot's servants arose early in the morning to stake out the best pasture for their flocks. On the following morning there was trouble because Abram's servants slept in the field overnight, and they were first the following morning. When Lot's servants finally arrived they were told,

"This field belongs to Abram's servants."

But bitterness escalated during the day. Some of Lot's servants spied on the field. When Abram's servants went to help retrieve a lamb that had fallen in the ravine, they returned to see that their sheep were being driven away by Lot's servants.

*"You can't do that...we were here first today."*

*"We were here yesterday..."*

Harsh words turned into shoving, threats, cursing.

Abram came running as fast as his old knees would carry him. Because Abram was the eldest, he asked for silence to hear both sides of the dispute.

"Today we were first."

"Yesterday we were first."

Abram tried to smooth the raw nerves suggesting they divide the pastures. A servant who was uncomfortable with their squabbling said,

"The Canaanites live in this land. They should not see us fighting."

Turning to Lot, Abram explained that God had made them both rich, that God had taken care of their needs. Putting his hand on younger Lot's shoulder, Abram suggested,

"We are brothers..."

Abram didn't finish the sentence for Lot knew what his uncle would say. The older and more generous Abram told the younger nephew,

"You choose first."

Abram was the greater of the two; he had not given into selfishly possessing the better land. Because servants reflect their leader, Abram's servants agreed to give Lot first choice. Lot didn't feel gracious by choosing first, rather he felt vindicated to stake out the better options. Lot announced his choice almost as if he won a great victory,

"I choose the well-watered plains."

He pointed down to the lush valleys below. "I want the well-watered plains."

Abram was left with the hill country, it was second choice for the flocks, but in God's providence, it was the best choice whereby to develop one's spirituality. That evening Abram walked out from his camp to the highest peak; after all, the highlands were his because Lot chose the valleys. God met with the aging patriarch to tell him,

"Lift up your eyes...northward...southward...eastward...westward," Abram saw all the Promise Land from the high vantage point. "I give this land to you and to your children," God told Abram, "walk through all this land, it is yours forever."

## My Time to Pray

- Lord, Abraham's lack of trust in You exposed Lot's greed. First Abraham wouldn't trust You in the land to which You led him, and second he lied in Egypt and wouldn't trust You to protect him. Strengthen my faith in You, without which I can't please You.

- Lord, Abraham humbly let Lot choose first, even though You promised the land to Abraham, not Lot. Teach me humility and trust in all my decisions.

- Lord, give me eyes to see all the spiritual blessings You have for me, just as You allowed Abraham to see the land You promised to him.

# Genesis 14:1-24

## ABRAM RESCUES LOT

The four kings from the Euphrates River Valley, from Shinar, Ellasar, Elam
and the nations made war on the five kings of Sodom, Gomorrah,
Admah, Zeboiim and Bela. They fought near the Salt Sea, the
Dead Sea. Because they lost, they paid tribute to Hammurabi their
leader for 12 years, but quit paying taxes in the 13th year. In the
14th year Hammurabi swept through the Jordan Valley with four
kings and defeated the five kings at the clay pits near the Dead Sea.
The remnant fled into the hills. The five kings went through Sodom
and Gomorrah, ransacking the cities, taking everything with them.
They also took Lot, Abram's nephew and his goods. One person
escaped to tell Abram that his nephew was taken captive.

*Lord, Lot should have known better. Teach me that*
*Mistakes have consequences and help me*
*Make wise choices.*

When Abram heard about Lot's predicament, he took 318 men and chased
after the enemy to the northern part of the land of Canaan. Abram
divided his armed men and attacked them by night, and won a
decisive victory, chasing the army of the four kings, back to
Damascus.

Abram brought back all the possessions captured by the four kings,
including his brother Lot and Lot's possessions.

Two kings went out to meet Abram when he was returning victoriously.
First, it was the king of the wicked city of Sodom who said,
"Give me the people of my city, but keep the possessions." Abram

responded, "I have lifted my hand to the Most High Lord—
El Elyon, Possessor of Heaven and earth—I will not take even a
string that ties your sandals."

A second king—Melchizedek, King of Salem—met Abram at the Kiddron
Valley below the future city of Jerusalem. Melchizedek gave Abram
bread and wine and blessed him saying, "May El Elyon, Maker of
Heaven and earth, bless Abram who gave a great victory in battle."
There, Abram gave Melchizedek a tenth of all he had.

Amen.

### Background Story of
### Abram Rescues Lot

### Genesis 14:1-24

Place: The Promised Land ↶ Time: 1911 B.C.

"**T**HERE'S A MAN RUNNING UP THE VALLEY," someone yelled.
All of the servants reached for a weapon. Abram went to the door
of his tent to stare intently to the opening in the woods where he knew
soon a figure would soon appear. Shortly an exhausted man stumbled
through the trees. His frantic eyes and a large gash on his forehead told
Abram something was wrong. The battered man was almost naked and
barefooted, unusual for walking in the hot plains. The man ran straight to
Abram, falling before him, refusing a drink until he announced,

"Abram…your nephew Lot has been taken captive…"

Abram listened carefully to the story of how an invading army had swept
up the Jordan River Valley seeking money, cattle, and slaves. The vicious
army killed anyone who opposed them. As Abram heard the description

of their clothes, he knew the invading army was from Mesopotamia, his home. Abram knew the mean-spirited soldiers had absolutely no respect for their captives.

"Lot and his family have been taken prisoners..."

"When?" Abram asked.

"Last night."

Abram's eyes flashed with anger. He knew that if the invading army got back to Mesopotamia, Lot and his family would be lost in one of the thousand places where slaves are sold. Abram knew that he had to strike quickly, before the invading army got too far away. Standing to his feet, Abram announced to the scared people around the fire,

"Lot is family...we must go rescue him."

Three other nomadic tribes, those who lived like Abram and believed like Abram were recruited to help. In all, Abram gathered an army of 319 men. They were quickly rounded up to his campfire where Abram announced,

"If we march through the night, we can catch them by sundown tomorrow."

The men around Abram were not soldiers; they were shepherds and house workers. They were not trained in war, nor had they the taste of blood in their mouths. Abram announced,

"The army that we will be attacking is full of vicious murderers. We must be quicker...we must strike without warning...we must be merciless!"

Abram explained that there were 100 enemies for every one of them. He also explained that they could not win a hand-to-hand battle. Abram challenged his motley band,

"We will run fast...strike them unexpectedly...hit them hard...." He explained that a night attack would scare them so badly that they would run away.

The following night Abram caught up to the enemy army—technically four nations—they were camped at the foot of Mount Hermon. The spies crept in closely to find that the enemy was drinking, laughing, and had set almost no night sentries. They were not expecting a counter attack.

The battle went just as Abram had planned. They struck quickly...hard...unexpectedly. Thirty thousand soldiers ran wildly in every direction. Abram's men hit them so hard that they thought it was a much larger army than they. In the early morning light, Abram's soldiers began gathering up the booty; money, clothes, thousands of heads of cattle, and all of the slaves who were chained in shackles. When the enemy scattered in the night, they took nothing.

Two days later, Abram returned home, leading a large parade of treasure. Rich Abram had become richer; but with the accumulation of more wealth, Abram was now a king in his own right.

When Abram reached the Kidron Valley, he looked up to the top of the mountain to see the city of Salem (the future city of Jerusalem), safely quartered behind large gates and a massively high wall. The gates opened to Abram, the conquering hero. The king of Salem invited Abram to a feast. The king of Salem—Melchizedek—greeted Abram with the dignity afforded a conquering king. The two men sat together at a table in the green grass, underneath the towering walls of Salem. Melchizedek offered to Abram wine and bread, symbols of friendship and respect.

Melchizedek had prepared an altar for a sacrifice. When men go into battle, they may needlessly kill or maim an opponent; they may have sinned even in fulfilling their obligation to defend their people. Melchizedek wanted to sacrifice for any sin unintentionally done by Abram. Then taking the young lamb that had been set aside, Melchizedek sacrificed the innocent animal upon the altar, spilling its blood, symbolic of the Lord's forgiveness for Abram and his men. Melchizedek prayed for Abram,

"To the Lord...Possessor of Heaven and earth."

Both Abram and Melchizedek were worshipers of the God of Heaven. They led their people in righteousness, purity, peace. They recognized each other as brothers and cotravelers in the faith journey to please God.

While they were eating, a ragged figure stumbled out from the rocks. He carried no weapons, but his wild, blinking eyes reflected a nervous self-consciousness. His frail body showed signs of starvation. He had been lost in the hills since the invading armies swept through the Jordan Valley. He was the king of Sodom, and his frail health reflected his sexually inspired disease.

Abram and Melchizedek sat in dignity behind the table. While the king of Sodom ran over to the cattle pen, searching for animals that had belonged to him. He began pointing to thousands of cattle that came from Sodom. Then he spied some of his servants and neighbors also from the city of Sodom. He ran over to hug the men passionately, kissing them disgustingly. Returning to the table where Abram was sitting, the king of Sodom said,

"Keep all of my money...keep all of my cattle...keep everything that belongs to me; only return my servants." Then in a magnanimous gesture he pointed to Abram, "I give all my wealth to you."

Abram was repulsed at the show of false compassion. The riches were his because he conquered the enemy. The king of Sodom who had been hiding in the rocks could not give them to Abram. Abram didn't want anything to do with Sodom because he knew the word Sodom stood for filthy sexual sins. Rising in dignity before the king of Sodom, Abraham said,

"I have lifted my hand to the Lord...the Possessor of Heaven and earth...I will not take anything that is yours, not so much as a thong of a sandal."

## My Time to Pray

- Lord, Abraham didn't take tainted money, and You blessed him for his actions. Help me to always follow his example.

- Lord, Abraham helped his nephew, even though Lot caused his own predicament. Teach me to help friends and family, even when their sins get them in trouble.

- Lord, I will tithe to You everything I receive, just as Abraham gave tithes to You through Melchizedec.

# Genesis 15:1-21

## THE LORD REAFFIRMS HIS COVENANT WITH ABRAM

Lord, after these things You came to Abram in a vision saying, "Do not be afraid, Abram, I will protect you from harm. Also, I am your great reward."

*Lord, I know You will protect me from satanic counter attacks and his evil revenge.*

*Also, when I give You everything—as Abram gave to You—You will be my reward.*

Abram also prayed, "Lord God, what will You give to me seeing I am childless without an heir and Eliezer of Damascus will inherit my possessions?"

Lord, Your Word came to Abram, "This man will not inherit your possessions. Your heir will come from your physical body."

You brought Abram outside, "Look into the heavens, can you count the stars? You shall have more descendents than the stars."

Lord, Abram believed Your promise to him, and You declared Abram was righteous before You." Then You told Abram, "I am the Lord God who brought you out of Ur of the Chaldees to give you this land for an inheritance."

You answered Abram, "Bring Me a three-year-old cow, a goat, a ram, a dove, and a young pigeon." Abram cut each animal in half and separated them on either side of a path. He put one dead bird on either side of a path but didn't cut them in half. Before You came to accept the sacrifice, scavenger birds descended on the sacrifice, but Abram scared them away.

Lord, about this time the sun went down, You put Abram into a deep sleep and the horrors of hell fell on him. Then You said, "Your descendents will become slaves and be held captive in a foreign land for 400 years. But I will judge that people and you will leave that nation with many possessions."

"Your people will stay in captivity for 400 years until the sins of the Amorites be ripe for judgment."

"But you, Abram, will live a life of peace and be buried after a long good life."

Lord, after the sun set, You came in a thick darkness and smoking lamp, and passed between the meat offered in sacrifice. You went by Yourself without Abram so it was sealed as an unconditional covenant.

Lord, You reaffirmed Your covenant with Abram, "I am giving this land to your descendents—from the Nile River of Egypt to the Euphrates River in Babylon. You will have all the territory of the land of the Canaanites and their descendents."

Amen.

## Background Story of
## the Lord Reaffirming His Covenant With Abram

### Genesis 15:1-21

Place: Hills of Palestine ᕁ Time: 1910 B.C.

A few days later, Abram and his servants were back in his campsite, everyone was tense, afraid of a counter attack from the army that Abram had defeated. Then a sound from the darkness,

SNAP!

Everyone jumped when they heard the sound of a servant stepping on a branch in the darkness. Those in the light of the evening flames jumped for a weapon. A mother had quickly gathered her children to run into a tent. The servant who had broken the branch stepped into the light to announce,

"It's done."

The servant had taken half of Abram's cattle high up into a mountain pasture, a green field, unknown to most. The field was hidden up in the mountains. Abram expected a counter attack so he hid some cattle for their future livelihood. Everyone agreed that if they were attacked and scattered; they would gather in that mountain pasture.

Abram walked away from the campfire, needing time alone with God. Praying always cleared his mind. A few days ago Abram returned from winning a decisive battle with the four great kings from Mesopotamia. Out of that battle Abram gathered a tremendous amount of wealth—cattle, clothing, slaves, and gold. It was wealth that belonged to the king of Sodom and Gomorrah and other Canaanite kings. But Abram gave the money back to them, even though the custom of war awarded the spoil of battle to the victors. Abram didn't want anything from the evil Canaanite culture in his camp, it might contaminate him.

Walking that night outside the camp, Abram talked with God. He heard God's audible voice speak out of the black night,

"I am the Lord who is your Shield..."

God promised He would shield Abram from a counter attack from the enemy. All Abram had to do was trust God. Then the voice spoke again in the night,

"I am your Exceeding Great Reward..."

God reminded Abram that He could provide more money to Abram than he gave back to the king of Sodom. Since money is nothing but a tool of happiness and security, God promised Abram more happiness and security than he could get from money. Hearing God's voice, Abram knelt, threw both hands into the air,

"Lord, I believe You..."

## My Time to Pray

- Lord, I know I can't see You, not even the thick darkness that passed between the sacrifices. Help me follow in life what I know is right in my heart. Help my blind faith have outward confidence.

- Lord, I believe You will give the Jews the land of Canaan because You promised it to Abraham. Help me see Your unfolding plan in the modern-day conflict in the land of Israel.

- Lord, You declared Abraham was righteous because of his faith. Thank You for preparing me for Heaven and declaring me righteous because I believe in Jesus Christ.

# Genesis 16:1-16

## THE BIRTH OF ISHMAEL

Sarai was embarrassed because she did not have a son but she had an
Egyptian maid, so she said to Abram, "Because the Lord has not
given me children, go sleep with thy slave-maid, she'll have your
son."

Abram listened to his wife because he had been ten years in the land
Without a physical heir,
So he took Hagar and had sex with her.

When Hagar realized she was pregnant, she treated Sarai with distain.

*Lord, may I never take a short cut to Your will*
*When it involves an outwardly wrong action.*

Sarai got mad at Abram and blamed him; Sarai acknowledged giving Hager
to her husband, but now she hated the fact that Hager hated her;
Sarai said, "The Lord will decide who is right."

Abram told his wife, "She's your slave, do what you have to do." Sarai
treated Hagar so roughly that the slave girl ran away.

Lord, Your angel found Hagar by an oasis in the desert on her way home
to Egypt. Your angel asked, "Where have you come from and
where are you going?"

Lord, Hagar answered, "I'm running away from my mistress;" Your angel
told her, "Go back to Sarai and submit to her."

Lord, You also told her, "I will greatly increase Your descendents; there will
be so many you can't count them. You are pregnant with a son, call

him Ishmael, which means wild horse. He will be against everyone and everyone will be against him.

Lord, Hagar called You El Roi, the God who sees me. She said, "I have seen God and stayed alive." Then Hagar named the well Beer-Lachai-Roi, the well of one who sees me. It is between Kadesh Barnea and Beer-sheba.

Hagar bore Abram a son when he was 86 years old; Hagar named him Ishmael.

Amen.

## Background Story of the Birth of Ishmael

### Genesis 16:1-16

Place: Judean Highlands ᴄ Time: 1909 B.C.

Abram and Sarai sat around the evening fire discussing how God led them to the Promised Land. Abram remembered the Lord promised he would have many children who would bless the world. He remembered that God promised a Savior for the world would come from his children. Sarai reminded her husband,

"But you don't have a son..."

"Hush," Abram didn't look up from the fire as he spoke, "We must be patient."

"We're not getting any younger." Sarai was always practical with her observations, she said, "God helps those who help themselves...I have a plan to get children."

Hagar, the Egyptian servant girl, came out of the tent to bring them an evening drink. Sarai smiled, Hagar was her plan. She waited until the Egyptian slave left, then said,

"Why don't you take Hagar as a slave wife?" Sarai explained, "Hagar can give you a son in my place. The other tribal chiefs have children with a servant girl."

Sarai explained that Hagar was a trustworthy servant. Being from Egypt, she was meticulously clean and conscientious about small details. Of all the servants Sarai observed,

"I trust Hagar…besides she is young, healthy, and pretty."

Abram did what his wife suggested. He slept with Hagar, and she conceived. Everything seemed to go just as Abram intended. But after Hagar was pregnant, things didn't go as Sarai planned.

Hagar was uncomfortable with normal problems that a woman experiences in her first pregnancy—morning sickness, back pains, she was too tired to do her chores around the tent. So Hagar asked Sarai,

"I'll need a maid to wait on me…the son of Abram deserves the best." Sarai gave Hagar a maid, then Hagar asked,

"I'll need new clothes. Since I'm going to have Abram's son, I ought to look my best." Sarai got new clothes for Hagar, then she asked for more,

"I'll need a new tent," Hagar told Sarai, reminding her, "Nothing is too good for the son of Abram." That irritated Sarai, but she arranged for the tent. She wanted Hagar out of her sight, so she moved Hagar to the other side of the camp.

Every time Sarai gave Hagar what she asked, Hagar wanted more. Then one day Abram came into camp and walked to Hagar first, before greeting Sarai. Abram patted Hagar's tummy commenting,

"He'll be a fine son."

After Abram left, Hagar made the mistake of saying to Sarai, "Abram loves me more than you."

"THAT'S IT!" Sarai flew into a rage, and bitter words passed between the two women. That night Sarai told Abram what happened and demanded that something be done with Hagar. She demanded,

"The two of us cannot live in the same camp."

"Take Hagar, and do what you need to do," Abram answered.

Sarai sent Hagar away. Hagar was given food and a water bottle. Naturally Hagar began returning to her home in Egypt. But God knew about the squabble between the two women, and God followed Hagar on that dusty road. She found herself sitting by a wall when the Lord asked her a question,

"What are you doing here?"

"My mistress Sarai has mistreated me."

God asked a second question,

"Where are you going?" Again God knew the intentions of Hagar's heart. God knew she was heading home, but God had a plan for the child of Abram and Hagar. He told her,

"Return to Abram and Sarai...." The Lord instructed her to go back to Abram's camp to raise her son there. He gave Hagar this promise,

"I will multiply this son; call his name Ishmael, multitudes will come through him. He will be a wild man, he will be against every man, and they will be against him."

Hagar returned to Abram's camp and gave birth to a healthy baby boy that was nervous and hyperactive. She named him Ishmael as God commanded, the name means wild horse. For 13 years there was a cobelligerent truce in Abram's camp. Sarah didn't go near Hagar's tent, nor did she have anything to do with little Ishmael except what was absolutely necessary.

## My Time to Pray

- Lord, Abraham tried to do Your will the wrong way. Keep me from making mistakes. I will do Your will in Your way.

- Lord, today the children of Ishmael hate the children of Isaac. Teach me that mistakes have consequences.

- Lord, You have tender compassion for even a slave girl like Hagar; have mercy on me who is the least of Your servants.

# Genesis 17

# ABRAM IS RENAMED ABRAHAM

Lord, when Abram was 99 years old, You appeared to him and said,
"I am El Shaddai (God Almighty);
walk in my presence and be blameless."

Lord, You reminded Abram of Your covenant, "I will make an agreement
with you and I will increase your children greatly."

Lord, Abram fell on his face to worship You; You said to Abram,
"I will re-affirm my covenant with you. You will be the father of
many nations. Your name will no longer be Abram (Great Father)
but Abraham (Father of Nations). You will be fruitful, kings and
many nations will come from you."

Lord, You said to Abram, "I am establishing this covenant between Me and
you, and all your generations after you. It will be an everlasting
covenant, I will give to you and your descendents the land
where you now dwell, it will be yours for a permanent possession
and I will be the God of your descendants."

Lord, then You told Abraham to be circumcised, both he and his
descendants as a sign of this covenant. Every male is to be
circumcised—generation after generation—when they are eight days
old. This includes every slave born in Abraham's house and every
slave that he buys. All are to be circumcised in the foreskin of their
flesh. Therefore Your covenant will be "cut" into Abraham's flesh,
and in the flesh of all generations that follow him. Any male
who is not circumcised will be cut off from his people because
he has not fulfilled the covenant.

Lord, then You said to Abraham, "Do not call her Sarai any longer, from now on her name is to be Sarah (princess). I will bless her and give you a son by her. She will be mother of nations and kings. Many people will come from her.

Lord, Abraham fell on his face before You laughing, "Will a son be born to a man who is 100 years old? Will Sarah give birth when she is 90 years old?"

*Lord, I laugh with Abraham at Your mighty grace and power. Surely the miracle you did for Abraham and Sarah was greater than anything they ever thought.*

*Lord, teach me to expect miracles in my life greater than I can conceive.*

Lord, Abraham said to You, "Let Ishmael live before You." You answered, "No, Sarah your wife will bear you a son, and you must call him Isaac (laughter). I will make my covenant with Isaac as an everlasting covenant, and to all his descendants who come from him.

Lord, You told Abraham, "I have heard your prayer for Ishmael. I will bless him and give him many descendants. Twelve sons shall come from him and he will lead a mighty nation.

Lord, You made it clear, "I will establish My covenant with Isaac who will be born to Sarah next year." You left when You finished speaking with
Abraham.

Amen.

## Background Story of
## Abram Is Renamed Abraham

### Genesis 17

Place: Judean Highlands ↶ Time: 1897 B.C.

As little Ishmael grew from a baby into childhood, Abram became a permissive father in his old age, giving Ishmael everything he desired.

"Hold your bow and arrow like this," Abram yelled to his son Ishmael. This was the most wonderful day in his life. He was teaching his 12-year-old son how to hunt. His dreams were being lived out in his only son.

Although weak, frail, and 89-years-old, Abram could still stretch the bow. His arrows hit the tree 50 yards away…most of the time. He laughed,

"When I was a young man, I never missed." Abram was hunting and fishing with Ishmael to celebrate the boy's entrance into manhood. A few days later Abram announced,

"This animal is yours," Abram gave him a beautiful, white Arabian colt. "You and this young stallion can grow together. This horse is wild like you." Abram inwardly remembering that the name Ishmael meant *wild horse.*

"You'll be a great prince…" Abram told his son Ishmael. "People will respect you, and you can lead my people…."

But someone was listening when Abram said Ishmael would lead his people. God who hears everything, listened to the dream that old Abram had for his young son born to Hagar. But God disagreed with what He heard. Ishmael was not God's plan for the Deliverer to save the world. That night as Abram walked out among the trees to fellowship with God, his old ears heard the audible voice of God speak, just as he had heard in Ur of the Chaldees, just as he heard in Haran. God spoke to him again saying,

"I am Almighty God. Walk before Me and be blameless."

"Yes, Lord," Abram knelt before the Lord Who answered him,

God answered, "I made a covenant with you twenty-four years ago that your seed would bless the world, and I will keep my promise." As Abram fell on his face, the early evening dew wet his prickly ancient beard. God informed him,

"Your name will no longer be Abram…'he who loves his father,' but your name in the future will be Abraham, 'father of many nations.'" God told him to get up and walk to the tallest peak.

"Look, Abraham, at the land about you…"

Abraham squinted into the red setting sun over the western hills. From the heights of Hebron one could see the setting sun over the great Mediterranean Sea in the west. Then turning to the darkened Jordan River Valley behind him, Abraham surveyed the land—North, South, East, and West. God promised,

"I will give this land to you as an everlasting possession to you and to your sons."

Immediately, Abraham thought about his wild son Ishmael. His thought of the handsome son brought a smile to the crinkle-lined face. But God was not happy with the smile because He knew Abraham's heart. God said,

"Sarai, your wife, will have a son."

The eyebrow of Abraham arched. He was not sure what he heard. God had just said that his 89-year-old wife would get pregnant. Sarah has been barren all of these years, and now she is too old to get pregnant. Nevertheless, God had just said she would have a child. Abraham's gravelly voice bellowed victoriously,

"Ha…ha…ha…!" Abraham laughed triumphantly. His infectious laughter worshiped God. "Shall a baby be born to a man who is one hundred years old? And shall a baby be born to a woman who is ninety years old?"

God wanted to make an agreement—a covenant—with Abraham to prove He would keep His word. God wanted Abraham to do something to prove he would keep his part of the bargain. God instructed Abraham to take all of the male children and circumcise them. Abraham knew that the word *covenant* meant, "to cut." When two men made an agreement, they cut their forefinger or wrist, so that blood touched blood. The cut was a covenant that the agreement was bonded. But here God wanted to make an agreement between Himself and His servants. He wanted every male to be circumcised in the foreskin of his flesh. God said,

"Your wife will no longer be called Sarai, she will be called Sarah." The new name meant *princess*. Just as Abraham was given a new name, Sarai was given a new name with her new position.

God had just promised the most wonderful promise to 99-year-old Abraham. God promised a son by his beloved wife, Sarah. Then Abraham's conscience pricked him, he remembered Ishmael, the wild stallion, the hunting lessons, and his dreams for the handsome son. Abraham prayed to God,

"Oh, that Ishmael might live before You...and You might bless him."

God was not pleased that Abraham was compulsively hanging on to Ishmael. For God had just said that his son by Sarah would give him the seed to save the world. But God accommodated Abraham's request,

"Ishmael shall be a strong prince, and nations shall come out of him, but I will make my everlasting covenant with your son through Sarah."

## My Time to Pray

- Lord, Abraham spent his old age playing with the fruit of his flesh—Ishmael—when he should have been claiming Your promises in prayer. Keep me from loving the flesh.

- Lord, when I stray from Your perfect will—as did Abraham— speak to me as You did to Abraham and bring me back into fellowship with You.

- Lord, teach me to worship You with laughter as did Abraham when he appreciated Your mighty miracle.

- Lord, You are El Shaddai—God More Than Enough—I trust Your sufficiency for my life.

# Genesis 18

# GOD PROMISES A SON TO SARAH

Lord, you appeared to Abraham at the Oaks of Mamre as he sat at the opening of his tent during the hottest part of the day. He saw three men coming toward him, and he ran to greet them in the Near-Eastern manner.

Then Abraham asked if he had found grace in their sight, that he might feed them before they continued on their journey.

The men agreed, so Abraham ran quickly to tell Sarah to bake some cakes with the best of flour. He ran to the herd and took the best young calf and told a servant to prepare it. Then he set milk with the rest of the meal for the three men to eat. Abraham stood near as they ate.

Lord, you said to Abraham, "Where is your wife?" Abraham said, "In the tent." You said, "About this time next year, she shall have a son." Sarah was old and beyond the age of child-bearing. She was behind them in the tent when she heard, so Sarah laughed, saying, "I am too old, and so is my husband."

You said to Abraham, "Why did Sarah laugh? Is anything too hard for God to do?" Then God You continued, "At the right time next year, according to the time of pregnancy, she shall have a son."

Lord, Sarah denied laughing saying, "I didn't laugh;" but You told her, "No, you did laugh."

*Lord, may I never sarcastically laugh with unbelief*
*When faced with the need of Your great power.*

The next morning, the three travelers set out for Sodom,
    Abraham went with them for a short way.

You said, "Should I hide from Abraham the thing I am about to do? He is
    the leader of a great nation and all the nations of the earth will be
    blessed by him. He gives commands to his household and they obey
    My ways, to do the right thing in the right way. He walks with
    Me to bring about what I have promised him."

Lord, You said, "The cry against Sodom and Gomorrah is great and their
    wickedness is so great, that I must go see if their cry demands I
    judge the cities."

Lord, the two angels turned and went to Sodom, but You remained and
    Abraham stood in intercession before You.

Lord, Abraham approached You and said, "Will you judge the righteous
    with the wicked? If there are fifty righteous, will you forgive the
    city?" Abraham said, "I know You will not judge the righteous with
    the wicked, I know that is not like You. I know You will do the
    right thing."

Lord, You said, "If I find fifty righteous people in Sodom, then I will forgive
    and save the whole city from judgment."

Abraham said, "I am but dust and ashes, yet I have come to intercede for
    the city. Will You destroy it if You find forty-five righteous?"

Lord, You said, "I won't destroy it if I find forty-five there."

Abraham said, "What if you find forty?" You said, "I won't destroy it for
    forty."

Abraham said, "I don't want You to be angry, but will you destroy it if you
    find thirty?" You said, "I won't destroy it for thirty."

Abraham said, "I have become audacious to ask You, but will you destroy it
for twenty?" Lord, You said, "I won't destroy it for twenty."

Lord, Abraham said, "Don't be angry if I ask one more time, will you destroy
the city for ten?" Lord You said, "I will not destroy it for ten."

Lord, You went Your way when Abraham quit asking, then Abraham
returned to his tent.

Amen.

## Background Story of
## God Promises a Son to Sarah

### Genesis 18

Place: Judean Hills ⌒ Time: 1897 B.C.

A braham was sitting in the afternoon shade of his tent door. The tent was pitched under a scrub oak tree. The temperatures had soared to over 100 degrees; not a trace of breeze to drive away the heat. A fly buzzed around his head. Abraham nodded, half-asleep, only tolerating the blistering heat. The dozing Abraham was awakened by a yell,

"THREE STRANGERS ARE COMING UP THE PATH..."

Abraham was living high in the hills where travelers never took the strenuous road through the mountains, but rather most walked the flat road in the valley from Jericho on their way to Egypt. Hearing the yell, Abraham's ancient knees creaked as he sprang into action. Being hospitable was as important as being human, and Abraham wouldn't let strangers pass his tent without bringing them a cup of cool water. He invited the strangers to sit with him in the shade of a tree. Abraham asked,

"Will you eat a meal with me this evening?"

"Yes," the leader responded.

Running through his large Bedouin tent, Abraham barked orders to different servants; to one, "kill the special calf!" to another, "bake fresh bread," to another, "get cool milk for the evening meal!" A few minutes earlier the heat immobilized them from moving, much less working. Now, a compelling purpose overrode any desire for their physical comfort. Everyone worked feverishly preparing an evening meal.

After a delicious meal, the servants and women retired, leaving Abraham and the three strangers to talk by the smoldering fire at the door to his tent. The sun disappeared over the western horizon; a cool evening breeze drove away the sultry remains of the day. The first stranger asked Abraham,

"Where is Sarah your wife?"

Abraham jerked his head. No one knew Sarah's new name but God. Only a few days ago God changed Sarai to Sarah; yet this stranger knew her new name. Abraham thought to himself,

"Is this stranger from God...is this God?"

"I will make Sarah's body young again," the first stranger said to Abraham. "Sarah your wife will have a baby. It will be a son."

When men talked around the fire at night, the women customarily sat inside the tent door, out of sight, listening for news from the outside world. Travelers usually told wonderful stories about what was happening in the outside world. The women, not trusting their husbands to remember everything, eavesdropped on the conversation. When Sarah heard that she was going to have a son, she laughed,

"Ha..." she sarcastically thought, *"I'm too old to get pregnant, and Abraham is too old to have a son."*

"Why did Sarah laugh?" the stranger looked deep into Abraham's eyes with his question.

Abraham had not heard Sarah laugh, but Abraham realized that God knew everything; wise Abraham knew he was in the presence of deity. Calling Sarah out of the tent to the fire, she responded,

"I didn't laugh…"

"Yes…" the first stranger said. "You did laugh."

Then turning to Abraham, God asked a question—not for His information—the question was to teach Abraham the purpose of God. He asked,

"Is anything too hard for God?"

# Genesis 19

# SODOM AND GOMORRAH DESTROYED

Two angels came to Sodom at evening as Lot was sitting at the gate of the city. Lot went to greet them in Near-Eastern fashion. He invited them to come spend the night at his house. There they could wash, get up early and be on their way.

The angels said they would sleep in the square, but Lot insisted they go home with him. He made them a meal which they ate.

Before the men could go to sleep, the Sodomizers of Sodom surrounded Lot's house. They represented every area of the city, both young and old. They yelled to Lot, "Where are the men who are staying with you? Bring them out so we can have sex with them."

Lot went out, closing the door behind him. He said to the crowd, "Please don't do this wicked thing, they have the sanctuary of my home. I have two virgin daughters. I will bring them out. You can do what you will to them."

The men of Sodom told Lot, "Get out of the way, you came to live with us, now you are our judge. We'll treat you worse than we'll threat them." They rushed at Lot to break in the door.

The two angels reached out and pulled Lot inside and shut the door. The angels blinded the men outside, both young and old, so they couldn't find the door.

The angels said to Lot, "What people do you have in this city beside yourself—sons, daughters, sons-in-law? The angels told Lot, "Leave

this city and bring them with you because God has sent us to
destroy it."

Lot spoke with his sons-in-law who had married his daughters and said
"Leave this city because God is going to destroy it."
But they wouldn't listen to him.

The next morning, the angels told Lot to "Hurry, take your wife and two
daughters and leave before you are destroyed when this city is
punished." But Lot didn't leave immediately, so the angels grabbed
the hands of Lot, his wife, and his two daughters and pulled them
out of the city.

*Lord, You were merciful to them;*
*Thank You for Your protective mercy in my life.*

When they got out of the city, the angels said, "Run for your life! Don't
look back, don't stop anywhere, but hide in the hills. Otherwise
you'll be judged with Sodom."

Lot pleaded, "No, you've already been kind to me by saving my life. I can't
run to the hills. I'm afraid. I don't know how to live there. Look,
there's a small town. Let me escape there. I can live there."

The angel answered, "I approve what you ask, but hurry, because I am
about to destroy Sodom and I can't do it until you are safe. Because
of this, the town is named Tzoar (small)." When Lot reached the
town, the sun was up.

Lord, You caused fire and sulfur to rain down on Sodom and Gomorrah to
destroy the cities, its inhabitants, and everything that was therein.
Lot's wife looked back and she was iodinized.

Lord, Abraham got up early that morning and went to the place where he
interceded with You. He looked on the Jordan plains and saw smoke
from Sodom and Gomorrah bellowing up like a huge furnace.

Lord, You remembered Abraham by saving Lot from destruction when You destroyed Sodom and Gomorrah.

Lot left Tzoar and went into the hills to live in a cave with his two daughters. The older one said to the younger, "Our father is old and there isn't a man on earth to marry us and have children. Let's get our father drunk with wine and sleep with him, so that we will have descendants. That night they got their father drunk and the older one slept with him and he didn't know when she came in or left. The next night they got their father drunk again. The younger one slept with him and he didn't know when she came in or left.

Both daughters got pregnant by their father, the older one gave birth to a son and she called him Moab, the father of that nation. The younger gave birth to a son, and she called him Ben-Ammi, the father of the Ammon nation.

Amen.

## Background Story of
## Sodom and Gomorrah Destroyed

### Genesis 19

Place: Judean Hills ↶ Time: 1895 B.C.

The following morning the three strangers prepared to leave Abraham's camp. Abraham knew that the first stranger was from God, but he was not sure if He was the angel of the Lord or some other physical manifestation of God. Then the Lord asked,

"Shall I hide from Abraham the thing I'm going to do?"

The Lord knew that Abraham would become a revered man, and that his children would obey him, but He wondered if Abraham could understand the enormity of what was about to happen. Then the Lord told Abraham,

"The people of Sodom and Gomorrah have cried out to me because the sin of that city…it is very evil."

The Lord explained to Abraham that He was going to send His two angels down to examine the cities, to see if the sin was as grievous as the complaints coming from many of the people. As the two angels turned to leave, the Lord stood momentarily with Abraham. Because Abraham felt deeply for Lot and his family, he fell on his face to beg for his relatives that lived in Sodom. Should the Lord destroy the city, He would destroy part of Abraham's family. So Abraham asked the Lord,

"If You find righteous fifty people in the city, will You save the city?"

"I will not destroy the city if I find fifty righteous people there."

Abraham was relieved that the Lord listened to him, so he stepped over his reluctance and asked again,

"Suppose You find only forty-five righteous people, will that be enough for You to save the city?"

"I will save the city for forty-five righteous people."

Abraham had doubts if there were 45 in the city. He knew that Lot was righteous, but he was not sure how many others were in the city. So Abraham asked,

"Will You spare the city for forty righteous people?"

"Yes."

"Will You spare the city for thirty righteous people?"

"Yes."

"Will You spare the city for twenty righteous people?"

"Yes."

"Will You spare the city for ten righteous people?"

"Yes."

Abraham had pushed his boldness past the point of reluctance, and he couldn't ask anymore. Knowing he had already asked for too much, Abraham bowed his head before the Lord and said,

"Thy will be done."

It took all day for the angels to walk from the hills near Hebron down to the plains of Sodom. They entered the city as the sun was going down, shadows darkened the streets of the city. Lot happened to be sitting on the stage at the gate of the city. This was the stage where official business was conducted; and during the night, entertainment was provided for the people. Recognizing the two men were strangers, Lot had learned hospitality from Uncle Abraham.

"Let my house be your lodging for this evening." Lot invited the two young men home with him to sleep for the evening.

"No...we will stay in the city square this evening," the two angels answered.

Lot was concerned because the men were youthful and innocent looking. They didn't appear to be hardened workmen, nor had sin exacted its toll on their appearance. To Lot the men were almost angel-like. He knew the dangers of the open city of Sodom. The Sodomites preyed upon young, impressionable men—raping them, destroying them, and leaving them on the trash heap of humanity.

"No..." Lot insisted that the men come home with him that night. He would hear no excuse. As they entered his home, Lot bolted the door behind them. Lot treated the men royally, washing their feet and preparing a feast for their supper. When it came time for them to go to sleep, the men of the city—Sodomites—banged viciously on the door, yelling to Lot,

"WHERE ARE THE MEN...BRING THEM OUT...WE WANT TO KNOW THEM."

Lot would not allow the two young men near the door, but unbolting the door he slipped out, telling his family to lock the door after him.

"Don't do wickedly with these visitors…" Lot sternly spoke to the mob gathered in front of his door. It would be a terrible reputation upon Lot for the men of the city to violate the visitors entrusted to his care. The angel-like men had accepted his protection, and Lot was raising a barrier around them.

"STAND BACK," the Sodomites threatened Lot. "BRING THE MEN OUT IMMEDIATELY…!"

The mob began to accuse Lot that he was not one of them, that he was only a visitor in the city, that he had no right to judge them. They reached out with their fists. Another waved a stick in the air. Others were ready to attack the door yelling,

"LET US IN!"

Suddenly the door flew open, startling the Sodomites. The two visitors reached out, grabbed Lot by both arms, jerking him in the house before the startled mob could respond. The door slammed in the face of the mob, and the lock was thrown. Then an angel turned to warn Lot,

"We are going to destroy this place because of the cry of many innocent people who have been harmed in this city."

The angels blinded the eyes of the mob so they couldn't find the door. During the night the heavy door held back any other intruders. At the first light, the two angels awakened Lot and his family, commanding,

"Quickly leave the city because it will be destroyed today."

Turning to Lot an angel said, "Take your wife and your daughters and get as far away from this city as possible."

Lot wanted to prepare for the journey, to pack at least a bag of belongings. Lot's wife wanted to prepare food and to take some of their valuables. Two daughters began putting things in a sack to take with them. But knowing judgment was imminent; the angels grabbed them, forcing them out of the house. Lot was not sure whether his danger was from the men of the city or whether it was from God in Heaven. The angels continued pushing,

"Hurry up…don't look to the right or left…run for your life…run to the mountains."

"But I don't want to go to the mountains." Lot complained. "I'm afraid of the animals and danger of the mountains. There is a little city called Zoar," Lot tried to reason, "Why can't I stay in that little city?"

Before they had gotten far away, fire fell from Heaven. Like pouring water from a gigantic bucket, liquid fire splashed over the city of Sodom, burning up everything. The city sat on a rich load of sulfur, phosphate, and salt. When mixed with liquid fire from Heaven, the minerals liquefied, and the earth boiled like a gigantic caldron. Lava and molten rock erupted to hell's burning inferno. Burning sulfur exploded, hurling globs of fireballs into the sky; globs of burning sulfur went hurling through space.

"Hurry…" the angels warned. "There is danger if we tarry."

But Lot's wife stopped, turned, and looked back at her city…at her home…and at the destruction of her friends. An angel tugged at her hand, but she shrugged him off. She would not be moved. Her constant gaze at the city reflected her heart's grief at the loss of life she didn't want to give up. Sodom was still in her heart.

"Hurry."

"No."

The angels, pulling Lot and the daughters, left Lot's wife standing on the brow of the hill overlooking the city of Sodom. Out of the sky came a hurling glob of burning sulfur, phosphate, and salt, inundating the place where she stood. Lot's wife died instantly, becoming nothing but hardened, crusty salt.

That night Lot found refuge in the mountains that terrorized him. He made his way into a cave that frightened him. This was the only safety he could find, he was still afraid of flying liquid fire. As far as Lot and his daughters were concerned, they were the only ones left on earth. They remembered that God destroyed the world by water because of its sins in the days of Noah. But they also remembered that God said next time the world would be destroyed by fire, and they were sure that it happened that day.

Lot and his two daughters thought they were the only ones left on earth. To preserve the human race, the first daughter got her father drunk, and had sex with him to conceive a child. Even though incest was wrong, she rationalized her actions, thinking that it was the only way to repopulate the world with the human race. She was willing to do it. The next night the other daughter did the same thing.

Eventually the first daughter gave birth to a baby boy, calling him Moab. The young boy had the blood of Abraham's family flowing in his veins, but he grew up to become a nation that hated the children of Abraham. The second baby was also a boy; he was named Ammon. He too followed the path of his brother Moab. The two nations tormented Abraham's children forever.

## My Time to Pray

- Lord, there is coming a day of judgment when You will destroy the entire world's population by fire. Thank You that I am safe in Jesus.

- Lord, I believe in guardian angels; may they protect me from evil, even when I don't now what's happening around me.

- Lord, even though Lot compromised his faith and was attracted to sin, You saved him because he was Your child. Thank You for forgiving my sin and taking me to Heaven in spite of my failures.

# Genesis 20

# ABRAHAM DECEIVES ABIMELECH

Abraham traveled toward the desert and lived between Kadesh and Shur. While Abraham was a foreigner in Gerar, he told everyone Sarah was his sister. Abimelech King of Gerar sent men and took Sarah.

Lord, You came to Abimelech in a dream and said, "You will soon die because you took a man's wife." Abimelech had not had sex with her. The king said to You, "Will you destroy a righteous nation? The man said to me, 'She is my sister' and she said, 'He is my brother.' My heart is innocent and my hands are honest."

Lord, You said to him, "Yes, I know your heart is innocent, so I kept you from sinning against Me. I did not let you touch her. Return the woman to the man. He is a prophet, he will pray for you, and you will live. But if you don't restore her, you and everything you have will die."

Abimelech got up early and told his men these things. They were afraid.

Abimelech called Abraham and said, "What have you done to me? You have made me and my people commit a great sin, you've done something that should not be done. Abimelech continued, "What made you do this to me?"

Abraham answered, "Because I thought there was no fear of God in this place. I thought you would kill me to get my wife. Actually, Sarah is my sister, she is the daughter of my father, but not the daughter of my mother; but I married her. So I asked her when we live among this people, to tell everyone you're my sister!"

Abimelech gave Abraham sheep, cattle, male and female servants and
returned Sarah to Abraham. Then Abimelech said to Abraham
"Look, my whole land is before you, live where you like." To
Sarah he said, "I have given a thousand pieces of silver to your
brother. Everyone will understand he is your husband."

Lord, Abraham prayed to You, and you healed Abimelech's wife and slave
girls from their infertility, for You had closed up all the wombs
because of Sarah, Abraham's wife.

*Lord, Abraham was Your follower when he sinned,*
*Forgive all my sin as You forgave Abraham;*
*Keep me from sinning against You.*

Amen.

# Genesis 21

# THE BIRTH OF ISAAC

Lord, You remembered the promise You made about Sarah, and she conceived in her old age and delivered a son at the time You promised.

Lord, Abraham called his son that Sarah delivered Isaac (Laughter). Abraham circumcised him on the eighth day as You had commanded. Abraham was 100 years old when Isaac was born.

Sarah said, "God has given me a good reason to laugh, now everyone can laugh with me. Who would have believed I would nurse a son. Nevertheless I have delivered a son in my old age."

Isaac grew and when he was ready to be weaned, Abraham gave a great banquet to celebrate the child's weaning. But Ishmael, the son born to Abraham by Hagar, mocked Isaac and treated him roughly.

Sarah told Abraham, "Kick this slave girl's son, Ishmael, out of the camp. I will not have this slave girl's son living with my son Isaac."

Abraham was upset because of his son. But You said to Abraham, "Don't be upset because of the slave girl and Ishmael. Do what Sarah tells you must be done, because your descendants will come through Isaac. But, I will make a nation from the son of the slave girl, since he is your descendent."

Abraham got up early in the morning and gave bread and a skin of water to Hagar, and sent her and the son away. She wandered in the desert near Beer-sheba; when the water was gone, she put her son under a bush, and went about the distance of a bow shot. She cried and said, "I can't stand to see him die." You heard the boy's voice, and the angel of God said to her, "Don't be afraid, God has heard the voice of the lad. God is going to make a great nation for him." Then You opened her eyes and she saw a well of water. She filled her skin with water and gave to her son to drink.

*Lord, You protected the boy and he grew up in the desert and became an archer. He lived near Paran and his mother took a wife for him out of Egypt.*

*Lord, You love everyone and have a plan for their lives,
Even unsaved people.*

*Just as You had a plan for Ishmael,
You have a plan for everyone.*

*That means You have a special plan for me,
Show it to me and help me fulfill it.*

About that time Abimelech and Phichol, the captain of his Army, said to Abraham, "God is with you in everything you do, now swear to me by your God that you will never deal falsely with me, my son, or my grandson, but you will show me the kindness that I have shown to you as you live as a foreigner among us."

Abraham said, "I swear it." Now Abraham had complained to Abimelech about a well that was taken from him by Abimelech's servants.

Abimelech answered Abraham, "I don't know anything about the well. I only heard about it today when you told me." So Abraham gave sheep and cattle to Abimelech and they made a covenant about the well.

Abraham had put seven female lambs in a spot by themselves. Abimelech asked, "Why have you put these seven female lambs by themselves?" Abraham said, "You are to accept these seven female lambs as tokens that my servants have dug this well." To this day the well is called Beer-sheba, i.e., the well of seven and the well of the oath.

After they made a covenant, Abimelech and Phichol returned to the land of the Philistines. Then Abraham planted a grove of trees at Beer-sheba, and there called on You by name, El Olam (the Everlasting God). Abraham lived a long time as a foreigner in the land of the Philistines.

Amen.

## Background Story of
## The Birth of Isaac

### Genesis 21

Place: The Southern Desert ↶ Time: 1894 B.C.

Abraham strutted around camp, a feeble 100-year-old man prancing like all other fathers of a newborn, bragging about his new baby boy. He told everyone,

"Isaac...my baby's name is Isaac, which means "laughter." The proud father told everyone; he laughed in gratitude when God told him about the coming miraculous birth. Abraham loved the name Isaac. At the same time, Abraham was careful not to embarrass Sarah's laugh of unbelief.

Everyone rejoiced with Abraham, except Hagar and Ishmael. The young slave girl who bore Abraham a child was still as possessive and stubborn as ever. While she wouldn't dare do anything outright to disrupt Abraham's joy over young Isaac, she filled her son Ishmael with venom. She purposely drove a wedge between Isaac and Ishmael.

When baby Isaac played in front of the tent, Ishmael constantly hit the child. When the teenaged Ishmael was confronted, he denied any intent to hurt Isaac saying, "I wanted to make him tough." When Ishmael pushed Isaac to the dirt, he quickly rationalized, "I just wanted to make Isaac run faster."

"We'll have the greatest baby dedication ever," Abraham told everyone when Isaac turned three years old. That was the age that mothers weaned their children from breast feeding. Abraham announced his plans for a banquet much more elaborate than the one he gave for Ishmael. "Invite everyone," Abraham instructed the servants, "Prepare the greatest feast ever." Hagar didn't have anyone who would listen to her grumbling, so she complained to her son Ishmael, telling him that he was being treated like a second-class family member.

On the night of the festivities, it was customary for each visiting family head to bring a gift for young Isaac. Some brought a small chest of gold coins, or a bottle of rare perfume. Some brought animals, sheep, rams, cows. Then Abraham stood with his arms outstretched for silence. This was the moment when the father gave the child a gift. Ishmael listened to hear what Abraham would give to his rival Isaac. Abraham had given Ishmael a beautiful tan-colored dog that became the boy's childhood friend when he was weaned. Ishmael stood in the darkness outside the firelight, watching to see what Abraham would give Isaac.

Abraham smiled triumphantly, then clapped his hands. A servant led a prancing white Arabian stallion into the glow of the fire. Everyone shouted approval and applauded. Everyone but Ishmael, the green passion of jealousy blinded him. He didn't get his white stallion until he was 12, then Abraham gave him only a colt. This stallion given to Isaac was elegant enough for a king. Ishmael ran to his tent to get a gift for the child Isaac. Then walking slowly to the fire with a basket, Ishmael asked his aged father,

"May I give a gift to baby Isaac?"

"Yes, my son Ishmael," Abraham beamed with delight as the other chiefs appreciated the graciousness of Abraham's other son. Ishmael opened the lid and threw a serpent on Isaac. Everyone shrieked. Ishmael laughed saying,

"Because you're a snake," Ishmael danced with delight at the commotion. Abraham tried to get up to protect Isaac, but his old knees failed him. A servant rushed up to brush away the snake, then relieved everyone's anxiety announcing,

"It's not poisonous!"

The crowd breathed a sigh of relief.

Hagar smiled with evil glee as she viewed the episode from the edge of the light. Just as the face reveals the intent of the heart, Sarah saw Hagar's fiendish delight and decided to do something that evening. She was through making compromises for the slave girl and her teenage menace. Later that night when the party was over, Sarah confronted Abraham to demand,

"Get rid of Hagar and her son or else."

Abraham tried to overlook the incident claiming, "Ishmael was only having fun in an immature way."

"OR ELSE," Sarah demanded; she would not be denied.

Abraham couldn't sleep; he went for a walk in the fields to talk with God. A large harvest moon lit up the path, even though it was past midnight everything seemed midday. Abraham loved the wild spirit of Ishmael, yet in his heart knew what Sarah asked was right. Then God spoke to him,

*"Don't let this thing grieve you. Do what Sarah said, cast out the slave girl and her son for through Isaac will come your children and My Deliverer. But don't worry; I will make a great nation through Ishmael because he is your son."*

Hagar and Ishmael left Abraham's camp, going the wrong way to Egypt, they headed toward Beer-sheba the desert oasis and last spring of water before launching out into the desert. Again, they made a wrong decision, heading straight across the sand toward Egypt, not taking the longer road around the edge of the desert by the Mediterranean Sea. Their water gave out and Ishmael fainted of heat exhaustion first. Hagar crawled a little distance away, she didn't want to see him die. While Hagar wept, unknown to her, Ishmael was praying. Then she heard the Lord speak,

"Don't fear, I have heard your son praying." When Hagar crawled back to her son, she saw a spring of water in the desert. Whether God created it for her or it had been there previously doesn't matter. She filled the water bottle and gave Ishmael to drink. Eventually they both lived, Ishmael became a chieftain of a great family living in the land of Midian in the southern Sinai Peninsula. His descendants were called Ishmaelites after his name and Midianites after their territory.

## My Time to Pray

- Lord, thank You for choosing and protecting Isaac, because through his line was born Jesus Christ, my Savior.

- Lord, just as Isaac was conceived supernaturally when Sarah was too old to have a son, so the virgin Mary conceived Jesus supernaturally. Thank You for the miracle of life given to them so Jesus could live without sin and in death takes away my sin.

- Lord, Abraham prayed to You El Olam (the Everlasting God). You are without beginning and without end. You are from everlasting to everlasting. I worship You for Who You are.

# Genesis 22

## ABRAHAM'S FAITH IS TESTED

Lord, after all these things, You tested Abraham, calling to him,
"Abraham." He replied, "Here I am." You said "Take Isaac, your
only son, whom you love to the land of Moriah. Offer him there
to Me as a burnt offering on a mountain that I'll show to you."

Abraham got up early in the morning, saddled his donkey,
cut wood for the burnt offering, took two young men and Isaac
his son, and headed toward the place God directed. On the
third day, Abraham saw the place God told him about.

Abraham said to the young men, "Stay here with the donkey.
I and the boy will go and worship, then return to you."

Abraham put the wood on Isaac's shoulder, then he took
the knife and fire and they both went together. Isaac
said, "My father," Abraham said, "Here I am." The son asked,
"Here is the fire and wood for a sacrifice, but where is the lamb for
the sacrifice?" Abraham answered, "God will provide Himself for a
burnt offering."

*Lord, I praise You for providing Your son on Calvary*
*As the sacrifice for my sin.*

*This was the same mountain*
*Where Abraham offered His Son.*

Lord, they came to the place You showed them. Abraham built the altar
and placed the wood in its appropriate place. He then bound his

son Isaac, and laid him on the wood on the altar. Then Abraham took the knife in his hand to slay his son.

*Lord, when You took Your son up the same mountain,*
*You had Him bound to the cross to die as my substitute.*

*But You, Lord, didn't stop the sacrifice, as You stopped Abraham;*
*You allowed Your son to die for my sins.*

Lord, You called out of Heaven, "Abraham, Abraham." He answered again the same way, "Here I am." You said, "Don't lay your hand on Isaac; don't do him any harm, because I now know you fear Me, and you wouldn't withhold your son, your only son, from Me."

Abraham looked up and saw a ram caught in the bushes by its horns. Abraham went and sacrificed the ram as a burnt offering in place of his son.

Abraham called this place Jehovah-Jireh (The Lord Provided), as it is called this day, "On this mountain the Lord provided."

Lord, You called out of Heaven to Abraham a second time, saying, "I have sworn by Myself that because you have done this and not withheld your only son from me, that I will bless you and increase your descendants as the stars of Heaven and as the sand of the sea, and your descendants will possess the gates of their enemies and through your descendants I will bless all the nations of the earth—all because you obeyed Me."

Abraham and Isaac returned to the young men, and together they returned to Beer-sheba, and Abraham lived in Beer-sheba.

Abraham was told that Milcah had delivered children to his brother Nahor. She bore him eight children, the important one was Bethuel that bore Rebekah (Isaac's future wife).

Lord, You show us this picture in Scripture
>    Of a father's love for his earthly son,
>    Yet Abraham had a greater dedication to You.

May I have just as great allegiance to You
>    As did Abraham and may I have
>    The faith of Abraham to believe in You.

Amen.

## Background Story of
## Abraham's Faith Is Tested

### Genesis 22

Place: Mount Moriah (in the future city of Jerusalem) ⌒ Time: 1814 B.C.

God's people seldom have the solitude they seek. Just when everything is going well, God has another mountain to climb. When Abraham was walking one evening, God spoke to him,

*"Take your son—your only son Isaac—and offer him to Me on Mount Moriah. I know Isaac is the son you love but give him to Me as a burnt offering on one of the peaks that I will show you."*

Abraham wrestled with God as he walked back to the camp. His old ears recognized God's voice, and he understood what he heard. Abraham had decided to always do what God told him to do, but this was the most difficult thing he had ever been asked. Abraham thought, *I know Isaac was a miracle baby and that the Deliverer of the world will come through this boy...but why?*

Abraham couldn't understand why God would give him a son miraculously, then take the son away. Abraham had such deep faith in God's plan that he decided,

*If Isaac were to be sacrificed as a burnt offering, God would raise him from the dead.* So Abraham prayed to God as he returned home to the camp.

"Your will be done." As far as Abraham was concerned, his son had already been raised from the dead, even before the act was done.

"Sh-h-h," Abraham put a finger to his mouth as he awakened Isaac the next morning. "Get up...we have a three-day trip ahead." Abraham whispered so Sarah wouldn't hear. The servants had everything packed and ready to go. Abraham wanted to leave before Sarah awoke—he didn't want to explain his trip to her. He didn't want any hassle.

"We didn't wake anyone," Abraham told Isaac when they were a long distance away. "We're going to sacrifice to God," was all Abraham could tell Isaac as they began the journey. He couldn't tell his son what he knew. Three days later Abraham stopped to point, "There it is." He pointed up to Moriah, the mountain near the city of Salem. When they got ready to climb Moriah, Abraham told Isaac to carry the wood; he brought the fire and knife. He told the servants,

"Isaac and I will both go sacrifice at the top of the mountain," then with a great statement of faith, Abraham added, "then we will both come down together." The old man had walked with God for 75 years, Abraham knew God could be trusted, that's why he emphasized "both come down together."

Isaac and Abraham climbed slowly, it's difficult for a 125-year-old man to climb a mountain. When they stopped to rest, Isaac asked,

"I have the wood for the sacrifice and you have the fire," the boy looked in all directions before asking, "where is the animal?" Abraham had faced many difficult questions in his lifetime, but none as sensitive as this one. *How can I answer? Lord help me say the right thing,* he prayed.

Abraham then answered, "God will provide Himself a sacrifice." He didn't know how God would solve his dilemma, but Abraham still trusted God.

Father and son arrived at the top of Moriah. It took all the faith that Abraham could muster to go through with his part of the sacrifice. The old man had done it hundreds of times, but this time was epic-making, it was the moment for which he was born—this event determined his destiny. But Isaac also displayed faith, for he was much stronger than his feeble father—but Isaac submitted himself to God.

The wood was arranged and the fire was ready; Isaac lay on the altar. As Abraham drew the knife back, God shouted,

"ABRAHAM...ABRAHAM."

The old man dropped his knife hand to his side, then bowed his head in response, "Here am I." God answered,

"Now I know you fear God...because you have not withheld your son—your only son—from Me."

SNAP! At that moment Abraham heard the crackle of an animal caught in the bushes behind him. A ram was caught by its horns. The elderly father knew that God's timing was perfect. God had provided a sacrifice. He named the spot *Jehovah-Jirah*, "God Will Provide."

## My Time to Pray

- Lord, I know You expect total obedience to You, You don't want us to put anything in our lives in place of You. Maybe Abraham had put Isaac in Your place, I don't know. But You required explicit obedience from Abraham and You got it. Help me give that same kind of obedience to You.

- Lord, nothing much is said about Isaac in this story, he must have had great faith to let older Abraham do this to him. Give me the faith of Isaac.

- Lord, You are El Shaddai; I trust You to provide everything I need to grow in Christ and serve You.

# Genesis 23

# THE DEATH AND BURIAL OF SARAH

Sarah lived 127 years and she died in Hebron, also known as Kirjath-Arba, which is in Canaan. At first Abraham mourned inwardly, then everyone saw his outward grieving.

Abraham left the body of Sarah to go say to the sons of Heth,
"I am a foreigner, living as a stranger among you.
Let me have a burial site so I can bury my dead wife."

The sons of Heth said to Abraham, "Listen, we consider you a prince of God, choose any tomb to bury your wife. None of us would refuse you a tomb to bury your dead."

Abraham stood, then bowed before them in Near-Eastern fashion and said,
"If it is your decision to let me bury my dead, then ask Ephron, son of Zohar to give (sell) me the cave of Machpelah that he owns at the end of his land. Then I'll own a burial site for my dead."

Ephron was sitting among the sons of Heth, and answered Abraham in the presence of them. They were the ruling council of the area. He said, "No, I'll give you the field and the cave as a gift in the presence of the ruling council."

Abraham stood before the council and again bowed. Then he said to Ephron, "Listen to me please, I will pay the price of the field, I must pay for it, so the property will be mine."

Ephron answered, "The land is worth 400 shekels, but what is money between friends, just go bury your dead."

Abraham understood what Ephron wanted. So he counted out 400 shekels to Ephron before the council, the current coins accepted by the merchants.

The field of Ephron, along with the cave and trees, were deeded to Abraham in the presence of the council, so that Abraham could bury his dead. So Abraham buried Sarah his wife in the cave in the field of Machpelah, by Mamre, which is known as Hebron in the land of Canaan. The field and cave had been purchased by Abraham from the sons of Heth for a permanent burial site.

*Lord, no matter how much the Palestinians fight Israel over the Promised Land, no matter how much the United Nations and the powers of the world debate the future of Israel, I know You promised the land to Israel and one day they will occupy it in peace.*

Even so come, Lord Jesus.

# Genesis 24

## A Bride for Isaac

Lord, when Abraham was old and You had blessed him many ways, that he
said to Eliezer, his most trusted servant, who managed everything
for him, "Swear by the Lord God of Heaven and earth that you will
not let my son Isaac marry a Canaanite woman from around here,
but you will go to my relatives to find a wife for him."

Eliezer replied, "If the woman I find is not willing to come to this land to
marry Isaac, should I take your son Isaac there?

Abraham answered, "No, don't take my son Isaac to the land of my
relatives. The Lord God of Heaven who brought me from my father's
house and who led me away from the place where I was born, and
who spoke to me, and who swore that He would give this land
to me and my descendents; He will send His angel before you
to help bring a wife to my son. But if she will not come with
you, then you are no longer obligated to your oath."

Eliezer swore this oath with his hand.

*Lord, may I always be so trustworthy that people will*
*Believe my word whether I swore with an oath or not.*

Eliezer took camels for the trip and many gifts and headed toward
Mesopotamia, the place of Abraham's home. He arrived there at
evening time when young women came to draw water. He had his
camels kneel down.

Then Eliezer knelt to pray, "Lord God of my master, Abraham, give me
success today. I am here by the well where the young women come

to draw water. I will choose a woman and say, 'Please use your jar to draw water for me to drink.' If she answers 'Yes, I will draw water for you and your camels,' then I will know that she is the one for your servant Isaac."

Before Eliezer had finished praying, Rebekah, the daughter of Bethuel, son of Milcah, the wife of Abraham's brother, came to the well with a jar on her shoulder. She was beautiful and a virgin. She went to the spring and filled up her jar.

Eliezer ran to meet her and said, "May I please have a drink from your jar?" She lowered her jar from her shoulder and said, "Sir, please drink." When he was finished, she said, "I will draw enough for the camels." She poured water into the trough, and continue drawing water until all the camels had enough.

Lord, Eliezer watched her carefully but didn't say anything. He wondered if You, the Lord God, had guided him to the right girl.

*Lord, help me see Your hidden hand guiding me*
*Through the maze of this life.*

*When I know Your providence works in my circumstances,*

*I will praise You, as did old Eliezer.*

Eliezer gave the young girl some expensive jewelry and asked, "Whose daughter are you? And is there room in your father's house for us to spend the night?" She answered, "I am the daughter of Bethuel, the son of Milcah, who was born to Nahor." Then she added, "We have a room to lodge in and straw for the camels."

Lord, Eliezer bowed prostrate in worship before You, the Lord God, praying, "Blessed be You, Lord God of my master Abraham, because You didn't leave my master to fend for himself, but You guided me to the relatives of Abraham."

Rebekah ran to tell her family what happened. She lived with her brother Laban. When he saw the expensive jewelry that was given to her and heard his sister explain what happened at the well, Laban ran to meet Eliezer who was standing by the camels at the well. Laban said, "Come to my house, you who are blessed of the Lord God. Why are you waiting here when I have prepared a room for you and a place for your camels?"

Eliezer came into the house and unloaded the camels and gave straw to them. Water was brought for him to wash his feet, and for the men with him to do likewise.

When food was set before Eliezer, he said, "I won't eat until I tell you why I've come this far." Laban answered, "Please, tell us." Eliezer said, "I am Abraham's servant. The Lord God has blessed my master with many riches, having given him flocks, herds, camels and donkeys, silver and gold, men and women servants. His wife, Sarah, bore a son when she was old, and Abraham has given everything to his son. Abraham made me swear that I would not choose a wife for his son from among the Canaanites, but that I come here to Abraham's relatives to choose a wife for Isaac. When I answered Abraham, 'Suppose a woman will not come with me?' he said, 'The Lord God— in whose presence I live—will send His angel before you and you will find the perfect wife for my son. If she refuses to come with you, or if the family refuses to let her come, then you are released from this oath.'"

Eliezer told them, "Today when I came to the spring I prayed to the Lord God, 'If You are leading me, then as I stand by the spring, let the right girl give an answer positively when I ask, "Give me a drink of water," that she will say, "Yes, drink and I will draw water for your camels."' Even before I finished praying, Rebekah came with her jar on her shoulder. When I asked for a drink of water, she lowered her jar and told me, "Drink." Then she drew water for my camels. When I asked, 'Whose daughter are you?' she said she was the daughter of Bethuel, the son of Nahor to whom Milcah gave birth. Then I gave her the jewelry and bowed my head and prostrated myself on the ground before the Lord God and worshiped Him for leading me to the perfect girl for my master's son."

Then Eliezer asked, "If you intend to be merciful to my master Abraham, then let me know. If not, tell me so I can go search elsewhere."

Laban and Bethuel answered, "This thing is from the Lord God of Heaven, but we can't answer you yes or no. We can only do God's will. Rebekah is here, take her, let her be your master's wife as God has planned."

Lord, when Eliezer heard what they said, he again prostrated himself on the ground to worship You, the Lord God of Heaven.

Eliezer then presented gold, silver and clothing to Rebekah. Next, he gave valuable gifts to her mother and brother. Finally, he and the servants ate and drank and stayed the night.

When they got up in the morning, Eliezer said to the family, "Send me back to my master Abraham." But her mother and brother wanted Rebekah to stay a few days, at least ten saying, "After that, she can go."

Eliezer answered, "Don't hold me back since the Lord God has prospered me. Let me go to my master." The mother and brother said, "We will call Rebekah to see if she is ready to go." So they called Rebekah and asked her, "Will you go with this man?" She said, "I will." So they sent them away, Rebekah, her servant, Eliezer and the servants. They gave her the blessing,

"Our sister, may you become
The mother of countless millions.

May your descendents overcome
All their enemies."

Rebekah and her servants then mounted the camels to begin their journey with Eliezer, Abraham's servant.

Isaac had left the family home in Beer-Lahai-Roi and was living in the desert. As he was walking and meditating in the fields, he saw camels coming. At the same time Rebekah saw Isaac and asked, "Who is that man walking though the field to meet us?"

Eliezer replied, "It is my master." She quickly got off the camel and covered her face with her veil. Then the servant told Isaac the whole story of how he met Rebekah. Isaac took Rebekah into his mother's tent. She became his wife, and he loved her deeply. Thus Isaac was comforted after the death of his mother.

Amen.

### Background Story of
### A Bride for Isaac

---

### Genesis 24

Place: Near Ur of the Chaldees ⟋ Time: 1874 B.C.

"**E**liezer...come here!" the gravelly voice of Abraham called his trusted manager into his tent. "I want you to do the most important job that you've ever done."

Eliezer had never failed him. Abraham was going to send Eliezer on a long trip because he was too feeble to make the journey, and he dare not send Isaac. Abraham explained,

"My son Isaac must have a wife...a godly wife."

Abraham explained that the Canaanite women could not give birth to a son who was to be God's seed. Abraham knew the Canaanites were guilty of sexual sins—as though wickedness ran in their blood—no Canaanite woman could give birth to God's Deliverer to save the world. Abraham instructed Eliezer,

"Go back to my family in Ur of the Chaldees—on the Euphrates River— go to my people." Eliezer was entrusted with the task of finding a young woman worthy of Isaac and worthy to give birth to the children of God. Old Eliezer had a question,

"Suppose I can't find a wife...suppose the wife I find won't come...should I take Isaac back to Ur of the Chaldees?"

"No," was Abraham's firm answer. "God has called us to this land...God has given us this land...Isaac must not live among the Chaldeans...he must live here."

The old servant chose ten of Abraham's sturdiest camels. Eliezer packed well. The journey was one cycle of the moon—a month—to get there and another month to return. Eliezer knew that the young woman would require a dowry, so he packed clothes, gold, and many jewels. Choosing his strongest and bravest servants as protection, he set off on a journey into the unknown.

"Jehovah go with you..." was Abraham's parting prayer.

After one phase of the moon—a month—Eliezer's caravan arrived near the village where Abraham had lived some 90 years earlier. The old servant looked about for ancient landmarks that Abraham had described, but he didn't recognize anything. Houses were destroyed in earthquakes and some people had torn them down to build bigger houses. However, the old servant thought, *The well will be at the same place.* He went to the well in the town, knowing that young ladies would come to draw water in the cool of the evening. Everywhere he looked he saw young girls of marriageable age, and he thought, *Which one?* There were so many young girls from so many families, and he thought further, *Who knows the spirit of a young girl?* Bowing with his face to the ground, he prayed,

"Lord Jehovah, guide me...guide me to the right young woman...I'm going to ask a young woman to draw water for me...may Your choice be the one who offers to draw water for my camels."

As old Eliezer arose from his knees, a young girl approached the well, took a water pot from her shoulder and attached it to a rope. She then lowered it into the black hole in the earth until the refreshing splash of water was heard. Old Eliezer quickly walked to the well,

"Would you draw water for me?"

She dropped her black eyes in humility, as though it were a privilege to serve the old man. Her nimble fingers quickly pulled the water pot to the surface, and with both hands she held out the vessel to the older man.

"Drink my lord."

Eliezer tipped the water pot to the sky and let the refreshing water flow down his parched throat. More than quenching his spiritual thirst, the Spirit of God told him this was the one. He uttered a prayer, *"Thank You, Lord, for leading me here."*

"I'll draw for your camels," she quickly dropped the water pot back into the well. Then pointing to the trough, "Bring your camels here, and I will water them until they are full."

*"She's not only a hard worker,"* thought Eliezer, *"she's beautiful."*

A lock of black hair curled from under her shawl and circled her cheek. The girl's olive skin was the same texture as Sarah's skin, so Eliezer nodded his approval. When she finished, Eliezer held out a gift for her, golden earrings and two bracelets.

"These gifts are for you." Then the wise Eliezer looking to see if she had a spirit of hospitality asked,

"Do you have a place for us to lodge tonight?"

The bare-footed young girl flew home to tell her brother Laban what had happened. When the older brother saw the earrings and bracelets, he immediately ran to the well and in a loud show of hospitality insisted,

"Come to my home..." pointing down the street, "bring your camels and herdsman. I have straw for tonight and a place to sleep."

A little while later, the meal was set on the table. Laban was ready to feed his guests a wholesome but simple meal. But Eliezer interrupted the invitation,

"Before we eat, I must tell you why I am here." Eliezer announced, "My master Abraham is your relative. You are family..."

The candle on the table flickered in the faces of the household as they listened intently to old Eliezer's story. He told how Abraham had sent him to this country to find a wife. He told them that Abraham served the one true God and that God had given Abraham the land—the Promise Land—that would one day belong to the seed of Abraham. He told them that Abraham was very wealthy and that the bride of Isaac would become the mother of the Deliverer who would save the world. But most importantly, he told of praying by the well for the guidance of Jehovah and how he asked for a sign that the girl would not only give him water, but also water his camels. Then he said,

"Rebekah is that girl, because she did what I asked of God."

Laban was deeply impressed with the story. He nodded his head as old Eliezer told him of God's leading. The jewels and riches enticed him. He knew the dowry would be big, and it would be his. The old servant ended his explanation by saying,

"I have been on the road for thirty days, and the Lord has led me here."

The festive meal went late into the evening. Eliezer told stories of Abraham's conquest and how God had spoken to him. Not to be outdone, Laban told his stories of life in their city. He knew about Abraham, even though he had been gone for 90 years. A few people remembered the faith of Abraham, they remembered that Abraham believed in the

God who created the moon, not the moon god at the top of the ziggurat in Ur of the Chaldees.

After the meal was over, Eliezer smiled then clapped his wrinkled hands. At that signal, the servants brought in a chest. Reaching over, Eliezer's shriveled finger lifted the lid.

Gold, silver, and jewels sparkled in the subdued candlelight. *She will say yes,* Eliezer whispered to himself. Then lifting an earring, the one Rebekah admired, he handed the earrings to Rebekah. As she tried them on, old Eliezer knew, *She will go with me.*

As the family retired that night to sleep, Laban dreamed of his riches and slept comfortably. Rebekah thought of her new husband and dreamed visions of love. Eliezer thought of a job well done and slept soundly.

The morning sun poured in through the cracks in the wooden door. Eliezer was dressed early, and walked into the great room of the house. Having his strength refreshed with a good night of sleep and his mission accomplished, Eliezer was ready to go home. He announced to Laban and the family,

"I want to leave today…Abraham and Isaac wait for me, and I must take them the good news."

"Not today…" Laban protested. "Let us enjoy Rebekah for ten days…" Laban let his words trail off into nothing. To Laban, ten days was the first step in a number of delays. He wanted to keep Rebekah at home as long as possible. Also, he knew that the longer Eliezer and his servants stayed in his home, the more gifts he might receive from them. So he pleaded,

"Give us just ten days…"

"No, I want to leave today."

"Let's ask the girl," Laban suggested. "Let Rebekah make the decision."

But Laban didn't know that Rebekah had dreamed all night about the man with whom she was going to live the rest of her life. She was not looking back at her past home life. She was looking across the desert to the Promise Land. She was looking to her promised love. She immediately said,

"I will go today."

It was not long before Rebekah was prepared to leave. Her bags were tied tightly to the camel, and two servant girls were sent with her. Since she was going to be the princess of a nomadic tribe—a woman of importance—she needed servants to take care of her in the difficult days ahead.

That evening after the sun sank over the western desert, Rebekah and Eliezer sat in front of the smoldering, red coals of a dying fire. They had eaten their dinner. This was her first time alone with Eliezer. She had some questions.

"What does he look like?" She blushed, not wanting Eliezer to think her immature.

"What does he like to do?" A second blush rolled over the first.

That evening around the fire, old Eliezer told stories of how Abraham taught Isaac to fish, to hunt game, and the great, white stallion that he rode. Eliezer described Isaac's wise handling of people, and Rebekah liked what she heard about Isaac's tender compassion about his mother's death. But most of all Eliezer told Rebekah that Isaac loved God and followed the one true God, who created everything. Rebekah responded,

"I want to follow the Lord also."

After 30 days they approached Hebron, and they began looking for Abraham's camp.

"We'll see it in the morning," Eliezer said.

But unknown to the two of them, Isaac anticipated their return. Each evening he went into the fields to meditate on the glory of God that he saw in the heavens. As Adam had walked with God in the cool of the day, and every other Godly man had fellowshipped with God in the evening, so Isaac went out into the fields to meditate on God. In the distance through the red setting sun, Isaac saw ten camels coming. He couldn't be sure that it was Eliezer, but his heart wanted it to be his bride. So he quickened his steps to meet the caravan.

"Who is that man coming toward us?" Rebekah asked Eliezer.

The old servant smiled; he knew the passion of love when seeking one another. He knew that it was Isaac looking for his wife. He answered,

"It is my master...it is Isaac."

Quickly Rebekah placed a veil on her face, for it was the custom of unmarried ladies that her husband not see her until the marriage was consummated. Isaac and Rebekah were married shortly thereafter. They made a pledge to follow the Lord and to love each other. Isaac took her to his tent and loved her.

## My Time to Pray

- Lord, thank You for working through the details of circumstances to lead Eliezer to the right girl for Isaac; I trust You to work all circumstances in my life to Your glory.

- Lord, may I always praise and thank You for Your guiding hand in my life, as did Eliezer.

- Lord, I thank You for the willingness of Rebekah to quickly and willingly do Your will. May I always respond to You as she did.

# Genesis 25:1-34

## THE DEATH OF ABRAHAM
## AND
## ESAU SOLD HIS BIRTHRIGHT TO JACOB

Abraham married Keturah after Sarah died and she gave birth to Zimran, Jokshan, Medan, Midian, Ishbak, and Shuah. Jokshan had two sons, Sheba and Dedan. Dedan's children were called Asshurites, Letushites, and Leummites. Midian's children were Ephah, Epher, Hanoch, Abidah, and Eldaah.

Abraham left all his possessions to his son Isaac. But before he died, he gave some possessions to the sons of his concubines, then sent them away from Isaac.

Abraham was 175 years old when he died. His sons Isaac and Ishmael buried him in the cave of Machpelah next to Sarah his wife. This was in the field he purchased from the Hittites. Then God blessed Isaac who settled near the oasis Beer-Lahai-Roi in the desert.

Ishmael, the son of Abraham by Hagar had 12 sons: Nebajoth, Kedar, Adbeel, Mibsam, Mishma, Dumah, Massa, Hadar, Tema, Jetur, Naphish, and Kedemah. These 12 sons became heads of 12 tribes that were known by their names. They were scattered across the country from Hariloh, to Shur—east of Egypt—and they camped close to each other. Ishmael died when he was 137 years old.

Isaac married Rebekah when he was 40 years old. She was the daughter of Bethuel from the land between the Tigris and Euphrates Rivers, the sister of Laban. Because Rebekah was childless, Isaac pleaded with God for a child. God answered his prayer and Rebekah became pregnant with twins. Because the two struggled with each other in the womb, she asked God, "Why is this happening to me?"

Lord, You told her the sons in her womb were two powerful nations but rival nations, "One will be stronger than the other, and the children of the older will serve the children of the younger." When the twins were born, the first baby was covered with red hair, so they called him Esau, which means "hair." The second was born with his hand holding Esau's heal, so they called him Jacob which means "grasping." Isaac was 60 years old when his twins were born.

The boys became more different as they grew older. Esau loved to hunt in the open field. Jacob stayed around the tents. Isaac loved Esau because of the game he brought home to eat, but Rebekah loved Jacob.

One day Esau came back from hunting, exhausted and hungry. Jacob had some stew cooking on the fire. Esau asked for some of the red stew to eat (because of this incident Esau was also named Edom, meaning red). Jacob answered, "Only if you will give me the birthright (spiritual leadership of the family) for it." Esau reasoned that he was starving to death, what good was a birthright if he were dead? Then Jacob made his brother swear to him on the spot. So Esau did it, giving Jacob the birthright. Then Jacob gave him something to eat, and Esau went on his way. This showed how little value Esau put on the birthright.

*Lord, may my children and grandchildren realize the imperative Nature of their spiritual heritage that is given them.*

*May they place supreme value on their walk with You and may they always guard their integrity and faith.*

Amen.

## Background Story of
## the Death of Abraham and Esau Sold His Birthright to Jacob

### Genesis 25:1-34

Place: The Southern Desert ↶ Time: 1812 B.C.

Isaac and Rebekah had been living for several years in their own Bedouin tent on the edge of Abraham's camp. He loved her as much as she loved him, so much so that they spent little time with Abraham in his tent. But no wonder, Abraham had married Keturah after Sarah died. Old Abraham was in love again. The servants laughed at the spring in their master's step and the gleam in his eye. Was it possible that Abraham approaching 150 years in age could be young again at heart?

"Your father Abraham has another baby…" Rebekah said wishfully to Isaac. "They named this boy Medan." Rebekah stared at the dying coals in the fire. She didn't want her love for Isaac to die, but she felt something dreadfully wrong in her body. She should have had a child by now. She asked herself, *Am I barren?* Not having a child caused Rebekah to doubt her womanhood; and to make matters worse, Keturah was giving old Abraham one son after another.

Abraham and Keturah continued to have sons, but none for Isaac and Rebekah. Finally the young couple talked about their fears—what they were afraid to admit—Rebekah could not have children. To make matters worse, Abraham gave Isaac the birthright, the Messianic line was to go through him. Except there was no son to carry on the heritage. Isaac often walked in the field to meditate on God. One night he stopped, looked at the sky, and asked specifically,

"Lord…give me a son."

The prayer was simple, and yet filled with faith to overcome physical barriers. Isaac asked for God to do for him what He did for his father

Abraham. Isaac didn't know what to pray, and he didn't know how to tell God to overcome barriers; he just prayed,

"Lord, give me a son." Because God sometimes answers abundantly above all that is asked, Rebekah joyfully conceived, but her conception was double...unknown to her, Rebekah would give birth to twins.

The pregnancy was agonizing, almost from the beginning. Rebekah thought it was only one baby that constantly kicked...poked...and leaped within her womb. She couldn't sleep; she couldn't keep food down; she was constantly uncomfortable. Finally Rebekah had as much as she could stand. She prayed,

"Lord, why am I having difficulties?" She continued to pray. "You gave me this child in answer to prayer, why am I having such a hard pregnancy?"

God told Rebekah that there were two children in her womb. These two sons would become two nations; one would be much stronger than the other, and the two nations would constantly fight just as the two boys were constantly struggling in the womb. Then the Lord told her that the older boy would serve the younger one.

On the eventful day when the labor pains became intense, Isaac was sitting on a stool in front of his tent. The midwife was helping Rebekah in the tent. Isaac could hear the moans, but he could do nothing but pray. Finally, he heard it.

"Slap!" followed by "Waa...waaa..."

Isaac waited for the second slap, because he knew there were two boys in the womb. Then he heard it.

"Slap!" followed by the inevitable "Waa...waaa..."

"Your first baby has red hair on his body, like a grown man..." the midwife came out to tell Isaac who was anxiously waiting at the tent door. They wouldn't let the father go in until the babies were cleaned. Isaac yelled out,

"Call the first boy Esau." There's something about a first-born son that makes a man stand tall. "Call him Esau because it means *red*."

"The second boy came out holding the heel of the first boy," the midwife told Isaac, "the second boy wouldn't let go of the first one." Then the midwife asked,

"What is the name of the second?"

"Jacob..." quickly Isaac laughed, "the name *Jacob* means someone who is trying to take another's place. This second boy grabbed his brother's heel and wants to take his place."

Inside the tent Rebekah heard what her husband said and agreed with the name Jacob. She remembered that God had told her,

"The older boy will serve the younger one."

Isaac and Rebekah never intended to make the boys hate one another, but father and mother steered the boys into a lifestyle that reflected the parent's ambition for each. Isaac naturally taught his muscular son Esau to use a sling, "Hit that tree with this stone," he told his oldest son. But it was only natural that the father pushed Esau into physical exploits. Esau was a large, hairy man, stronger than any of the other servants his age, with quick athletic ability to use the bow, sling, and he was adept at trapping animals for food.

Jacob was just the opposite, quiet, withdrawn, and sensitive—like his mother—Jacob stayed with his mother around the tent. Because he did not have any body hair, some called Jacob a "smooth man." Jacob didn't care for the outdoors; hanging around the tent, he became an outstanding cook. He experimented with peppers, spices, and he wanted things seasoned just right. Whereas Esau wanted meat—a hunk of roasted meat—Jacob wanted it sliced, steamed, seasoned and tasty. Jacob learned to cook from his mother, the way her people back in Mesopotamia prepared food.

As Isaac got older, diabetes set in. His eyesight began to fade, and he lost circulation in his arms and feet. He could no longer go hunting with his son Esau. His diabetes confined him to the tent, and the greatest thrill to the old man was feasting on roasted venison that Esau, his first-born son, had provided.

As Esau became more productive, the deer herds thinned out; Esau had to go on longer and longer trips just to find venison for his father. Then the eventful day came when he saw no game, he went farther than usual, and returned home exhausted. Esau's hunting bag was empty. As he approached the camp, Jacob was stirring peppers into a pot of red beans, a few chunks of meat simmered in the broth. The aroma of the seasoned meat reached Esau on the outskirts of the camp, his nostrils flared. Never had he smelled meat that enticing, enhanced by red peppers and his famished appetite.

"Gimme some of that stew," Esau demanded, sitting down near Jacob's fire.

"Why should I give you any of my delicacies?" Jacob snapped back with an added conviction, "You never give me any of the venison you kill. You give it all to Father." Then to add to his irritation, Jacob poured out the challenge, "You're Father's pet."

"No, I'm not."

"He gives you everything…"

"No, he doesn't."

Esau spit on the ground and cursed at his father's special treatment explaining, "Father can't do anything for me now—he's sick. I do everything for him…"

Jacob had never heard his older twin speak irreverently of his father. Jacob always wanted the approval of his father that Esau had, but never got it. Jacob wanted the blessing of his father on his life, just as Abraham had blessed his father, Isaac. Jacob was envious that Esau would carry on his father's name. With an evil strategy in mind, Jacob scooped a bowl of bean stew slowly, then sat down beside Esau, smacking his lips after each spoonful, "Mmmm…Mmmm…good."

"I'll die if I don't get some of that stew…" Esau lusted for the beans in the pot.

"You can have all the stew you want..." Jacob's eyes squinted in anticipation, "if you'll give me your birthright."

"Why do you want my birthright?"

"Why do you want my bean stew?"

"All right...you can have it." Esau dropped his shoulders, agreeing to give Jacob the most prized inheritance in life—his birthright.

"That includes the walking stick," Jacob eyed the most prized possession of his father—the family rod. On the top was carved the signet of Abraham, he's the father of them all. Next was carved the signet of Isaac. Both boys had heard their father tell when the signet of Isaac was carved on the walking stick.

*One day, my signet will be carved there,* Jacob silently thought to himself. As of yet, Jacob's deceitful nature disqualified him from the stick, yet his desire to be the spiritual head of the family was not lost to God's intention.

As the two boys argued over red bean stew, God saw them arguing over the spiritual destiny of his people, the Hebrew nation. Esau was first born but cared little for God's people; Jacob was the fleshly son who deceived everyone, but he wanted God's blessing. It's as though God said, "One day Jacob will grow into spiritual maturity."

Then the eternal destiny of two boys was decided over something as meaningless as red bean stew. So Jacob demanded,

"Swear." Jacob drove a hard bargain. "You must swear eternally that the birthright is mine that I'll carry on the family name that the Deliverer will come through my children."

"I swear."

That day Jacob didn't get the walking stick, but one day it would be his and the signet of Jacob would be carved under his father, Isaac.

## My Time to Pray

- Lord, such great decisions are made over little things like red bean stew. Help me realize every decision determines my destiny and help me always decide with eternity in mind.

- Lord, You are not controlled by time as I am. You are now present at all times from the beginning to the end. Guide me so I'll become a greater spiritual person than I am right now. Help me grow in Christ.

- Lord, children are Your heritage to all of us, I pray for my children, grandchildren, and great grandchildren. May they follow You, Lord, more than I do.

- Lord, I'm so controlled by this earthly life, help me develop eternal values, and help me see Your plan for my life.

# Genesis 26:1-35

## ISAAC DECEIVES ABIMELECH

A famine spread across the land, just as during Abraham's life. Isaac moved to Gerar, where Abimelech was king of the Philistines.

Lord, You told Isaac not to go to Egypt, which was the place Abraham got into trouble. You told Isaac to stay among the Philistines and that You would bless him and be with him. You reminded Isaac of the promise that all the land would eventually be his and his descendents. You said, "I will make your descendents as numerous as the stars in the skies and I will give them this land, and through your offspring I will bless all nations. I will do this because Abraham obeyed all I told him to do."

Isaac stayed among the Philistines, but he committed the same sin of his father Abraham. When the Philistines asked Isaac about his wife Rebekah, he said, "She is my sister." Isaac thought they would kill him to take his wife because she was very beautiful.

After Isaac was there for a time, Abimelech looked out a window and saw Isaac caressing Rebekah. Abimelech charged Isaac, "I see she is your wife, why did you tell me she is your sister?'

Isaac told Abimelech that it was because he was afraid they would kill him to get her.

Lord, You protected Isaac because Abimelech only lectured Isaac, "You have done a terrible thing to us. Someone could have slept with her and you would have caused us to do a terrible sin." Then Abimelech told everyone, "Anyone who hurts Isaac or Rebekah will die."

*Lord, thank You for protecting Your people from harm*
  *Even when they don't have faith that You can do it.*

*Thank You for keeping the line of Messiah from being polluted,*
  *Even though Your people didn't guard it as they should.*

Lord, You blessed Isaac so that he had a great harvest,
  At least 100 times more grain than he planted. He became rich with
  a large number of sheep, goats, cattle, and many servants.

When the Philistines became jealous of Isaac, they filled in his wells with
  dirt; these were the wells dug by Abraham's servants. Abimelech
  told Isaac to leave because he had become too prosperous for them.

Isaac set up camp in the Gerar Valley and reopened the wells that Abraham
  his father had dug because the Philistines had filled them in after
  Abraham died. The workmen discovered an artesian well. But the
  herdsmen of Gerar quarreled with Isaac's herdsmen claiming it was
  their well. So Isaac named the well "Argument."

Isaac was not a fighter, so he moved and dug another well and called it
  Rehoboth (a large open space) and declared, "Here is where the
  Lord has made room for us to prosper."

Lord, then Isaac moved to the oasis Beer-sheba and You appeared to him
  that night and promised, "I am the God of Abraham, your father.
  Don't be afraid because I will be with you, and bless you, and give
  you many descendents because of my promise to Abraham. It was
  there Isaac built an altar to sacrifice to You and he pitched his tent
  there. Isaac called on You and dug a well there.

Abimelech, the king, and Phichol, the army commander, came to see
  Isaac. Isaac asked, "Why have you come, you've been hostile to
  me?" They answered, "We see God is with you. Let's make a peace
  pact that you will not harm us and we will not harm you. We

have not harmed you but sent you on your way in peace. Now God has blessed you."

Isaac served them a banquet and they ate and drank together as part of preparing to make a treaty. Early the next morning, they swore that they would not attack each other.

Late that day Isaac's servants told him they had struck water in the well they were digging. So Isaac named the well Shevah (oath) and it is known to this day as Beer-sheba (the seven wells of an oath).

When Esau was 40 years old, he married Judith, a Hittite. Next, he married Basemath, also a Hittite, but Esau's wives irritated Isaac and Rebekah.

*Lord, You blessed Isaac because he was a peace-loving man;*
*You made even his enemies respect him.*

*Teach me to turn the other cheek to receive your blessings*
*As You blessed Isaac.*

*Teach me to fight (Genesis 14) when it is appropriate*
*As You blessed Abraham, the warrior.*

Amen.

# Genesis 27:1-46

# JACOB STEALS ESAU'S BLESSING

When Isaac got old, he also could barely see. He called Esau his oldest son and told him, "I have gotten old and expect to die any day soon. Take your bow and arrows and go hunt some wild game for me. Cook it spicy, the way I like it and let's have an important feast before I die. I want to give you the family blessings (financial inheritance)."

Rebekah was listening to everything her husband said. She quickly said to her son Jacob, "Your father is planning on giving the financial blessing to your brother Esau. He has gone hunting for wild game and when he comes back, they'll have a big feast where your father will pledge to Esau the family inheritance in the Lord's presence." Rebekah told her son her plan, "You go get two choice young kids and I'll cook it spicy the way your father likes it. You carry the meal into your father and get the blessing instead of Esau. Your father is about to die and you should have the family inheritance."

Jacob answered his mother, "Father won't believe I'm Esau; my brother is a hairy man, I am smooth-skinned. When he touches me, he'll realize I'm trying to trick him. He will curse me and not bless me."

Rebekah said, "The curse is my responsibility! Go do what I told you." So Jacob got the goats and Rebekah prepared a spicy meal, the way Isaac liked. Then Rebekah took Esau's clothes and had Jacob put them on. Finally, she prepared a tightly fitted goat's skin coat to cover Jacob's arms and shoulders.

Jacob took the meal into the tent and said, "Here is the food, my father,"
Isaac answered, "I am ready to eat, who are you? Esau or Jacob?"
Jacob answered; "I am Esau your first born. I have the meal you
wanted. Now sit down, enjoy the meal. Then pledge to me the
financial inheritance of the family."

Isaac said, "My son, how did you get it done so quickly?" Jacob answered,
"God brought the game to me." Isaac answered, "Come close to me
so I can touch you, that way I'll know you are my son Esau. As
Jacob approached his father, Isaac touched him and said, "You
have Jacob's voice, but Esau's arms." Then Isaac pledged to
Jacob the family inheritance, and asked, "Are you really my son
Esau?" Jacob answered, Yes, I am Esau."

Isaac asked for the food saying, "I will eat the food, then I'll make the
blessing." Isaac ate the meal and drank the wine his son served
him. Then the father said, "Come and kiss me, my son." When
Jacob kissed him, Isaac smelled his clothes and was convinced it
was Esau. He said,

*My son has the smell of an open field. May the blessing of the Lord*
*God be upon you.*

*May God always give you plenty of dew for crops and a prosperous*
*Harvest for food and wine.*

*May many nations become your servants,*
*May you become lord over your kin.*

*Cursed be everyone who curses you,*
*And blessed be everyone who blesses you.*

As soon as Isaac promised Jacob the family inheritance—the blessing—
Jacob left his father's tent. He had just left when Esau came in with
the food he had prepared. He said, "Father, come eat the meal you
requested, and then pledge to me the blessing." Isaac said, "Who

are you?" Esau answered, "I am your son Esau, your first born." Isaac trembled uncontrollably and said, "Who was it that brought me spicy wild game? I ate it and pledged to him the financial blessing of the family. It's an irrevocable bond. I can't take it back."

When Esau heard it, he cried loudly, "My brother Jacob came in deceitfully and stole the blessing. His name—Deceiver—fits him well. He's stolen from me two times. First, Jacob took my birthright (spiritual leadership), now he's taken my blessing (financial inheritance). Then Esau asked his father, "Have you any blessing for me?"

Isaac answered, "I have made Jacob lord over you and I have given him all our kinsmen as servants. I have promised him grain, and wine in harvest. What else can I give to you?"

Esau cried, "Do you only have one blessing? Please bless me also." Esau continued crying, and his father answered,

*Your home will be the land on which you live,*
  *You will live by the dew that makes the earth rich.*

*You will live by the sword*
  *And you will serve your brother a long time,*
  *Then you will break his yoke and be free.*

Esau hated his brother Jacob because he stole his father's inheritance. Esau plotted, "The time will soon be over for mourning for my father. Then I'll kill Jacob." Rebekah heard what Esau was planning to do. She sent for Jacob and told him Esau's plot. She told her son, "Go, escape to my brother Laban beyond the Euphrates River and live with him a little while until Esau's anger goes away. When he forgets about all this, I'll send for you."

Then Rebekah said to Isaac, "These local women make me sick. I'd rather die than see Jacob marry one of them." That's how she planned to protect Jacob by sending him back to her family.

*Lord, this family is split by hatred and dissension;*
  *Give me a family that loves one another and loves You.*

*I know that I'm a part of Your family*
  *And that You love me and will take care of me.*

*I count on Your love to satisfy me*
  *And Your power to protect me.*

Amen.

## Background Story of
## Jacob Steals Esau's Blessing

### Genesis 27:1-46

Place: Southern Desert ❧ Time: 1759 B.C.

Isaac, the bed-ridden father had a special message for his first-born son, Esau. Rebekah overheard the servant giving the message to Esau, and she quickly ran to the back of Isaac's tent to eavesdrop on the conversation. She picked up some leather hides, pretending to clean them; but she was really listening to the conversation between her husband and oldest son. Isaac, crippled with arthritis and blinded by diabetes, said to Esau,

"I think I'm going to die…" Rebekah was not alarmed at that statement. Isaac was depressed over his physical condition and had complained frequently about dying. Isaac told his son, "I want one last meal of venison killed by you…we will eat it together."

"I'll do it," Esau replied. The blinded father could not see the indifference in Esau's eyes. If Isaac could see, he would have realized the lack of concern that his son had for him. Esau did what his father asked out of obligation, not out of love. As he was leaving the tent, Isaac said,

"I'll pledge to you the family inheritance when you return."

Esau grinned a fiendish smile. He knew that the financial blessing meant a double portion of the inheritance. He would get twice as much money as his brother Jacob. He knew that when his father died, he would control the estate, and could cheat Jacob out of everything. He would be a wealthy man.

As Esau left the tent, he was thinking, *Let Jacob have the spiritual blessing, let his name be carved on the walking stick, I'll get the money.* Esau ran quickly to get his bow and arrow and to find some deer. But Rebekah also heard, and she ran quickly to find her son Jacob, telling him,

"Hurry," she prodded him into action, "we must act quickly before Esau gets the blessing. If Esau gets the financial blessing, you won't inherit anything."

Rebekah knew that her younger son had stolen the spiritual birthright from Esau with a pot of red beans, but that didn't alarm her. She remembered that God promised when the boys were in the womb that the older would serve the younger. Now she wanted to make sure that Jacob got the money. She explained her plan to Jacob,

"Kill a lamb, we'll cook it immediately; we'll use spices so your father will think it is venison..."

"What about my arms and shoulders?" the young son Jacob complained. "When Father puts his hands on me, he'll know I'm a smooth man."

"I'll sew a goat-skin coat with long sleeves. Your father will think he's touching his hairy son Esau."

Rebekah and her son worked feverishly, praying that Esau might not find the venison before they could complete their deceptive task. While the lamb was being roasted and seasoned, Rebekah's nimble fingers sewed the goat-skin coat, and with laces she pulled it tightly around his arms, shoulders, and chest. As Rebekah ran her fingers over the arms and shoulders of her son, she felt the hair of Esau. As soon as the meat was done, Jacob carried the savory dish to his father, his arms covered with false hair.

"Who's there?" Isaac asked.

"I'm Esau," the younger brother lied.

"Your voice doesn't sound like Esau," old Isaac's voice trembled.

"Your hearing has gone bad with your eyesight," Jacob lied to his father. Then to drive his point home, he added, "Also your voice quivers, and you don't sound like Esau."

"Come closer, and let me feel you." Isaac put his hand on the shoulders of Jacob, feeling the hairy texture of the skin. He knew his fingers would not mislead him. Then in a moment of weakness cried,

"The arms are Esau's, but the voice is Jacob's."

Jacob knelt before his father, and with Isaac's hands on his head, he received the pledge of financial blessing. Isaac said,

> *"May God give you the dew of heaven and the fatness of the earth and always plenty of corn to eat and wine to drink. May many people serve you, and may nations bow down before you, and may you be lord over your brothers. Let everyone who curses you be cursed of God, and let everyone who blesses you be blessed of God."*

After Isaac had finished eating the seasoned meat, Jacob cleaned up the utensils and quickly left the tent. Scarcely was Jacob back to his own tent when Esau appeared with his savory venison for his father to eat. Entering the tent, he realized what happened when his father asked,

"Who are you?"

"I am Esau, your first-born son. I have come to receive your pledge of the blessing."

Isaac trembled with fear—he was afraid of God—for Isaac knew that Jacob was God's choice to receive both the spiritual birthright and the financial blessing. In selfish determination, Isaac had planned to disobey God and bless his favorite son Esau. But now God had intervened, and

Isaac's hands shook not with diabetic weakness, but with fear that he had almost thwarted God's plan. Isaac answered,

"I cannot bless you with the family inheritance because I have pledged it to your brother."

Isaac explained to Esau that Jacob had brought in seasoned meat, and when he felt his hairy arms, he was deceived into thinking he felt Esau.

"Oh no, my father...," Esau could feel his wealth slipping between his fingers. All of the money that should have been his was going to his brother.

"Take it back from Jacob," Esau begged.

"I can't do that." The aged Isaac was weaker now than he had been all day. His spirit was crushed. With a whisper that was barely heard, the quivering voice said, "The blessing is irrevocable."

"Do you not have one blessing for me?" Esau asked.

Esau left his father's tent in a rage, cursing Jacob...cursing his father...cursing Jehovah for the turn of events, not caring if any heard him; he promised,

"I'll kill Jacob...soon as father dies...I'll kill Jacob with my own hands."

Rebekah overheard the threat, and she knew her son's temper. She knew Esau's strong will, that he would kill her son Jacob. Rebekah told her youngest son that he would have to go away to Mesopotamia, to Laban her brother. There Jacob would be safe. What Rebekah didn't know was that she would die before Jacob would return. She would never see her favorite son again.

## My Time to Pray

- Lord, when there's money on the table, families fight. Teach me to seek the spiritual blessing in life, and trust You to take care of me financially.

- Lord, it's never right to do the wrong thing to accomplish a right purpose. May I never be deceitful as was Rebekah and Jacob.

- Lord, the money Jacob sought to get by lying was lost to him, he never got the money and he never saw his mother again. Help me understand the consequences of dishonesty.

- Lord, old Isaac was deceived because he was deceiving his family and doing his selfish thing. I know the consequences of my sin are punished by the crimes I've committed. Keep me honest with all, but most of all with You.

- Lord, family should never be deceitful, angry, and rebellious. Help me love my physical brothers and sisters and make me lovable so they in turn will love me.

# Genesis 28

# GOD CALLS A DECEIVER TO HIMSELF

Isaac prepared to send his son Jacob away by blessing him
and saying, "Do not marry a Hittite girl, but go beyond
the Euphrates River to the house of Bethuel, your grandfather, and
marry one of the daughters of Laban, your mother's brother.

Lord, Isaac asked for You, El Shaddai, to bless Jacob and make him
fruitful, and give him many children so they become a nation.
Isaac asked for You to give to Jacob the blessing You promised
Abraham, so that he would possess the land promised to Abraham.

Isaac sent Jacob away to the Euphrates Valley to live with his uncle Laban,
his mother's brother. When Esau heard that Isaac had blessed
Jacob and told him not to marry a Hittite woman, Esau visited his
uncle Ishmael, the son of Abraham and Hagar, and married one of
his daughters. Esau did it because his father despised the women
of the tribes around them. His new wife was named Mahaleth.

Jacob left Beer-sheba in the desert and traveled toward Haran. At
sundown, he set up camp in the hill country for the night. He took a
stone for his head, and lay down to sleep. In his dream he saw a
ladder reaching from Heaven to the earth, with Your angels going
up and down that ladder.

Lord, Jacob saw You standing at the top of the ladder, saying, "I am
the Lord God of your grandfather Abraham, and the God of your
Father Isaac. I will give you the land on which you are living
to you and your descendants. Your descendents will be as
numerous as the grains of sand on the earth. You will expand to the

West, East, North, and South. All the people of the earth will be blessed by your descendants. I will be with You and protect you wherever you go. One day I will bring you back safely to this land. I won't leave you until I have done everything I've promised.

Jacob awoke from his sleep and said, "Truly You, Lord, are in this place and I didn't realize it." Then Jacob became afraid because he realized he was at the door to Heaven—an entrance to the house of God.

Lord, Jacob awoke early in the morning and stood the stone up that was under his head up and poured olive oil on it and named the place Bethel (House of God) even though the place was originally called Luz.

Lord, Jacob vowed to You, "If You, God, will be with me and protect me as I travel, and give me bread to eat and clothes to wear, so that I can return to my father's house, then You, God, will be my Lord, and this stone will be the place of Your house, and I will give You 10 percent of everything You give to me.

*Lord, it's an awesome thing to encounter You and face Your promises*
*As Jacob faced You at Bethel.*

*May I live holy as You command, and may I pray as I should,*
*And I will give You 10 percent of all You give me.*

Amen.

## Background Story of
## God Calls a Deceiver to Himself

### Genesis 28

Place: Near Hebron ↶ Time: 1759 B.C.

B efore dawn Jacob left his father's home with nothing but the walking stick. His father Isaac had given Jacob the family genealogical rod—not Esau—because Isaac realized the promise of God, "The elder will serve the younger."

Jacob fingered the prized walking stick, again rubbing his fingers over Abraham's signet. Then he looked again at his father's signet. Jacob asked, "When will I carve my signet in the family rod?" Even though Jacob got the staff with deceit, he treated the walking stick with respect. It was his most prized possession. It was his only possession. He decided to wait until his father, Isaac, died before carving his name on the stick.

The faint glow behind the Eastern mountain barely gave him light to see. He headed toward the land of his grandfather Abraham, and beyond that to the home of his mother, Rebekah. At first his stride was brisk and purposeful; he was running away from his twin brother. He was escaping with his life. But also, he was excited about his future in Mesopotamia. But as the day grew hotter and longer, his steps halted with doubts. He wondered, *When will I see my mother again?* He was concerned for his safety, constantly looking over his shoulder asking,

*Will my brother Esau track me down to kill me?*

That evening he was still traveling high among the rocks in the hill country. Not knowing where to sleep, he suddenly stopped and laid down on a large flat rock where it would be difficult for his twin brother to track him on rocks that left no footprints. Finding a smaller stone for a pillow, Jacob slept fitfully; every sound in the distance scared him. In a dream he saw a golden ladder reaching up into Heaven. Angels were ascending and descending on the ladder. At the top of the ladder the Lord stood and spoke to him,

> *"I am the Lord God of Abraham, your grandfather, and Isaac, your father. I will give you the land that you are sleeping upon and the land through which you are walking. You will have more children than the sand of the earth, and through your children the Deliverer will come who will bless all people of the earth. I will go with you to keep you and will bring you back to this land, and you will live in this land, I will accomplish the things I am promising."*

Jacob awoke and sat upright, looking in every direction, then peered into the sky. He knew it was a dream…a dream from God, and suddenly Jacob was more afraid of God than he was of his brother. He thought, *This is the house of God,* and he named the place *Bethel,* which meant *the house of God.* Not knowing how to sacrifice to God, Jacob took oil and poured it upon the stone that had been his pillow. Then kneeling before God, he looked into Heaven with outstretched hands saying,

"I promise that if You will be with me and keep me and give me bread to eat and clothes to wear, I will return to this place and to my father's house. I will make You my Lord and God, and I will give a tithe of all I have to You."

The next morning Jacob with walking stick in hand continued his trek toward his destiny.

## My Time to Pray

- Lord, help me to hold money loosely in my hand and yield all finances to Your use. Jacob deceived his father to get the family inheritance and ended up with nothing.

- Lord, help me realize Your call on my life and Your presence with me is greater than any money I can accumulate.

- Lord, when Jacob met You at Bethel, he vowed to follow You and to give You 10 percent of all he received. I now make the same pledge.

- Lord, Jacob saw You at the Gateway to Heaven. I'm thankful Jesus is the door to eternal life and that I've entered by Him.

# Genesis 29

## Jacob Arrives in Mesopotamia

When Jacob arrived at the land east of the Euphrates, he saw a well with a
stone on it and three flocks of sheep lying next to it waiting to be
watered. The shepherds waited until all the flocks arrived before
removing the stone. Jacob said to the shepherds, "Are you from
here?" They answered, "Yes." He then asked, "Does Laban, the son
of Nahor live near here?" They answered, "Yes," and they added,
"here comes Rachel his daughter with the sheep." As Jacob
continued speaking, Rachel arrived.

Jacob went and removed the stone and watered the sheep of his Uncle
Laban, his mother's brother. Then Jacob told Rachel that he was her
father's relative and that he was Rebekah's son. Then Jacob kissed
Rachel. She ran to tell her father all about it.

When Laban heard, he ran to the well to meet Jacob, hugged him and
kissed him and brought him to the house. When Jacob told him all
that happened, Laban said, "You are my flesh and blood."

After Jacob had been there a month, Laban said, "You are my relative, you
shouldn't work for free, tell me how much I should pay you."

Laban had two daughters, the eldest was Leah who had poor eyes. The
second was Rachel who was very beautiful, and shapely. Since
Jacob was in love with Rachel he said, "I'll work seven years for you
in exchange for Rachel your youngest daughter." Laban answered,
"It's better that you marry her than someone else." So Jacob
worked for Laban seven years, but it seemed only a little while
because his love for Rachel was so strong.

Jacob said to Laban, "I've finished seven years, now give me
Rachel as my wife so I can live with her."

Laban gave a wedding feast to all the men of the area. Then
he put Leah in the wedding tent instead of Rachel. Jacob went in
and slept with her. In the morning Jacob saw it was Leah and not
Rachel. He said to Laban, "You've tricked me. I didn't work for
Leah, I worked for Rachel." Laban answered, "Our tradition
demands that we marry off the older girl first." Then Laban
suggested, "Spend the marriage week with Leah, then I'll give you
Rachel if you will work another seven years for me." Then Laban
gave Jacob Zilpah a slave girl to wait on Leah.

Jacob agreed and a week later married Rachel. Laban also gave him
Bilhah, the slave girl, to wait on Rachel. Because Jacob loved
Rachel more than Leah he served his uncle for another seven years.

Lord, when You saw that Leah was unloved, You gave her a son, Reuben,
while Rachel was childless. Leah said, "You Lord, have seen my
state, now my husband will love me." But it didn't happen. She
became pregnant again and Simeon (hearing) was born. Again she
said, "The Lord gave me another son so my husband will love me."
Again, it didn't happen. Once more she conceived and said, "Surely
my husband will love me now because I've born him three sons."
She named the third Levi (joining). Then Leah conceived a fourth
time and bore Judah (praise) and said, "I will now praise the Lord."
Then she stopped having children.

*Lord, I know the family is important to each person,*
*Please help me and my family live for You.*

*While You don't approve of two wives for any family,*
*You work in the lives of people as they are.*

*Thank You that the children of Israel came from Jacob,*
*And that Jesus Christ came from the line of Judah.*

Amen.

## Background Story of
## Jacob Arrives in Mesopotamia

### Genesis 29

Place: Mesopotamia ↶ Time: 1759-1739 B.C.

A month later, Jacob arrived in Mesopotamia, following the Euphrates River toward the land of his relatives. His mother had only given him sketchy details of what to look for, but in his heart he knew he was near the home of his family. Up ahead he saw shepherds in a field. There were three flocks grazing nearby, the shepherds were waiting for the evening when the owners of the well removed the large stone over the mouth of the well. Then the shepherds would water their sheep. Jacob, a stranger to the area, yelled to them,

"Do you know Laban, son of Milcah?"

"Yes."

"Is Laban well?"

"That is his daughter bringing her sheep to the well now..."

The shepherds pointed to a young girl leading her sheep to the well. Jacob saw the most stunning girl he had ever seen. As she led her flock of sheep to the well, Jacob saw disappointment cross her beautiful face. The large stone sealed the well. She was unable to water her sheep. Jacob was no different than the young boys are today, they like to show off their strength to young girls. Seeing the problem, and not thinking about the consequences, Jacob ran to the stone,

"I'll remove the stone for you..."

With a strong, sturdy back he slid the rock away. She admired his muscular body, but not as much as he admired her beauty. Then young Jacob helped her water the flock. But he kept spilling water; he couldn't keep his eyes off Rachel's eyes. The young girl's cheeks blushed a rosy pink because of the young man's obvious attention, and she encouraged his advances.

"You are my cousin…," Jacob said to the young girl, studying every line of her beautiful face. Her flashing black eyes and infectious grin told Jacob she was attracted to him. Just as love is addicted to its object, Jacob couldn't keep his eyes off her beauty.

"I am looking for Laban…your father…," Jacob explained that his mother was Rebekah—sister to Laban.

"We're cousins," Jacob quickly added, giving her the customary welcoming kiss. "Oh!" her laugh captured Jacob. Her feminine voice melted the last fear in his heart. From this moment he knew she must be his wife. Jacob asked,

"Where is Laban, your father?"

Rachel left the well, running quickly to tell her father about this strong, young relative who moved the stone from the well. Laban awoke from his nap in the afternoon sun hurrying down to the well. He rubbed his puffy hands in glee—hands that were not used to hard manual work. The most difficult thing Laban did with his hands was count the coins his many servants brought him.

Laban was delighted with the thought of another relative from Abraham's tribe. Why? He remembered the old visitor who brought jewels and gold years ago from Abraham. Laban expected to see ten camels and a multitude of servants, just as he saw years ago, but all he saw was this lone young man with his walking stick, sitting on the stone as though he owned the well. Laban greeted Jacob,

"Come to my house…make it your house…you are family."

Laban embarrassed Jacob, wrapping both arms around the young relative, but his hypocritical sincerity was looking over the young man's shoulders for the camels. Not to be outdone, Jacob with mocking enthusiasm for his uncle was looking over his uncle's shoulder at Rachel.

"You don't have any money?" Laban asked that evening at supper. His fat jowls obviously dropped. Young Jacob didn't have a dowry for a wife, all he had was his walking stick. Laban began to size up the situation; he wanted to make some money off this newfound relative.

"Stay with us for as long as you wish," Laban told his nephew Jacob, "but I'm not running an orphanage. You can look after one of my flocks, to earn some money."

For the next few months Jacob birthed lambs, fought off wolves, killed snakes, and went searching for strays. At a family meal, Jacob kept asking,

"When will you pay me?"

Laban was craftier than the young Jacob. The old uncle had seen his young nephew staring at Rachel. He had observed them talking every available chance. Sitting at the meal, Laban smiled. Then with obvious intention, Laban moved his eyes to Rachel, knowing Jacob's eyes would be naturally drawn to Rachel. Laban was setting a trap. Then he asked,

"What do I have that you want from your uncle?"

Jacob blurted out his deepest heart's desire without thinking,

"I want to marry Rachel."

"But you have no dowry." Laban put both empty hands in the air, as though the situation were out of his hand. Before old Laban could speak again, young Jacob blurted out,

"I'll work for her…"

"It will take a long time," the old uncle was crafty.

"I'll work forever." Those infected with love often exaggerate.

Laban slyly suggested, "Seven is God's number. Would you work seven years for my most beautiful daughter?"

"Yes!"

Laban slyly smiled again because he knew there was a daughter older than Rachel—an ugly daughter that no one wanted—a daughter with fat puffy eyes and black moles on her eyelids that made her all the more repulsive. Leah was the daughter who should be married first by their custom. Laban was willing to give Jacob his beautiful daughter—Rachel—but if the older daughter—Leah—were not taken in seven years, Laban would force the young impulsive nephew to marry the ugly one. But Laban didn't tell young Jacob his plan, he simply said,

"Agreed!" Laban responded vigorously, but in his wicked heart Laban thought, *We'll see when the time comes.*

"Agreed," an eager Jacob nodded his head vigorously.

At the end of seven years, Jacob had served faithfully, the herds of Jacob had prospered more than the other herds that belonged to Laban, more than even the son's of Laban who began with the best flocks and had the best locations. Laban was doubly blessed, free labor from Jacob and a greater increase in the flock Jacob tended. But Jacob was not being cheated, he was getting something in return that was greater than Rachel; he was being prepared for the leadership of God's people. For if he could lead sheep, he could lead people. Jacob slept in the freezing desert nights and worked faithfully in the searing sun of each day, he learned to make the desert serve him. He provided food for his flocks and he drank milk from its herds and ate meat from its abundance. He clothed himself with wool cloth that he spun, and wore leather sandals that he made.

His love for beautiful Rachel made his sacrifice as nothing. Every time Jacob saw Rachel, he dreamed of a tranquil tent where they would sit in perfect happiness. Every time Jacob saw Leah, he thought how ugly her countenance, and Jacob called her "Bad Eyes," a derogatory name his children would one day regret.

Since the older sister Leah hadn't married, Laban was going to out-trick younger Jacob, the trickster. The ugly one would go first, and if everything developed as he planned; he'd get rid of both and become a rich man because Jacob was making him wealthy.

The wedding feast was set; friends were invited; vows were exchanged; food and drinks were consumed, and Jacob was blinded with anticipation to what was happening around the banquet table. Jacob couldn't keep his eyes off Rachel; the young man didn't see Laban whispering to the older ugly girl. Jacob didn't hear what his uncle said to Leah.

"Wait in the marriage tent...don't say anything when Jacob enters...keep quiet until morning...consummate the marriage...."

Unknown to Jacob, Laban had servants gag Rachel and take her to a shepherd's camp for the evening. Jacob slipped into the darkness of the bridal tent into the arms of love. He tenderly removed the veil from her face that symbolized she was single and unmarried. He made love to the wrong woman, and because he was tricked, Jacob never loved Leah.

For years, Jacob didn't realize Leah was a good woman; she was God's choice for Jacob. Leah was the mother in line of the Deliverer and Leah was buried next to Jacob.

Jacob was not only blind to the goodness of Leah, he was also blinded to the deceitful ways of Rachel. Because like attracts like, the deceptive Jacob was drawn in love to the deceptive Rachel. It would take years for Jacob to discover this fact.

The next morning a verbal tornado swept through the family compound, destroying the frail peace of Laban's home. Jacob came storming out of the marriage tent yelling,

"YOU LIAR...," Jacob yelled for all to hear, "YOU TRICKED ME!"

"HOW DARE YOU INSULT MY HOSPITALITY," Laban yelled back at his nephew. Everyone ran for cover, mothers picked up their children to disappear behind the flaps of tents. Servants watched to see if either man reached for a weapon. Jacob kept demanding that his uncle give him Rachel,

"Where is she? I worked seven years for Rachel, she is my love." Laban kept repeating the family custom of marrying off the older sister first. Uncle Laban pleaded innocently, "I couldn't give you the youngest daughter first!" After several hours of an on-going feud, Laban finally tried to pour oil on the troubled waters. It was a solution he dreamed would make him even wealthier.

"Maybe you can also have Rachel...." When Laban began to explain the scenario, Jacob began to cool down. "First give Leah a good honeymoon—seven days—after a week you can have Rachel."

Jacob's voice toned down, his rage subsided. He scratched the stubble on his chin questioningly. He didn't trust his father-in-law. He innocently said,

"You mean I can have Rachel after seven days?"

"On the same basis as Leah," Laban's sly grin returned. "You'll have to work another seven years in the future for Rachel, just as you worked seven years in the past for Leah."

During the next seven years, the flocks of Laban continued to increase, he became prosperous. But Jacob was not without the blessing of God. Jacob loved the beautiful Rachel, but it was Leah who gave birth to his first son, Reuben. Then she gave birth to three more boys, but Rachel, beautiful on the outside, was barren on the inside.

When Jacob complained to Rachel about not having any children, she got angry and forced him to lie with her servant girl. Jacob had two sons with Rachel's handmaid. Not to be outdone, Leah forced Jacob to lie with her servant girl, two more sons were born. Now Jacob had eight boys, each one learning to be shepherds. Then Leah had two more—10 sons—a proud heritage. God looked down from Heaven to see the wives squabbling over the affection of Jacob. The boys had different birthmothers, and they hated one another as their mothers strove with one another.

God wanted one boy with a good heart to worship and obey Him. God knew Rachel was a good woman who would conceive a son with her good spirit, He opened her womb and she conceived a son, and bore Joseph.

After the 14 years of servitude was over, Laban asked Jacob to continue keeping his flocks for he was getting wealthier each day as Jacob watched his flocks. They made a deal. Jacob told Laban,

"You will get to keep all the regular ones that are born to your cattle." Laban liked the idea because most of the animals were born that way. "I'll keep the animals born with a ring around its neck, or the ones with spots or speckled."

"Agreed," Laban nodded his head quickly.

But God who controls the origination of life blessed Jacob and there were more born with rings, spots, or specks than ever before. Jacob took the animals that were his by birth and separated them so his sons could look after his flocks. Each time Jacob brought a speckled or spotted animal, he laughed with glee because his flock was now growing faster than Laban's.

Jacob forced the animals into fertility patterns at the water springs—thinking the ancient customs were helping the new births to have rings, spots, or speckles—Jacob didn't know God was blessing him in preparation for his return to the Land of Promise.

Each time Jacob boasted to his sons about his heathen fertility customs, the father didn't realize he was teaching his sons to be tricksters—just as he was the ultimate trickster.

When Laban realized his choice of regular animals at birth had backfired; he changed the agreement. Laban now wanted the animals born with rings, spots, and speckles. But no matter how Laban switched the agreement—they switched 10 times—God blessed Jacob; the nephew's flocks grew more rapidly than Uncle Laban's. Over a period of time, Laban continued switching the agreement, so much so; that Laban's sons complained and took their vengeance out on Jacob. Then God came to Jacob in a dream,

"I am the God of Bethel. Do you remember anointing a stone with oil and vowing to me? Return now to the land of your family."

Jacob had spent 20 years in Haran, the land of Laban. He came to the Euphrates River with nothing but a walking stick—a reminder of his roots—now he was ready to return home. Jacob was rich—11 sons, 2 wives, many flocks, and servants. But even to the end, Jacob was the trickster. He couldn't bring himself to tell Laban where he was going or when he was going. Jacob waited until Laban left his home to visit his sheep being sheared. Jacob knew Laban would be so busy counting his profits that he could get a three-day head start on his uncle.

On that eventful day, all Jacob's wives, sons, and servants were ready to go. Jacob climbed upon a camel, whacked his walking stick across the camel's neck, and Jacob's caravan moved out. Jacob didn't look back, but he couldn't get the black figure of vengeance out of his mind, Jacob knew Laban was ruthless; he didn't give up possessions easily.

## My Time to Pray

- Lord, Jacob's old nature made him deceive everyone, especially his family. Transform me! Make me honest and reliable.

- Lord, I'm amazed how You worked through the details to give Jacob what he wanted, yet Your perfect will was done. I yield to You; work Your perfect will in my life.

- Lord, even when Jacob tricked people, he was a hard worker. May I learn to work hard from Jacob.

- Lord, in spite of Jacob's weaknesses, he had a heart to please You. May I be like Jacob with a heart to do Your will.

- Lord, You use more power to work Your will through circumstances and people than You probably do when You do miracles. I ask for You to work Your will through the circumstances of my life.

# Genesis 30

# JACOB WORKS FOR LABAN

When Rachel realized she wasn't having children, and she was jealous of
her sister Leah, she demanded of Jacob, "I will die if you don't give
me children." Jacob angrily answered, "Do you think I'm God? He's
the only One who gives children." Rachel said, "Sleep with my
servant Bilhah to get me a child. Bilhah became pregnant and bore
a son. Rachel called him Dan (to vindicate). Then Bilhah bore
Jacob a second son. Rachel named him Naphtali (struggle), saying,
"I have struggled with my sister and won."

Leah realized she was no longer getting pregnant, so she gave her servant
girl Zilpah to Jacob. Zilpah bore a son and Leah named him Gad
(good fortune) saying, "I am fortunate." Then Zilpah bore another
son, Asher (happy) saying, "I have joy, the other women will see
my happiness."

During the wheat harvest, Reuben found some mandrakes (a narcotic
believed to have magical powers to overcome infertility) and
brought them to Leah, his mother. Rachel begged her for them, but
Leah angrily answered, "You've stolen the love of my husband, now
you want to steal my son's mandrakes." Rachel said, "I will let you
sleep with Jacob tonight if you will give them to me."

*Lord, Rachel was a conniving woman, mad at her husband and*
*Bargaining his sex like merchandise.*

*Keep me pure in my desires and obedient to Your plan.*

When Jacob came home, Leah met him and said, "You must sleep with me
tonight because I have traded my son's mandrakes for this

privilege." So Jacob slept with her and she became pregnant. God answered her prayers. She gave birth to Issachar (reward), saying, "God has rewarded me for giving my husband another son." She became pregnant again and bore Zebulun (honor) saying, "God has given me a son, now my husband will honor me." Later she gave birth to a daughter and named her Dinah (vindicated).

Lord, You answered Rachel's prayer. She became pregnant and bore a son, saying, "God has removed my shame." She named him Joseph (to add) praying, "May the Lord add to me another son."

After Joseph was born, Jacob said to Laban, "Send me back, so I can return to my home and my country. I want to take my wives for I have worked for them; let me go. You know I have served you faithfully."

Laban answered, "Please let me ask you something. I can tell by the results that God has blessed me because of you. Stay and work for me, name your wages, I will pay them."

Jacob answered, "You know I have served you faithfully and your livestock has prospered as I took care of them. You had only a few when I came, now you have much. The Lord has blessed you because of everything I do. Now, when will I provide for myself?"

Laban asked, "What do you want?" Jacob said, "Nothing, I will continue taking care of your flock and giving them pasture. I will go through the flock and pick out all the speckled, spotted, and dark-fleeced sheep. They will be my wages. You will be able to tell if I am honest. Go through my flock and if you find any that are not white, you will know I have stolen from you."

Laban said, "I agree to what you ask." But that day Laban took all the speckled, spotted, and dark-fleeced sheep and told a son to take them three days away.

*Lord, it seems no matter how hard we try to make other people act*
*Honestly to us,*
*Their sinful heart tempts them to lie and deceive us.*

*May I be aware of the constant temptation to lie and deceive;*
*Keep me honest and may I always act right.*

Jacob cared for Laban's flock. But Jacob took fresh-cut branches from poplar, almond, and other trees and peeled off the bark, making them light-colored rods. He set the rods up by the watering trough so the animals would see them when they drank. They mated when they drank. The animals that mated in sight of the rods bore speckled, spotted, and streaked young. Jacob divided those from Laban's flock and kept his flock separate from Laban's. Whenever the stronger animals were in heat, Jacob set up the rods at the watering troughs. The weaker animals became Laban's and the stronger ones were Jacob's though this is the way he became very rich in flocks, camels, donkeys, and male and female servants.

*Lord, Jacob practiced old wives' tales to produce productivity*
*Among the flocks, but wisdom tells us*
*There is no truth to what he did.*

*I believe you blessed Jacob even though he*
*Followed the superstitions of his day.*

*Lord, I will follow You with all the knowledge I have;*
*Please bless me, even when I followed ideas that are faulty;*
*I will always attempt to find the truth and follow it.*

Amen.

# Genesis 31

# Jacob Runs Away From Laban

Laban was annoyed when his sons complained, "Jacob has taken away the wealth of our father. Our father no longer prospers and is not respected by all."

Jacob knew something was wrong when he looked into the face of his father-in-law, Laban. He knew he had to do something.

Lord, it is then You spoke to Jacob, "Return to the Promised Land, the land of your fathers and I will be with you."

Jacob called Rachel and Leah to the field when he kept Laban's sheep, telling them, "I can see in your father's countenance that he has changed his attitude toward me. But God has been with me even though your father deceived me and changed my wages ten times. When Laban told me I could have the speckled cattle, the animals bore speckled. When he said I could have all the streaked cattle, they all bore streaks. God has taken your father's cattle and given them to me."

Jacob told them, "In my dream I saw what was happening. Then God said to me, 'Jacob,' and I said, 'Here I am.'" Then God said to me, "I have seen all that Laban has done to you. I am the God of Bethel where you anointed the rock and you vowed to be faithful to Me. Leave this land and go back to the Promised Land, the land of your fathers."

Leah and Rachel said to Jacob, "There's no reason for us to stay here. There is no inheritance for us in our father's house. He sold us for money, now there's no money left in our father's house. God has

221

taken all the money from our father and given it to you, so we'll go wherever you say."

Jacob packed his goods, put his wives and sons on camels, and carried away all the goods and cattle he had gotten in Mesopotamia and headed toward his father Isaac in Canaan.

Laban had gone to shear his sheep and didn't know Jacob was leaving. Rachel stole her father's idols and took them with her. Jacob crossed over the Euphrates River heading to the Promised Land.

Laban heard about it three days after Jacob left. Laban took his men as warriors and pursued Jacob. It took seven days to catch him.

Lord, You appeared to Laban in a dream saying "Be careful that you do not curse or bless Jacob."

Jacob was camped in Mount Gilead when Laban caught him. Laban said to his son-in-law, "Why did you sneak away without telling me you were going? I would have given you a big going away party. But you've sneaked away with my daughters like they were captives. I didn't get a chance to kiss my grandsons and grand daughter good-bye. I could fight you and inflict damage on you, but the God of your fathers appeared to me and said 'Do not curse him or bless him.' I understand your desire to go to your father's house, but why did you steal my idols?"

Jacob answered, "I was afraid because I thought you would take your daughters from me." Then Jacob addressed the accusation that Laban's idols were stolen, "You can kill anyone with me who has stolen your idols. And if you find anything that is yours among my possessions, take it." Jacob didn't know Rachel had stolen the idols.

Laban searched Jacob's tent, then the tent of Leah, and next the tents of the two handmaids. He found nothing. Then he went to Rachel's tent. She had hidden the idols in the camel's saddlebags and was sitting on them. She said, "Forgive me for not rising, but it's my woman's time of the month." He didn't find the idols.

*Lord, it's amazing how "like attracts like";*
*Rachel lied just as her husband Jacob had lied.*

*Help me become like You.*

Jacob was mad at Laban, arguing, "What sin have I done that you've chased me like a criminal? You've searched everything I have and haven't found your idols. Now your servants and my servants can judge which one of us is right. For 20 years I served you, and I haven't killed your animals to eat. If a wolf killed your lamb or one was damaged, I bore the cost of it. I watched your flocks in the heat of the day and the frost of the night. I went without sleep. I served you 14 years for your daughters and six years for my cattle; and you've changed my wages 10 times."

Lord, Jacob recognized Your blessings by saying, "The God of my father Isaac and the God of Abraham has been with me. If it hadn't been for God, you would have sent me away empty. God has seen my affliction and rebuked you."

Laban answered heatedly, "These daughters are mine, these sons are mine, these cattle are my cattle, all that you have is mine. But I can't harm these daughters and these children who are born to you."

Laban and Jacob agreed to make a covenant. Jacob took a stone and set it as a pillar. Then all the servants gathered many stones into a heap. They all sat down and ate a meal. Then Jacob called the place Galeed (Jegarsahutha, a heap). Then the two men covenanted together the Mizpah benediction,

*May the Lord watch between me and thee,*
*While we are absent, one from another.*

Laban said, "If you hurt my daughters, or you take other wives besides my daughters, God will see and God will judge you." Then Laban said, "This heap of stones is between you and me. It is a witness that I will not come over this heap to attack you, and you will not come over it to attack me. The God of Abraham, the God of Nahor, and the God of their fathers, judge between us."

Lord, Jacob swore this oath, then sacrificed to you. Then they ate a meal and slept the night. The following morning, Laban kissed his sons and daughters and returned home.

*Lord, You blessed Jacob, even though he was a deceiver;*
*You protected him because of Your promise to Abraham.*

*Thank You for protecting me throughout my life;*
*You have blessed me because of Christ.*

Amen.

## Background Story of
## Jacob Runs Away From Laban

### Genesis 31

Place: Mount Gilead ⌒ Time: 1739 B.C.

The two men stared defiantly at each other; a large jagged rock in the middle of the road separated them from physical assault. The roadbed was worn down on either side of the rock; countless animals of many caravans had aimlessly trod on each side of the rock.

The older of the two men, Laban, had chased down his foe and caught him at this rock. His hands were not armed, but they were clenched. It was his dedicated servants who had their weapons ready—swords, bows, and spears. Dozens of mean-spirited, dirty, and tired men had followed their angry master Laban. Now they were willing to fight at his word, only their aging leader stood silent.

The hot desert wind whipped up sand around their ankles, their tunics flapped around their bodies. The blistering sun burnt their tempers raw. A dirty beard and foul-smelling clothes from a hard chase didn't help old Laban's disposition.

Younger Jacob stared from the other side of the stone at his Uncle Laban. Neither man trusted the other. If anyone had lurched for a weapon, there would have been a battle. Laban's dozens of warriors had worked in the fields with Jacob; they didn't trust him, and they were ready to kill him.

Jacob had as many herdsmen to tend his large flocks, they were not warriors but they knew if a battle began, they would have to fight for their lives. Jacob's 11 sons stood behind their father.

Silence...except for the hot wind.

"Why did you take my daughters?" Laban's raspy voice finally broke the tension. "Why did you sneak off into the night with my grandchildren?"

"I knew you wouldn't let me go..." Jacob the son-in-law sheepishly answered. For the first time he dropped his eyes in guilt.

"They are my daughters," Laban's voice got more powerful. "These are my children..." he waved to make sure everyone knew he was referring to the 11 sons of Jacob. "You have gotten rich from my flocks." Laban pointed to the several flocks of animals milling around—flocks of goats, rams, camels, cows, bulls, and donkeys. They were the sign of wealth, and if Laban were correct, Jacob had stolen much from him.

God had visited Laban in a dream, telling him not to harm Jacob. If God had not warned the mean-spirited Laban, he would probably have killed Jacob when he caught him. Now, all Laban could do was warn his nephew.

"Let this rock…," Laban said as he pointed for all to see the gouged rock in the middle of the road, "let this rock be a division between us."

Jacob looked at the rock and nodded.

"You will not come on this side of the rock." Laban's loud voice carried for all Jacob's servants to hear. "I will not come on your side of the rock."

"Agreed!" Jacob quickly shouted for all to hear, "I AGREE!"

"Bring a knife," Laban demanded.

At first, Jacob flinched when he heard the word "knife," then he realized the nomadic tradition. Laban grabbed the knife, then quickly pierced his wrist until blood appeared. Laban threw the knife over the rock to Jacob. Quickly Jacob followed the example of his uncle. Then reaching out, they clasped hands to arms, the blood of one relative mingled with the other. Together they agreed by blood…blood touching blood. Together they said,

"May the Lord watch between you and me, while we are separated one from the other."

Laban kissed his daughters and children. Then as he prepared to mount his horse, he again pointed to the rock, "This rock is my witness, I will not cross to your side…"

Laban stopped his words in mid-sentence; then turning, he pointed to Jacob, "If you hurt one of my children…God is witness what I will do."

With that warning, Laban turned abruptly, still angry but now somewhat pacified; dug his heels into the side of his horse. They bolted down the road. His warriors fell into columns, following Laban eastward toward home.

## My Time to Pray

- It's so easy to be greedy in a world filled with advertisement for all kinds of stuff when I have a lustful old nature. Keep my eyes on You and teach me to be satisfied with the things You provide for me.

- Jacob and Laban pledge honesty to each other, yet they cheated one another. I pledge to You my Lord, that I will be honest, that's greater than pledging to another human. Help me keep my pledge.

- Lord, teach me to trust You at all times, about all things, in all types of circumstances.

# Genesis 32

# JACOB SENDS GIFTS TO ESAU
# AND
# JACOB MEETS GOD

As Jacob continued journeying, a host of angels met him. He called that place Mehanaim (two hosts: he and the angels). Then Jacob sent messengers to Esau his brother who was living in Edom.

The messenger was told to say, "Your servant Jacob has lived with Laban for 20 years; and has now come home. He has oxen, donkeys, cattle, men and women servants; now he wants to find grace in your sight."

The messengers returned to Jacob to tell him Esau was coming to see him with 400 men.

Jacob was afraid. He divided his band into two groups. He said, "If Esau finds one group and destroys it, then the other one shall escape."

Lord, then Jacob prayed to you, "O God of my father Abraham, and God of my father Isaac, and You Lord who told me to return to my homeland so You could bless me. I am not worthy of your mercies that You have shown to me. When I come this way, I had only my walking stick, now I have two groups of people and cattle. Deliver me from the anger of my brother Esau, I'm afraid of him. He will kill me and the mothers of my children and my children."

Lord, Jacob claimed Your promise when he prayed, "Lord, You promised to do me good, and make my seed as the sand of the sea, that cannot be numbered."

*Lord, Jacob had tricked his brother twice, so he deserved*
    *The punishment he thought he would get;*
    *But You showed mercy to him.*

*Lord, when I displease You, be merciful to me because of Christ,*
    *Bless me with Your eternal blessing.*

Jacob planned to offer gifts to Esau to soften his wrath. He put together
    200 she goats, 20 he goats, 200 lambs, 20 rams, 30 milk cows, 40
    cows, 10 bulls, 20 female donkeys, and 10 male donkeys. He put
    this many in each drove and started them toward Esau, but
    separated each drove from the sight of the others.

Then Jacob instructed the leader of each drove when they met Esau to tell
    him these cattle belonged to Jacob but he is giving them to you as a
    gift. And that Jacob was coming behind them. Jacob told each to
    say, "I will see your face." Each leader was to say the same thing to
    appease the anger of Esau. Jacob was planning to save his life
    this way.

Jacob sent each drove out before him, but he came to the ford over the river
    Jabbok with his two wives, his two maid servants, and his sons. He
    sent them over the river, but he stayed alone that night in a tent.

Jacob wrestled with a man (a theophany) all night until day break. The
    angel of the Lord said, "Let me go for it's daybreak." But Jacob
    said, "I'll not let you go unless you bless me." When he couldn't
    prevail, the angel of the Lord touched the hollow of his thigh.
    (Jacob's thigh was out of joint permanently). The angel of the Lord
    asked, "What is your name?" He answered, "Jacob." The Lord said,
    "Your name will no loner be Jacob, but Israel: for you are a prince
    who has power to prevail with God and with men."

Lord, Jacob called the place, "Penuel, for I have seen God face to face, and
    I didn't die." As the sun arose, Israel crossed the river, but he was
    limping. After that the children of Israel wouldn't eat the sinew in

the hollow of the thigh, because God touched the hollow of Jacob's thigh.

*Lord, I take encouragement in the example of Jacob,*
*He was a deceiver and liar as a young man;*
*Yet as he grew older, he became a man of God.*

*Overlook the sins and failures of my youth,*
*Make me godly and may I walk with You.*

Amen.

### Background Story of
### Jacob Sends Gifts to Esau
### and
### Jacob Meets God

### Genesis 32

Place: The Jabbok River Canyon ✢ Time: 1739 B.C.

All that day and the next, the words of Laban haunted Jacob. Even though his uncle promised not to pass the stone—he called the stone Mizpah (place of watching)—Jacob couldn't be sure that his uncle would not attack in the night, killing him, and taking his daughters and grandchildren.

The memory of an angry uncle reminded Jacob of an angry brother he left in the Promise Land 20 years earlier. Twenty years ago, Jacob had sneaked out of his father's tent because his brother Esau had threatened to kill him. Jacob couldn't forget the words of his brother,

"When Father is dead...I will kill you."

231

Jacob believed his brother would kill him. Jacob saw his brother's anger, so 20 years ago Jacob ran away from home and from his brother. Jacob had lived 20 years with his Uncle Laban. Jacob tried to put Laban out of his thoughts, but couldn't stop thinking about his brother Esau and his red beard, his red hair, and his fiery disposition. Would Esau still try to kill him?

Now Jacob was going home. He was a wealthy man—two wives, 11 sons, servants, and herds of cattle. He left empty, now he led a large nomadic tribe toward the Promise Land. Jacob was leaving an angry uncle; he was heading toward an angry brother.

"Will my brother Esau try to kill me?"

Jacob had tricked his older brother, Esau, out of the birthright, which meant Jacob became the family head, the family spokesman, the family priest. Next Jacob had tricked Esau out of the blessing. Jacob's father had promised him twice as much inheritance as his brother, only he never got anything; he ran fearing for his life.

*I'm still afraid Esau will kill me,* Jacob thought as he trudged the path back to his boyhood home. Going home was not a happy experience.

Early the next morning, Jacob sent servants to Esau. He gave them directions how to find Esau,

"Call Esau my master...tell him I'm returning home...tell him how rich I am...tell him I want to find grace in his eyes."

Jacob waited two days for their return. He sat mostly in the tent door. He prayed to the Lord, asking for grace. God had appeared to him 20 years ago and promised several things. Jacob remembered the voice of God,

"I am the Lord God of your fathers Abraham and Isaac...I will give this land to you and to your children...you will have many children...I will make you rich...I will protect you."

It was that last part about protection that Jacob remembered. He wanted God to keep him alive. He prayed that God would protect him from Esau his brother, just as God had protected him from his Uncle Laban. While

Jacob was praying, his thoughts were interrupted by shouts outside the tent.

"The servants are returning," was the cry throughout the camp.

The two servants who had been sent to Esau went directly to Jacob's tent. Jacob had been praying for a friendly message. He hoped that time healed old wounds; surely 20 years would cause Esau to forget. But the message Jacob heard from his servants was worse than his deepest fears,

"Esau is coming to meet you with 400 armed men."

"Enough to kill us all," was Jacob's first reaction.

There was no place to run, no place to hide. He couldn't return to Laban, the Mizpah rock stood in the middle of the road. Panic seized Jacob; it was difficult to think straight when you're scared to death. Jacob had heard enough to know that whatever frightens you, also is your master. And now Jacob was dominated by fear.

Slowly a plan developed in Jacob's mind. *I'll give Esau everything,* Jacob thought. *If I give him everything, maybe he won't kill me.*

Jacob was quick-witted; he could always scramble out of trouble. He was Jacob the supplanter, Jacob the trickster. He schemed to give Esau everything, it was an elaborate plan. It was more than just handing over to Esau all his riches, it was a plan that would take all day to unfold. It was a plan to confuse Esau.

Jacob separated his flocks into two divisions, he put some servants over each flock of animals, keeping the flocks separate from one another. Jacob then started the flocks journeying toward Esau, one flock at a time, each flock just out of sight of the other. First,

200 she goats...next,

20 he goats...next,

200 ewes...next,

20 rams...next,

30 milk cows...next,

40 cattle for meat...next,

10 bulls...next,

20 female donkeys...next,

10 male donkeys...each flock had the same number of animals.

Jacob instructed the herdsman of each flock of animals to say the same thing to Esau, they would immediately recognize Esau by his red beard. Jacob told them to bow to the ground saying,

"This is a present to you from your servant Jacob." He told the servants to tell Esau that "Jacob is coming behind us."

Twice that day the same thing would happen. Esau would see a cloud of dust approaching. Each time Esau would think the dust might be an approaching army, and each time, he would prepare for battle. Each time Esau would draw his sword...and each time his men would prepare for battle.

Each time Jacob tricked him.

Each time it was another gift of cattle to Esau. Each time the herdsman did the same thing, said the same thing. The driver bowed to the ground before Esau, offering elaborate gifts.

"These cattle are a present to Esau from your servant Jacob, (Jacob did not call himself his brother). This present is from your servant."

"If Jacob gives me this much..." Esau thought, "he must be very, very, very wealthy."

The herds of Jacob were like a gigantic snake crawling toward Esau, many miles long, and each herd separated from the other. It was impossible to see from the beginning cloud of dust to the end. Both herds did not reach Esau before nightfall. Esau camped for the night

"Tomorrow I'll see my brother Jacob." The redheaded Esau tried to sleep. "Tomorrow will climax 20 years of agony!"

Jacob camped for the evening near the small river Jabbok. Still he was up to his old tricks. Jacob pitched his big tent on the riverbank and entered with his two wives and children into the large spreading tent, a flat, white tent that stretched out over the soft Persian rugs, he provided for luxury, even in the wilderness. The servants were dispatched to sleep on the ground around the big tent. The fires were to burn through all the night. If Esau attacked during the night, he would capture the wives and the children and the servants. If Esau attacked that night, he would not capture Jacob.

The trickster still had one last trick up his sleeve.

As soon as darkness surrounded the massive tent, Jacob sneaked out from under the flaps. No one saw him, not the servants, nor his family. The moonless night painted dark shadows, it was easy to escape from the camp unseen. Jacob sneaked the opposite way, away from his brother Esau. The shallow river was ahead, he easily waded across the Jabbok, and in a cluster of trees, he found the small tent he had hidden from view.

"No one will find me here..." Jacob whispered to himself.

Inside, he knelt almost immediately. Wild thoughts raced through his mind. He wanted to pray to God, the quicker the better. A cold shutter ran up his back.

"Will Uncle Laban return to kill me?" his mind couldn't forget the hostile encounter with his uncle a few days ago, "or will my brother Esau kill me tomorrow?"

Jacob knelt before God, bowing his face to the ground. There was no soft rug in this small tent. It was not hidden among the trees for comfort or for luxury; the tent was there for safety.

He knew Laban's rage, would he return? Was his uncle in the dark shadows? Jacob wondered if Esau accepted his gifts yesterday. He wondered if Esau would sneak up to the large tent to attack his family. It is terrifying not knowing whether you sleep in danger or safety!

"O God of my grandfather Abraham...O God of my father Isaac..." Jacob reverently sought God. "I am returning to my country because you are sending me home," Jacob reminded God he was obedient to the vision God had given him to return to his home country.

"I am not worthy of Thy mercies," Jacob confessed his sins. Jacob knew he had deceived many in his young life. Jacob held his prized walking stick up to God. He tenderly caressed the signet of Abraham and Isaac. "I only had this staff when I crossed Jordan 20 years ago."

Tears came to Jacob's eyes as he gratefully remembered, "You have blessed me with a family, children, flocks, servants. Tonight I am divided from my family," Jacob didn't know what happened to the flocks he sent to Esau. He didn't know what happened to his wives and children left behind.

Lonely—20 years ago Jacob left his father and mother because he had deceived his family. Lonely—tonight he prepares to re-enter the Promised Land. Lonely—because he again deceived his family.

"Deliver me from my brother Esau because I fear he will kill me, and the children, and their mothers." Jacob could not bear the thought of no sons, no seed to Abraham's promise, God's promises cut off.

"Lord, You promised to do me good," Jacob reminded God, "You promised I would have more children than the sand of the seashore."

There was no wind that night, the silent trees were too frightened to speak. There was no moon, the dark shadows added to the terror of the evening. The dull gray clouds even blocked out the starlight. The silence was threatening.

Then Jacob heard the unmistakable crunch of footsteps in the sand outside the tent.

*What's that?* he thought, but couldn't speak. He listened as the sounds of steps ceased. Silence! Then the steps began again.

His eyes dilated, his heart rate doubled. He yelled,

"WHO'S THERE?"

Jacob first thought it may be Esau, he blinked his eyes to see the red beard of Esau, maybe not; he squinted to see the gray beard of Laban.

No one answered!

But Jacob knew someone was there, he could feel the presence of a person outside the tent. The tent flap moved. Next Jacob saw a hand pull back the flap, the figure entered the tent,

"NO!" yelled Jacob, he jumped, grabbing the figure, "I'VE GOT YOU!" Jacob yelled again.

The two men wrestled to the ground, Jacob reached for the man's arms, holding them lest he have a weapon. The men wrestled, both trying to hold the other, neither letting the other go free.

"Release me..." the intruder demanded.

"NO!" Jacob answered.

Almost immediately Jacob realized the man didn't have a weapon, it was strength against strength, will against will, stamina against stamina. The man was persistent, but of all the things Jacob knew about himself, Jacob knew he was stubborn.

"I have come to answer your prayers," the man pleaded for Jacob to listen, but the trickster thought he knew better. Jacob had wrestled many times, and had talked opponents into releasing their grip on him. He had won many wrestling matches against an opponent by using a trick like this.

"How do I know you have come from God?" Jacob grunted as he wrestled.

"You are afraid of being killed!" the opponent said to Jacob.

"That's easy to see," Jacob answered. "I'm hiding in this tent because I'm afraid."

"You've asked God to protect you," the opponent knew what Jacob had been praying.

"All my servants have heard me pray that," Jacob sneered.

Jacob would not believe his opponent came from God, but he didn't disbelieve it either. All he could do was hold onto anything, an arm, a leg, any part of the body. Jacob held on because that was the way he lived and fought. Jacob knew if he let go, he would lose. When he couldn't do anything else, Jacob could hang on.

"If you're from God..." Jacob refused to release the man, "if God sent you, then bless me."

As Jacob desperately hung on to his opponent, he begged, prayed, even pleaded,

"If you're from God...protect me from Esau...save my life...save my family...save my children...please help me."

They wrestled for what seemed like hours. From the tent came sounds of grunts and groans, but no one was there to hear the sounds. The moon never arose to let Jacob see his enemy. Through the black night he wrestled an unseen figure, one stronger than he. Jacob had finally met a person he couldn't beat and he couldn't trick. All Jacob could do was hang on.

"If you're from God," Jacob repeated his demand, many times during the evening, "bless me if you're from God."

"Let me go..." the figure continued to demand of Jacob.

"I will not let you go unless you answer my prayers," a stubborn Jacob answered.

Then the first light of a new day peeked over an eastern hill. The dayspring appeared over a clump of white birch trees, and with the faint light of morning, a dove spoke its language from the top of a birch tree. Another answered. The silent night was being awakened by the crickets.

Even the Jabbok River that had passed the tent silently in the night began to bubble over some wet moss stones.

"Let me go..." the figure demanded, "for the dawn is breaking."

"NO!" Jacob repeated the answer he had given all night, "I will not let you go except you bless me."

"What is your name?" the figure asked.

"Jacob…" When Jacob spoke his name, he knew the name meant supplanter, one who deceives.

"You will have a new name," the man told Jacob. "God will bless you…your name will be *Israel*…your new name means, 'a Prince with God'…you will be special to God for the rest of your life…and God will bless your children who will continue forever."

"Israel…" thought Jacob. "My new name means a new way of living."

"You will be called Israel forever," the voice answered Jacob, "because you have wrestled with God and would not let go…because you have always sought the Lord, in spite of your deception…because you have prevailed."

The figure touched Jacob's thigh, a wrestling move Jacob had never experienced in all his matches with other shepherds. When the figure touched Jacob's thigh, a pain shot down his leg to his toes, then up his nervous system into his brain…he felt excruciating pain.

"YEEIII!" Jacob yelled out. It was a cry he had not yelled since an older man had crushed him as a teen. It was a cry of pain beyond human experience.

"You will limp for the rest of your life," Jacob heard the voice say. "Everywhere you walk…you will walk with pain. You will remember this night…you will remember that you wrestled with God and would not let go."

The pain was so sharp that Jacob released his opponent instinctively without thinking. He shut his eyes to squeeze out the pain. Now his mouth was open, only a sound would not come. It was a silent scream.

"You will limp for the rest of your life," the figure told Jacob, "because you have prevailed with God, because you have power with God."

"Tell me your name…" Jacob's pain subsided. His first thoughts centered on the one who disabled him. He had to know who was this person.

"What is your name?" Jacob asked.

"Why do you want to know my name?" he answered Jacob. "You don't need to know my name! But I will bless you," the figure replied. "You have prayed to God for His blessing…I will bless you."

Jacob realized this person had heard his prayers, and only God can hear the prayers of men. This person had known his heart, and only God knows that heart of men. This person was going to bless him, and only God can bless an individual.

Jacob knelt before the figure, the experience of pain in his thigh was compensated by the awesome experience of God's presence. Jacob bowed his head, afraid to look up. Even though he could see traces of the man's face in the early morning light, Jacob was afraid to look. He was ashamed of his unbelief throughout the previous night.

The hand touched Jacob with God's blessing. Whereas the figure earlier touched Jacob's thigh to release his wrestling clutch, a touch that would make him lame for the rest of his life, this was a touch of spiritual healing and spiritual health. Jacob would never be the same, he had touched God, and been touched by God.

Jacob would walk with God, no longer relying on his human escapades. Jacob would be *Israel*, a Prince with God.

Jacob emerged from the small tent, the piercing sun was now shining over the eastern hill through the white birch trees. He blinked his eyes, and rubbed them with the back of his hands to adjust to the bright morning.

"I have seen God," Jacob spoke the words out loud, though no one was present to hear him. "I have seen God face to face and did not die."

Jacob took a step toward the River Jabbok, pain shot through his hip, it stopped him short. He reached back into the tent for his walking stick, the only thing he had when he left the land of promise 20 years ago. Now he needed the walking stick more than ever. He hobbled down to the

Jabbok River to wash his face, then his dirty body from wrestling all night on the tent's ground. A drink of cool water revived his spirit.

## My Time to Pray

- Lord, Jacob would not listen to You in the night, teach me to listen to Your voice and bow before You when I'm in Your presence.

- Lord, my heart is now completely pure because I am human like Jacob. Forgive me of my sins by the blood of Jesus (1 John 1:7) and prepare me for Your service as You prepared Jacob.

- Lord, Jacob was a trickster to the end, change my nature and make me honest.

- Lord, when Jacob grabbed to touch You, in return You touched him. Do the same for me.

- Lord, I want Your guidance and power in my life.

# Genesis 33

# JACOB MEETS ESAU

When Jacob saw Esau and 400 men coming toward him, he divided his
followers into groups, a group with Leah, and a group with Rachel.
He sent the two handmaids first, Leah second, and he came last
with Rachel and Joseph.

When Esau approached, Jacob bowed to the ground seven times.
Then Esau ran to Jacob and hugged him and kissed him. They
reconciled and wept. Finally Esau saw the women and children and
asked, "Whose are these?" Jacob said, "These are the children whom
God has graciously given me." Then the handmaids and their
children bowed to Esau. Next Leah and her children bowed to Esau.
Finally, Rachel and Joseph bowed to Esau.

Then Esau asked, "What is the meaning of all the droves I met?" Jacob
answered, "These are gifts to find grace in your sight." Esau
answered, "I have enough, my brother, you keep what is yours."
But Jacob replied, "No, if I have found grace in your sight, keep the
gifts because seeing your face is like looking into the face of God
when He is pleased with me." Again Jacob said, "Take these gifts of
mine because God has been gracious to me and I have enough." So
Esau took the gifts.

*Lord, thank You for the principle that*
*"Time heals all wounds."*

*Thank You for preserving the life of Jacob,*
*And that he repented, becoming a godly man.*

*Thank You for preserving my life through troubles*
*And for forgiving my sins.*

Esau and Jacob got ready to journey back into the Promised Land. Esau
said, "I will go before you." Jacob said to him, "My children and my
flock are young. If we drive them too hard, they will die. You, my
brother, Esau, go ahead at your speed. I will lead gently so the
young can endure and we will come to you at Seir (meaning rough,
hairy)." Esau wanted to leave some of his men to help Jacob, but he
refused. Esau left for Seir and Jacob didn't follow him, but turned
right toward Succoth (booths). He built a house there and pens for
his cattle with barns.

Next Jacob left Succoth and journeyed to Shechem (means city of liars and
drunks) and pitched his tent there. He bought land from Hampor,
Shechem's father, for 100 pieces of gold. There Jacob erected an
altar, and called it El-Elohe-Israel (The God of Israel).

*Lord, Jacob continually tricked his brother to get on his good side,*
*Thank You for using his cunning plots to save his life.*

*Lord, I'm amazed that You use human sinners such as Jacob,*
*But I'm even more amazed You would use a sinner like me.*

Amen.

# Genesis 34

# DINAH RAPED

Place: Shechem ☌ Time: 1732 B.C.

Dinah, the daughter of Leah, left Jacob's camp to meet the young girls of the area. Shechem, the son of Hamor, a Hivite prince, saw her, grabbed her and raped her. Later, he was sorry for what he did, and afterward loved her. Then he tried to speak kindly to her to make up for what he did. So Shechem asked his father, "Get her for me."

When Jacob heard what happened, he held his temper until the men of Shechem came to see him. The sons of Jacob came in from watching sheep to join the discussion because they were angry at Shechem for he brought reproach on Israel by raping Dinah.

Hamor told Jacob that his son loved Dinah and wanted her for his wife. He then proposed, "Let's make marriage. You give your daughters to us and we'll give our daughters to you. Live with us, trade with us, and add to your possessions."

Shechem said to Jacob, "May I find grace in your eyes; give me Dinah as a wife. Whatever you tell me to do, I will do. Whatever dowry you ask, I will give to you."

The sons of Jacob said, "We cannot do this! We cannot give our sister to one uncircumcised. This is a reproach. But we will agree if you will be circumcised as we are circumcised. Then we will give our daughters to you and take your daughters as wives and we will become as one people. But if not—if you won't be circumcised— we'll take our daughters and be gone."

Hamor and Shechem went to the gate of the city and told the men that the Israelites were peaceful people. They suggested the Israelites wanted to dwell among them, trade with them, give them their daughters, and take our daughters for their sons. Then they told the men the conditions of being circumcised as the Israelites were circumcised. Finally, they told the men, "When the Israelites live here, their cattle will be ours."

The men of the city consented to the suggestions of Hamor and Shechem and every man was circumcised who went in and out of the gate.

On the third day when the men of Shechem were incapacitated, Simeon and Levi took their swords and went through the city and killed all the men. Then the other sons of Jacob joined them and they took Dinah out of Shechem's house and took the wealth of the city because the Hittites had defiled their sister. They took all their cattle, children, and wives for themselves.

Jacob confronted Levi and Simeon, "You have made me stink among those who dwell here—the Canaanites and Perizzites. They will gather into a large army and come destroy my family and all I have." The boys answered their father, "Should we let them treat our sister as a harlot?"

*Lord, the laws of nature are true, whatever a person sows, that will they reap. Jacob tricked everyone, and his daughter was raped. You forgave Jacob's sins that blocked his fellowship with You, but he still suffered the consequences of a deceitful life.*

*Lord, forgive all my sins that would block Fellowship between me and You.*

*But concerning the natural consequence of a sinful life,*
    *Lord, have mercy on me.*

Amen.

# Genesis 35

## Jacob Returns to Bethel

Lord, You said to Jacob, "Now is the time to move to Bethel and live there. Construct an altar and worship Me, the God who appeared to you as you were running from Esau, your brother."

Jacob instructed everyone with him, "Get rid of your idols, purify yourselves and put on fresh clothes. We will move to Bethel where I constructed an altar to God who answered me in my anguish and protected me wherever I went."

Everyone gave Jacob all the idols in their possession, including their earrings, and he buried them under a tree near Shechem. As they traveled, a holy terror fell on the people in the cities around them, so no one attacked them.

*Lord, protect me as I travel through this life,*
*Just as You protected Jacob.*

*May others sense Your presence in my life.*

When they came to Bethel in Canaan, Jacob constructed an altar and called the place El-Bethel (the God of the house of God), because it was there God revealed Himself to Jacob when he was running from his brother Esau.

Rachel's nurse Deborah died there. She was buried beneath an oak tree in the valley below Bethel. After that the tree was called the Oak of Weeping.

Lord, after Jacob arrived at Bethel, You revealed Yourself and said, "Your name will no longer be Jacob, but you will be call Israel." You further said, "I am God Almighty (El Shaddai). Be fruitful and multiply. Become a great nation, indeed many nations will come from you. Kings will come from you. I am giving to you the land that I gave to Abraham and Isaac and to your descendants after you." Then You, Lord, went up from that place.

Lord, Jacob set up a stone pillar so he could remember the place You spoke to him. Then Jacob poured oil and a drink offering on the stone. Jacob called the place Bethel (House of God) because You spoke to him there.

Jacob left Bethel to go to Bethlehem, Rachel went into labor and she had great difficulty with this birth. When she was about to give birth her midwife said to her, "Don't worry, you're about to have another son." With her last strength, she named him Ben-oni (son of my grief), but Jacob called him Benjamin (son of my right hand). Rachel died and was buried on the way to Bethlehem. Jacob placed a stone pillar on her grave so he could remember the place.

Jacob continued traveling and camped on the other side of Migdal Eder. While there, Reuben slept with his father's concubine and Israel heard about it.

Jacob had 12 sons. The sons of Leah were Reuben, Simeon, Levi, Judah, Issachar and Zebulum. The sons of Rachel were Joseph and Benjamin. The sons of Bilhah, Rachel's handmaid, were Dan and Naphtali. The sons of Zilpah, Leah's hand maid, were Gad and Asher.

Jacob came to the home of his father Isaac in Mamre (Hebron) where Abraham had lived. Isaac lived to be 180 years old, then breathed his last and joined his people in death and Jacob and Esau buried him.

Amen.

# Genesis 36

## Descendants of Esau

Place: Seir ᖇ Time: 1730 B.C.

This is what happened to the descendants of Esau (Edom). Esau took two
wives from the women of Canaan: Adah, the daughter of Elon the
Hittite; and Aholibamah, the daughter of Anah and daughter of
Zibeon the Hivite. He also married Basemath, Ishmael's daughter
and the sister of Nebajoth. Adah gave birth to Eliphaz. Basemath
gave birth to Reuel. Aholibamah gave birth to Jeush, Jaalam, and
Korah. These sons were born to Esau in the land of Canaan.

Esau took his wives, his sons and daughters, and all his household, along
with his livestock and cattle—all his goods he had acquired in the
land of Canaan—and left his brother, Jacob. The land could not
support them both because of all the livestock and possessions. So
Esau (Edom) settled in the hill country of Seir.

This is the genealogy of Esau's descendants, the Edomites, who lived in the
hill country of Seir.

Esau's sons were Eliphaz, son of Adah; and Reuel, son of Basemath. The
sons of Eliphaz were Teman, Omar, Zepho, Gatam, and Kenaz.
Timna, the concubine of Eliphaz, gave birth to Amalek. These are
the sons of Adah. The sons of Reuel were Nahath, Zerah, Shammah,
and Mizzah. These are the sons of Basemath. Esau also had sons by
Aholibamah, Jeush, Jaalam, and Korah.

These are the sons of Esau who became the chiefs of various clans: The descendants of Esau's first-born son, Eliphaz, became the leaders of the clans of Teman, Omar, Zepho, Kenaz, Korah, Gatam, and Amalek; all descended from Eliphaz, descendants of Esau's wife Adah. The descendants of Esau's son Reuel became chief of the clans of Nahath, Zerah, Shammah, and Mizzah. These are the clan chiefs in the land of Edom who descended from Reuel, descendants of Basemath. The descendants of Esau and his wife Aholibamah were chiefs of the clans of Jeush, Jaalam, and Korah. These are the clan chiefs descended from Esau (Edom).

## Original Peoples of Edom

These are the sons of Seir the Horite, who lived in the land of Edom: Lotan, Shobal, Zibeon, Anah, Dishon, Ezer, and Dishan. They were the Horite clan chiefs. The sons of Lotan were Hori and Hemam. Lotan's sister was Timna. The sons of Shobal were Alvan, Manahath, Ebal, Shepho, and Onam. The sons of Zibeon were Ajah and Anah. (Anah was the one who discovered the hot springs in the desert while he pastured his father's donkeys.) The children of Anah were Dishon, and his daughter, Aholibamah. The sons of Dishon were Hemdan, Eshban, Ithran, and Cheran. The sons of Ezer were Bilhan, Zaavan, and Akan. The sons of Dishan were Uz and Aran. So these were the chiefs of the Horite clans: Lotan, Shobal, Zibeon, Anah, Dishon, Ezer, and Dishan. Each Horite clan was named after their chief who lived in the hill country of Seir.

## Rulers of Edom

These were the kings who reigned in Edom before any king ruled over
Israel: Bela son of Beor, who reigned in Edom from the city of
Dinhabah. When Bela died, Jobab son of Zerah from Bozrah reigned
in his place. When Jobab died, Husham from the Temanites reigned
in his place. When Husham died, Hadad son of Bedad reigned in
his place from the city of Avith. Hushan defeated the Midianites in
Moab. When Hadad died, Samlah from Masrekah reigned in his
place. When Samlah died, Saul from Rehoboth-by-the-River reigned
in his place. When Saul died, Baal-hanan son of Achbor reigned in
his place. When Baal-hanan son of Achbor died, Hadar reigned in
his place and reigned from the city of Pau. Hadar's wife was
Mehetabel, the daughter of Matred and daughter of Mezahab.

These are the names of the chiefs of Esau, who lived in the places named
for them: Timna, Alvah, Jetheth, Aholibamah, Elah, Pinon, Kenaz,
Teman, Mibzar, Magdiel, and Iram. These were the chiefs of the
clans of Edom, listed according to their dwelling places in the land
they occupied. They all descended from Esau, the father of the
Edomites.

*Lord, I realize a genealogy is kept in Scripture of those who refuse
To trust You and live for You.*

*Later, I'll read how the children of these people influenced Your
Chosen people—the Jews—to fulfill Your plan.*

Amen.

# Genesis 37

## JOSEPH'S DREAMS

Jacob settled in the land of Canaan where his father had lived. Joseph was a shepherd of his father's sheep, even when he was a young boy. At age 17 he told his father the wrong things that the sons of Bilhah and Zilpah were doing.

Jacob loved Joseph more than all his other children because he was the son of his old age. Jacob had a long-sleeved robe made for Joseph (coat of many colors). But his brothers hated Joseph because their father did more for him than he did for them. The brothers couldn't even talk to him in a normal way.

Joseph had a dream and he told his brothers, "We were tying bundles of wheat in the field, when my bundle stood up by itself. Your bundles gathered around me and worshiped me." They hated Joseph even more because of the dream. His brothers responded, "So you think you will be a king and rule over us." They taunted him and their hatred grew.

Joseph had another dream and told his brothers, "The sun, moon, and eleven stars bowed in worship before me." Then Joseph told his father, who rebuked him, "Do you think that your father and mother will worship you?" The brothers became more jealous of him, but Jacob didn't forget about it.

The brothers led the sheep to Shechem for pasture. Jacob said, to Joseph, "Go, see how everything is going with them, and bring me word." So Joseph left Hebron to go to Shechem. When Joseph got there he couldn't find them. A man told him, "I heard your brothers say they were going to Dothan." So Joseph went there looking for them. The ten brothers recognized Joseph a long way off, so they made plans to kill him, saying, "Here comes the boy with big dreams. Let's throw him in a deep pit, and then let's see if he has dreams of us worshiping him. Then we will kill him. When we are asked what happened to him, we will say, 'A wild animal killed him.'"

*Lord, the reason the ten brothers were jealous of Joseph was because Jacob was partial to Joseph.*

*The other part of the problem was Joseph who seemed to brag and Show off his position.*

*Teach me to be humble in all I do,*
*May I be sensitive to all I meet.*

Reuben said, "Let's not kill him. Why should we shed blood? Let's just throw him in the pit and leave him to die." Reuben was planning to rescue Joseph and let him go home.

When Joseph arrived, they stripped off his long-sleeved robe and then threw him into a deep pit without any water. As they sat down to eat, they saw a caravan of camels coming toward them. They were Ishmaelites (sons of Ishmael and Abraham) traveling from Gilead to Egypt carrying spices, healing resin, and myrrh (opium).

Judah said, "We won't get anything if we kill Joseph. We'll only end up being murderers, after all he is our brother. Let's sell him as a slave to the Ishmaelites." The brothers agreed and pulled him out of the pit and sold him for 20 pieces of silver. The Ishmaelites took Joseph to Egypt.

Rueben discovered Joseph missing when he returned to the pit. In anguish, he tore his clothes to show his mourning. He told his brothers, "The boy isn't here, what can we do?" The brothers killed a goat, dipped the long-sleeved coat in the blood and brought it to their father saying, "We found this robe, does it belong to Joseph?"

Jacob cried out, "It's Joseph's robe. A wild animal has attacked him, and eaten him. Joseph has been torn in pieces." Jacob mourned for Joseph for a long time (Jacob was still mourning years later when he found out Joseph was alive). Jacob's sons and daughter tried to comfort him but he refused to be comforted, saying, "I will mourn for him until I go to my grave."

In Egypt, the Ishmaelites sold Joseph to Potiphar, one of the Pharaoh's officials who was captain of the palace guard.

*Lord, even the family of your servants don't properly treat other*
*Members of the family;*
*May I properly love all those in my family.*

Amen.

## Background Story of Joseph's Boyhood Dreams

### Genesis 37

Place: The Hill Country of Judea *∞* Time 1712 B.C.

Jacob's two youngest sons, Joseph and Benjamin, were playing with a fluffy puppy at the tent door.

Joseph's olive skin and beautiful eyes—the eyes of his mother Rachel—crinkled when he smiled, making him attractive to all, except the ten half-brothers born to Leah and the handmaiden. They didn't like Joseph maybe because he didn't like them or trust them.

Joseph laughed at them behind their backs, calling the half-brothers "Bad Eyes," a nickname he picked up from his father. It was a cruel response to the eyes of their mother Leah. Everyone knew something was wrong with Leah's eyes; she was born with black moles on her eyelids. But even though she appeared ugly, Leah was a good mother who just happened to have rebellious kids…"Bad Eyes."

The father of them all, Jacob, arrived at the tent door as the setting sun dipped over the horizon. Joseph asked,

"Where do you go each evening?"

"I go to walk with God," Jacob explained that he wanted to be alone when he worshiped the God who created them. Jacob held up his walking stick in front of Joseph, then pointed to the signet carved at the top of the stick, it was the signet to remind him of his heritage. Jacob explained,

"Abraham is the father of us all…Isaac's signet is next, he was the son born to Abraham in old age…my signet is next." Jacob was proud, "I am the younger brother who took the place of Esau who sold his birthright." Joseph broke the silence,

"You have 12 sons…whose signet will be carved into the walking stick to carry on the family heritage?"

Silence shrouded the campfire. The sun was gone but the afterglow revealed stars in the sky. The distant valleys in the everlasting hills were black.

Jacob knew the family would explode if he answered—now—but in time he'd have to appoint a son to lead the family. So Jacob evaded the question.

"Look at the stars…" the boys and father leaned back to study the ever-darkening sky. "The Lord promised Abraham he would have more children than the stars of the night."

"Wow," Joseph thought, "there are thousands of stars."

Jacob explained that their family would be a great nation one day. He explained that some time in the future, "One star—a son—will be our Deliverer." Jacob explained that the Deliverer would be a seed of the woman—Eve—who would come to destroy evil. When the Deliverer comes, people would no longer get sick and die. "The Deliverer will be a Hebrew...our tribe...our blood...our future...."

Joseph stared at the stars, but he was not thinking about the stars he saw. Joseph determined to live godly in preparation for the coming Deliverer. He knew there were 12 sons. Joseph wondered if the Deliverer would come through him. Then Joseph blurted aloud,

"Our Deliverer can't come through "Bad-Eyes.""

"Hush," Jacob reprimanded Joseph.

Jacob went over and put an arm around Benjamin, the youngest of his 12 sons who needed more love than the other sons. Ten years ago Rachel had died giving birth to Benjamin. Now Jacob had to be both father and mother to this quiet, sensitive lad. Jacob sat for a long time with his arm around Benjamin and remembered the love he had for Rachel. For now the empty place in Jacob's heart could be filled with his young son Benjamin.

A few days later, old Jacob called Joseph into his tent. He had a surprise behind his back for him. Smiling through wrinkled eyes, Jacob looked beyond the beautiful face of Joseph, the father looked into the heart of his son. Jacob knew that Joseph shared his dream of the birthright and the blessing.

Joseph was sincere in his teenage years, as Jacob had been a rebellious youth. As a young man Jacob had tricked his brother out of the spiritual leadership of the family—and God approved what Jacob chose—but Jacob knew he couldn't appoint Joseph heir of all things. He knew there would be murder and hatred if he tried to make Joseph ruler over the family. Old Jacob knew Joseph could not be the next family ruler—Joseph was too young. But Jacob had a plan, the trickster had one more trick up his sleeve.

"Look…" Jacob brought the bright coat out from behind his back. It was a white tunic like the one the other shepherds wore, except it had brightly colored sleeves like those worn by the foreman. Working shepherds didn't have sleeves because they were constantly lifting sheep and lambs. They didn't have sleeves because they got dirty and sleeves were always in the way. But the foreman—in recognition of his rank—had long flowing sleeves on his garment. And the greater status of the foreman, the more colorful his sleeves. Joseph had never seen such a beautiful coat.

"Try it on, it's yours," Jacob instructed his teenage son. "You'll be foreman over my flock, because I can trust you."

When "Bad Eyes" saw the coat of colored sleeves, they were envious, then their envy slowly grew into hatred. "We'll not serve our younger brother." Rather than respect, "Bad Eyes" cursed Joseph, lied and physically abused Joseph.

Joseph began walking with God in the evening, thanking Jehovah for all his blessings. After a day of harvesting wheat in the field, Joseph had a dream where his sheaf of wheat stood upright; it stood taller and fuller than the other sheaves of wheat tied by his brothers, "Bad Eyes." Their sheaves of wheat were haphazardly thrown together and loosely tied. Joseph's wheat was taller…fuller…and impeccably arranged. Joseph's sheaf commanded attention because it stood taller than the others. Then in his dream, the 11 sheaves bowed in reverence to Joseph's dream.

The next day Joseph watched the harvest in frustration as "Bad Eyes" sloppily tied wheat sheaves in the field. Taking off his foreman's coat with colored sleeves, Joseph tied an immaculately sheaf of wheat, then commanded,

"Do it like mine!"

The brothers erupted in contempt at Joseph, ridiculing him for his arrogant attitude, "We'll never obey a son of Rachel." They threw a threat into his face.

"Yes you will!" Joseph's immaturity was struggling for prideful recognition. "One day you'll worship me," beautiful Joseph wasted his words on his ugly brothers. Joseph told them about his dream of 12 wheat sheaves, and he mistakenly told them that their sheaves bowed down to his sheaf.

"HA!" they sarcastically laughed at the preposterous idea of reverencing Joseph. From then on, they used the dream as an opportunity to mock Joseph, accusing him of arrogance and pride.

Joseph never forgot the night his father told him about the children of Abraham being as many as the stars. In his sleep Joseph dreamed that he and his brothers were stars—the stars of Abraham's sons.

The next time Joseph tried to tell his brothers what to do, "Bad Eyes" just glared at him in obstinance, refusing to do what their younger brother, Joseph, commanded. Joseph was naïve, he mistakenly thought if they knew what was right, they would do right; Joseph didn't understand the deep sinister urges of an evil heart. He thought his brothers would do God's will when they knew God's will, so he told them about his second dream.

"God gave me a second dream," he slowly unfolded the dream to them. But Joseph erred, not looking into the physical eyes of "Bad Eyes," for if Joseph had seen their contemptuous gaze, he would have known the eyes of their heart were blinded. Joseph told his stepbrothers that they were stars. Then he told them,

"The eleven stars bowed down to me," Joseph related the dream accurately, just as he saw it in his dream. He told how the sun and moon—his parents—bowed down to him. Rather than believing the dream, they spit on the ground and cursed Joseph. Then the brothers did what quarreling brothers always do—they ran to tell Father.

"What do you mean?" Jacob asked Joseph, his foreman son, thinking that the boy's job had gone to his head. "Do you think your mother and I will worship you?"

Joseph didn't know how to answer his father, so he said nothing. In dealing with them, Joseph didn't understand the wickedness of his brothers' intent because Joseph was good. He mistakenly thought everyone else was good. He naively believed in his brothers and tried to give good supervision to his brothers—never seeing their growing hatred for him.

A little time later, Jacob sent Joseph to check up on his brothers, they had gone two days away with the flocks. As they watched their flocks, they saw the bright sleeves coming over the horizon. There was no mistaking the coat. They hated him at a distance.

"Let's kill him," one of the "Bad Eyes" said to the others. "Let's see if his dreams can save him." They all laughed at the idea—except Reuben. Since Reuben was the oldest of the twelve, they sent him out to check on the sheep.

They didn't kill Joseph, but they did rip off the contemptuous coat. As he stood naked before his brothers, only then did Joseph realize how wrong he had been. It was then that Joseph was sorry for telling them about his dream. It was then that he was sorry for flaunting the foreman's coat with bright colored sleeves. It was then that Joseph's eyes were opened to understand the devious nature of his brothers' hearts.

Instead of killing Joseph, they threw him into a well—a deep pit—some shepherds had tried to dig for water but the pit was dry. Joseph had been held captive in the depths of his pure conscience, now he was captive in a hole in the ground.

With Joseph in the pit and their entertainment of retribution over, the brothers sat down to eat. But they moved far enough away so they couldn't hear the cries of Joseph. Reuben had been checking on the sheep, but he intended to return under the cover of darkness to release Joseph from the well. Reuben planned to let Joseph sneak safely away to home. After all, his brothers had made other vicious attacks on Joseph, and nothing came of them.

After dinner, the brothers were gloating in their success. The very thoughts about killing Joseph gave them immense satisfaction as though they had already accomplished the murder. As they bragged to one another, their boasting was interrupted.

"LOOK!" one of the "Bad Eyes" pointed to a camel caravan on the evening horizon. A group of traders were heading to Egypt. Then the fourth born—Judah—suggested to his brothers,

"We'll get nothing if we kill our brother." They all laughed. "Let's sell him as a slave, then we'll get some money for this dreamer of dreams."

"YES," they all laughed approvingly.

Joseph was sold for 20 pieces of silver—the price of a slave—the ten brothers divided the silver among themselves, two pieces for each. Benjamin the other baby brother born to Rachel was never with them. To compound the implication of their sin, the merchants were from Midian—Midianites—they were the descendents of Hagar and her son, Ishmael—Ishmaelites. They were blood relatives to Joseph because they were all descendants of Abraham. But the Ishmaelites didn't mind buying Joseph as a slave, the sons of Ishmael hated the sons of Isaac, so the Ishmaelites enjoyed locking the slave irons on a hated grandson of Isaac.

*"There is no evil so great as the evil done by family to family."*

## My Time to Pray

- Lord, remind me how deeply some people hate, then remind me to pray for them and return good for evil. Lord, don't let me act in a sinful way before them, and don't let me bring reproach on the name of Christ.

- Lord, help me to show equal time to all children, or grandchildren, or great grandchildren. Lord, then help them see my impartiality.

- Lord, You give dreams to guide us in this life, help me see the dreams You have for my life and service.

- Lord, thoughts of murder and acts of revenge are a terrible way to live; keep me from such plots, and help me always have pure motives.

# Genesis 38

# Judah and Tamar

Judah left his brothers and sisters and settled near Hirah who was an
   Adullamite. He married a Canaanite woman, the daughter of Shua.
   Judah was living in Kezib when his first son Er was born, his
   second son was Onan, and the third son was Shelah.

When Judah's oldest son Er grew up, he married Tamar. Because Er was
   evil, You allowed Er to die. Judah said to his next son, "Onan, go
   sleep with your brother's wife and preserve the family's line." Onan
   knew the child would not count as his (his signet wouldn't be carved
   on the family walking stick), so when he had intercourse with her,
   he spilled his semen on the ground, so his brother wouldn't
   have children. This was evil in Your sight, so You allowed Onan
   to die also.

Judah said to his daughter-in-law, "Don't marry but stay in your father's
   house till Shelah comes of age, then marry him to carry on the
   family line. (But Judah didn't intend to give Shelah to her because
   he was afraid Shelah would be killed like his brothers). So Tamar
   went to live with her parents. Lord, after a time Judah's wife
   died and he mourned for her. Then Judah went to supervise the
   shearing of his sheep in Timnah where his friend Hirah lived.

When Tamar heard where Judah went, she took off her widow's clothes and
   covered her face like a prostitute and sat at the entrance of a village
   named Enaim, which Judah would pass on his way to Timnah. Judah
   saw her and thought she was a prostitute, so he asked her to sleep
   with him. He didn't realize she was his daughter-in-law. Tamar
   asked, "What will you pay me?" He said, "I'll send a kid from my

flock." She said, "What will you give me to guarantee that you'll send the kid back?" Tamar asked for the family seal (signet) on a cord that was around his neck, and his family walking stick. So Judah gave her these things and they slept together. Then she returned to her family and put on her widow's clothes.

Judah asked Hirah to take a kid to the prostitute and get the items he left to guarantee his word. Hirah couldn't find her anywhere, so he asked the men of the city about the prostitute. They said, "There has never been a prostitute here." So Hirah told Judah he couldn't find the prostitute and that the men of the city said there was never a prostitute there.

Judah said, "Let her keep the things. I did my best to find her. This won't make me a liar."

About three months later Judah was told Tamar was pregnant and had acted like a prostitute. Judah said, "Bring her here, and let her be burned alive." She sent a message to Judah, "I am pregnant by the man to whom these belong. Tell me, who is the owner of the signet hanging on a cord and this walking stick?" Then Judah said, "She is more right than I was, because I didn't keep my promise to give my son, Shelah, to marry her. But Judah never had sex with her again.

In due season Tamar had twin sons. As they were being delivered, one reached out a hand and the midwife tied a scarlet cord around its wrist and said, "This one came out first." But the hand was withdrawn and the other child was born first. Therefore, the first born was named Perez (breaking out first); then the brother with the scarlet cord was born and given the name Zerah (scarlet).

*Lord, it seems sin influences sinners as well as*
*Your people. Judah and his sons didn't do right.*
*Thank You for working in mysterious ways that I don't understand.*

*Thank You that the Messianic line wasn't blocked, and that Jesus came through the line of Tamar and her son Perez.*

Amen.

## Background Story of Judah and Tamar

### Genesis 38

Place: Canaan ∼ Time: 1720 B.C.

Judah had a close friend, Hirah, a Canaanite. When visiting in the tent of Hirah, Judah was attracted to his daughter, Shua; and he married her. When they had sex, she conceived and Er was born. Next, Onan was born and the third son was named Shelah.

Shua had more motherly influence on her son Er than did his father Judah. Er followed the sexual sins of his mother's religion, the Canaanites. Er married a girl named Tamar but she was unlike her Canaanite ancestors. Tamar had character and was a godly woman.

Er died when he sinned against God. According to new Eastern practices, Judah told his second son, "Go marry Tamar, we must keep the family birthright going." Judah probably reminded his second son, "You'll have a son, but your name will be under Er's name on the walking stick, the family genealogical rod.

Onan didn't want to do the work without getting credit, so when Onan had sex with Tamar, he spilled his semen on the ground. God killed him, not so much because of birth control or a masturbation-type problem. No! Onan refused to recognize the family responsibility which included the promise of God to Abraham. God promised that from the seed of

Abraham would come a Deliverer and the children of Abraham would be a great nation.

Sex wasn't the issue. Onan refused to identify with the faith of Abraham and the promises of God. For all we know, Onan could be rebelling against God and the seed he spilled on the ground was cutting off the tribe of Judah. Also, for all we know, Onan could be cutting off the semen that would have produced the Deliverer, the Lord Jesus Christ. The Bible says, "The thing which he did displeased the Lord; therefore He [God] killed him also" (Gen. 38:10).

That sin was bad enough, but Judah compounded the problem by sinning on three levels.

Judah and Hirah went off to shear the sheep. It's probably like business-men today going on a business trip and since they are away from home and wife, they decide to have some sexual fun. "No one will know."

They saw a harlot at the entrance to a small town, Timnah. Judah was God's man who sinned by committing adultery. Perhaps he justified his adultery because his wife died. Having sex with a harlot is sin enough, but there is a second more condemning sin. Judah was to be the one through whom the Deliverer would come. His sexual sin was putting his semen in the body of a harlot.

When Judah met the harlot, he didn't know it was his daughter-in-law, Tamar. The Bible says, "She took off her widow's garments, covered [her-self] with a veil and wrapped herself" (Gen. 38:14).

When Judah begins negotiating the price of sex with this woman he thought was a prostitute, she wanted a high price. Judah agreed to give her a young goat, but his flock was not with him. Like a man who does-n't have cash or credit cards, he made a promise to pay later.

The prostitute—Tamar—agreed to have sex on the spot, but she wanted some proof Judah would send the goat back to her after the tryst was over. Tamar asked for his family signet that hung on a cord and his walk-ing stick. Now on some occasions such as this, the signet was worn around the neck and also carved into the genealogical walking stick. She wanted both to doubly convict Judah.

This is the third sin. When Judah leaves the signet and walking stick as a guarantee with the lady he believes is a prostitute, he is trampling the promises of God to Abraham and Isaac. God promised to expand the Jews into a great nation. But Judah had no respect for God's promises concerning a family and surrendered the signet and walking stick.

Did Judah know he was in the line of the Deliverer? No one knows for sure, but he along with the other sons of Jacob, all knew of the promises of God that a Deliverer would be born through their family who would crush the head of the serpent/satan. Each son must have thought, *Will the Deliverer be my son?* Later, God will prophesy through Jacob that the Deliverer would come through his son, Judah. God promised, "The scepter/staff will not pass from Judah until the Deliverer will come whom the people will obey" (Gen. 47:10 ELT).

Judah had sex with the woman and a few days later, Judah sends his good friend Hirah with the young goat to collect the signet and walking stick. If Judah had any respect for God, he would have gone himself. But no, he sends his "buddy" to do his dirty work.

Hirah explains to Judah that he couldn't find the prostitute so Judah excuses himself saying at least he tried to pay his debt. Notice Judah is more concerned with his reputation than with God's.

Later when Judah heard that Tamar is pregnant, Judah got mad and planned to enact family judgment on her. "She's had sex and she's a widow." When Judah came to confront Tamar with her sexual sin, she turns the tables and shows him the family signet and walking stick. He's the greater sinner.

Tamar did wrong to commit adultery to make a point that her father-in-law was not righteous. Maybe Tamar believed the Deliverer would come through the seed of Judah, and she did what she did to guarantee the continuance of the Messianic line. Anyway, Tamar's name and the name of her illegitimate son, Perez, are mentioned in the line of Jesus Christ (Matt. 1:3). When sin abounded, grace did much more abound.

## My Time to Pray

- Lord, the sins of Your people in Scripture are not much different from the sins of Your people today. I'm glad You are a forgiving God who understands our weaknesses and forgives us our sin.

- Lord, help me remember that where sin abounds, grace much more abounds. I must have Your grace for I am not perfect.

- Lord, keep me from sin; I promise to live as holy as possible. May I never excuse my sin because any other Christian sins.

# Genesis 39

# JOSEPH IN POTIPHAR'S HOUSE

When Joseph was brought down to Egypt by the Ishmaelites, he was purchased by Potiphar, an officer of Pharaoh, and a captain of the regiment that guarded Pharaoh.

Lord, You were with Joseph and blessed him abundantly as he served in the household of his Egyptian master. Potiphar saw that You, Lord, were with Joseph and blessed everything Joseph did. As Joseph pleased Potiphar, he was made manager of the household; and all possessions were entrusted to Joseph's management.

Lord, You blessed Potiphar's house because of Joseph, prospering the things in the house and fields. Potiphar gave Joseph complete control over everything he owned. He didn't worry about anything, except to choose what to eat.

*Lord, I know cream rises to the top,*
*Just as the superior wisdom of Joseph gave him leadership.*

*And I'll rise to the top if I*
*Continually do the right thing in the right way.*

Joseph was a handsome and strong young man. Potiphar's wife saw him and invited him to sleep with her. But Joseph refused saying, "No, my master has entrusted me with everything in his house. I have more authority than anyone here. He has withheld nothing from me, but you; because you are his wife. How could I do this wicked thing against him and sin against my God?"

She kept pressuring Joseph each day, but he wouldn't sleep with her or even be with her. One day while he was working alone inside the house, she grabbed his robe demanding, "Sleep with me!" When he ran away, she kept the robe.

She began screaming. When the servants gathered, she said, "My husband brought the Hebrew slave to embarrass me, he tried to rape me but I screamed for help. When he ran, he left this robe here."

She kept the robe and that evening she told her husband, "That Hebrew slave tried to rape me, but my screams scared him away. When he ran out of the house, he left his robe."

After hearing his wife's story, Potiphar threw Joseph in prison where Pharaoh's prisoners were kept.

Lord, You were with Joseph, and he found favor in the warden's sight. Joseph was made trustee over all the prisoners so that they did what he said. Joseph took care of all the problems so that the warden didn't have any worries. Because You, Lord, were with him, You prospered everything Joseph did.

*Lord, Joseph was righteous and he continually did the right thing,*
*Yet, You let circumstances go against him for Your purpose.*

*Help me trust Your long-range purpose in my life*
*When circumstances beyond my control go against me.*

Amen.

## Background Story of
## Joseph in Potiphar's House

### Genesis 39

Place: Egypt ↶ Time: 1720 B.C.

Joseph walked across the yard toward the owner's house, his olive skin was much fairer than the dark-skinned Egyptian slaves who worked with him. Each slave picked corn to fill a basket. Then with a long trek, each brought his harvest to the barn where they waited in line to stack the ears of corn tightly to store for the winter. Joseph approached his master Potiphar,

"We could harvest the corn much quicker," Joseph said to his master, "if a few just picked corn...if a few hauled corn...if a few stacked corn...."

Potiphar sat on his porch overseeing his slaves who worked his land. Potiphar's fields were surrounded with a high plastered limestone wall, as white as the ground was black. Potiphar owned choice land near to the Nile for water and near to Pharaoh's palace for prestige. Potiphar got the choice location because he was commander of the elite troops that guarded the palace, and were responsible for the protection of Pharaoh himself. Young Joseph appealed to his master's military organizational instincts.

"Organize your slaves to harvest your fields, just as you organize your soldiers to guard the palace." Joseph was obviously the most brilliant servant in Potiphar's household. Joseph continued to appeal to Potiphar's managerial instinct, "Choose those men to harvest who do it best, choose those to haul who are strongest. You'll get more work done when servants do the job they are best at doing. And your servants will work harder if you reward them with extra corn when they do extra work." Potiphar liked what he heard from the young Hebrew, then Joseph added,

"You'll make more money."

"Agreed," Potiphar was soldier-like in making decisive decisions. "I'll make you over-seer," Joseph was promoted on the spot. Potiphar told him, "Since you've conceived this plan, you know who is best qualified to do each task. You're in charge of the harvest."

Joseph smiled because his idea was accepted. But a dark corner of his conscience warned him not to make the same mistake that caused him trouble with his ten brothers..."Bad Eyes." An older and wiser Joseph bowed his head in submission as he told his fellow-slaves, "This is what Potiphar wants done," subconsciously he said, "not what I want." Because he was a fellow-slave, the others listened to Joseph, worked hard for Joseph, and their harsh circumstances improved. Because of an improved work-economy, fewer slaves were needed to harvest the crops. Joseph put the extra workers to building better houses for the slaves. Before the harvest was over, Joseph had improved the morale around Potiphar's home, and his barns were filled—Potiphar prospered.

But back of the scenes, God was prospering Potiphar's house because of Joseph; God had a plan for the young Hebrew's life. The Lord remembered His promise to bless Abraham and his seed. Those who obeyed the Lord would prosper, and even in slavery Joseph lived honestly according to what God would have him do.

Because of Joseph's efficient oversight, Potiphar didn't have to spend as much time with his servants. He trusted Joseph's leadership and the Hebrew slave rewarded his trust.

But this opened the door to other problems. Potiphar's wife had wandering eyes, with nothing to do each day but enhance her beauty and indulge her physical wants; she constantly reinforced her self-worth by capturing the affection of strong men. She captured the strength of men by trading her sexual pleasures for their bondage, casting them into the hell of their desires.

"Joseph…," she let the name of the Hebrew overseer drop gently from her lips. "Joseph, could you repair the door to my room?"

"I'll send a carpenter immediately," was his efficient reply. She tried to gain his attention the next day.

"Joseph, have the servants mix the fragrance of the orchids with some lotion." She seductively lifted her wrist to his nose to smell the mixtures from yesterday.

When Joseph dispatched the servant to prepare the aroma, the wife said to him,

"I admire the way you handle the servants, everyone willingly obeys your every word. How do you get everyone to do exactly what you command?"

"The servants do the will of my master—your husband—I am just the voice who gives them direction." Joseph did not claim any authority. Then the wife bluntly announced to Joseph,

"I've decided to reward you by having sex with you."

"I cannot do that." Joseph spoke without an emotional struggle, he had made a choice to always do the right thing. He explained, "My master has entrusted everything in the house to me, there is no one over me except your husband. He expects me to do the right thing. I cannot sin against him and God by doing this."

Joseph excused himself and left her presence. But his firm denial did not answer the problem. Every day the wife found an excuse to talk to Joseph, and every day she approached him with a different reason why he should lie with her. Every day Joseph gave the same answer,

"I cannot sin against my master and against God."

There was a day when Joseph was reviewing the records of the bed linens in the linen closet. When the records were not complete, Joseph went to his master's bedroom to check the records of the servant in charge, but the servant was not there, no one was there.

"Have you come for love?" Potiphar's wife spoke from behind the curtains. Before Joseph knew what happened, she grabbed his tunic and pulled him toward the bed, "Come lie with me..."

"NO!" Joseph threw off his tunic, running toward his private quarters. She began to scream and she continued screaming—with all her might she screamed. The servants came running, as well as the armed guards from the front gate.

"Joseph tried to rape me...," she gasped for words through sobs. "Run, get Potiphar...quickly." The house was filled with confusion. When Joseph heard the accusation, he stayed in his quarters. When Potiphar arrived, his wife's hysteria had calmed but her eyes were still puffy red, she constantly broke into tears as she falsely described the attempted rape. Then to convince her husband, she held out the damaging evidence.

"Here's Joseph's tunic I grabbed when he attacked me."

Potiphar doubted his wife. She had been unfaithful too many times. She had disappointed him too often. If Potiphar thought Joseph had tried to rape his wife, he could put Joseph to death. Slaves were not that valuable and Potiphar was a wealthy man. If he executed Joseph, it would be an example for all the other slaves to obey him.

*My slaves obey me,* Potiphar thought, *Joseph has taught them to obey me, I am wealthy because of Joseph.* Potiphar knew he couldn't execute Joseph, but at the same time he knew he couldn't leave Joseph as overseer of his house. The rumors of the alleged rape had spread throughout the palace as feathers from a pillow are scattered in the wind, never to be returned.

Potiphar threw Joseph in prison—not the slime pit of thieves who tortured one another and beat one another to death. Joseph was locked up with political prisoners; those considered a threat to the kingdom.

## My Time to Pray

- Lord, I know You see everything I do, just as You saw everything Joseph did. Keep me pure when I am tempted. I promise to be holy.

- Lord, give me a firm resolve against every temptation. Make me say "no" even if I feel weak.

- Lord, those who do right—like cream—rise to the top. Help me do the very best with every occasion in life. May I please You with my diligence.

- Lord, You were with Joseph in adverse circumstances and You helped him make the most of difficulties. Help me do the same.

# Genesis 40

## JOSEPH INTERPRETS TWO PRISONERS' DREAMS

At a later time, Pharaoh's chief cup bearer and baker were thrown into the same prison with Joseph. Potiphar, the captain of the guard, assigned them to Joseph. They remained there a long time.

One night, the cup bearer and the baker each had a dream with different meanings. In the morning Joseph saw they were dejected and asked, "Why are you so sad?" They answered, "We both had a dream and no one can tell us what they mean."

Joseph told them God was the One who interpreted dreams, then Joseph said, "Tell me the dream."

*Lord, I know You speak through dreams;*
*As You miraculously used a dream to predict the future.*

*Speak to my inner person with Your direction,*
*Then I'll do what You tell me to do.*

The chief cup bearer told Joseph, "In my dream I saw a vine with three branches that began budding, then blossoms appeared and finally clusters of grapes appeared. I had Pharaoh's cup in my hand, so I squeezed the grapes into the cup and gave it to Pharaoh."

Lord, You gave the interpretation to Joseph who said, "Three branches are three days. Within three days you will be restored and you will give Pharaoh his cup as you used to do when you were the cup bearer."

Then Joseph asked the cup bearer to intercede for him, "Remember me when you return to Pharaoh's presence to release me from prison. I was kidnapped from my homeland and I have done nothing to be in this prison."

When the chief baker saw the interpretation was good, he said, "I too dreamed and saw three baskets of white bread on my head, with all kinds of bakery goods for Pharaoh, but birds came and ate them."

Lord, You gave Joseph the interpretation, "Three baskets mean three days and within three days Pharaoh will cut off your life, hang your body on a pole and birds will eat your flesh."

Three days later on Pharaoh's birthday, he gave a feast for all his officials where he restored the chief cup bearer who then gave Pharaoh his cup. Pharaoh also had the chief baker impaled on a pole just as Joseph predicted. Nevertheless, the chief cup bearer didn't remember Joseph, but forgot about him.

*Lord, I know gratitude is the least remembered of all virtues*
*And that many good deeds I do are forgotten.*

*But Lord, remember all the good things I do;*
*I know you'll reward me in Your perfect timing*

Amen.

## Background Story of
## Joseph Interprets Two Prisoners' Dreams

### Genesis 40

Place: Egypt ☞ Time: 1722 B.C.

The keeper of the prison realized Joseph was an asset to him. Joseph had made friends with all the inmates, there was nothing the young Hebrew wouldn't do to make conditions better for the prisoners. He asked for lime to whitewash the walls, making the area smell better and sanitizing it against human filth. Because the Egyptians have a fetish about cleanliness, they granted Joseph's request. Because he organized the prisoners to get the job done, Joseph soon was trustee over all the prisoners. Next he supervised the distribution of food, then acts of violence died down. Again, unknown to prison officials, God blessed the prison because of Joseph.

But Joseph was learning lessons in prison that he hadn't learned when flaunting the coat of many colors over his brothers in his father's tent. Joseph never knew God was all he needed, until he was in prison in a foreign land and God was all he had.

When two of the most politically sensitive prisoners were thrown into prison, they were put in the same cell that Joseph supervised because the authorities didn't want any trouble out of them. Joseph became their friend, and one morning Joseph noticed his two friends—Pharaoh's chief butler and chief baker—were ashen-faced with fear.

"Why are you so scared?" Joseph asked his two important prisoners. "What happened?"

"We dreamed," both men replied, "we are afraid our dreams are sent to punish us."

"No," Joseph corrected the two men. "The interpretation of dreams belongs to God. Because I worship God, if you will tell me your dreams I'll give you the interpretation of your dreams."

The two high-ranking men were educated, yet they were superstitious, not wanting to offend any of the many gods of Egypt. They felt God spoke to people through dreams. Because they both had respect for Joseph, they agreed to tell their trustee what they dreamed. The butler went first,

"I dreamed a vine had three branches, and they blossomed before my eyes. The flowers turned to clusters of grapes—beautiful ripe grapes. I had Pharaoh's cup in my hand, so I squeezed the grapes into wine, filling the cup with delicious wine—so enjoyable I was able to give it into Pharaoh's hand."

Because Joseph walked with God, he trusted the Lord for its interpretation. Somehow, Joseph knew the correct interpretation would lead his freedom from prison. Joseph told the butler,

"The three branches are three days, within three days you will be restored to your previous position. Pharaoh will learn that you didn't try to poison him. You will again give the cup into Pharaoh's hand." Joseph added,

"When you get to talk to Pharaoh, make mention of me. I was kidnapped from my Hebrew family and sold into slavery. I have done nothing to be in prison—like you, I am innocent—tell Pharaoh I interpreted your dream."

"What about me?" the chief baker interrupted. "Can you interpret my dream?" Joseph nodded approval. The baker said,

"I was carrying three large white baking baskets on my head from which Pharaoh could eat. In the top basket were the best baked goods for Pharaoh, but birds came and ate them all up before I could deliver them to Pharaoh."

"Tell me the meaning of my dream," the baker begged. Joseph reminded them again that the interpretation of dreams came from God. Then Joseph shared a prediction of judgment on the chief baker.

"The three baskets are three days. Within three days Pharaoh will learn that you tried to kill him when you poisoned baked goods. Pharaoh will have you beheaded, and your body will be hung up for scavenger birds to eat.

"Ha, ha, ha!" that's ridiculous," the chief baker ridiculed Joseph's interpretation, "I love Pharaoh."

But three days later, Joseph's prediction came true. Pharaoh learned that the chief butler was loyal, people had lied about the butler; so the butler was restored. Just as quickly, the baker was executed and his body was hung out for the scavenger birds to pluck away its rotting flesh.

Joseph was right, but the chief butler forgot about his Hebrew friend back in prison. He didn't tell Pharaoh. Joseph languished in prison.

## My Time to Pray

- Lord, may I act graciously to all people, even if they are not grateful to me.

- Lord, I believe the predictions (prophecy) You have given concerning the coming of Christ and the destruction of the earth. Help me to live righteously because Jesus is coming back again.

- Lord, remind me to be grateful to all those who do kind deeds to me.

- Lord, I thank You for the example of Joseph who did right even when people around him lied and were ungrateful.

# Genesis 41

## JOSEPH INTERPRETS PHARAOH'S DREAM

Pharaoh dreamed two years later that he was standing beside the Nile River. Seven healthy cows came up out of the river and fed on the grass near the river. Next, seven skinny, miserable-looking cows came out of the river and ate up the healthy cows. Then Pharaoh woke up, but he went back to sleep and dreamed that seven fully ripened ears of grain grew on a single stalk. Next, he dreamed of seven more ears of grain that were shriveled by a hot eastern wind. The thin ears swallowed the seven fat ears. Then Pharaoh woke up.

The next morning Pharaoh was still upset by the dream so he called his magicians and wise men to interpret it for him. But none could do it.

*Lord, I know You speak through dreams to those without Scripture*
*Just as You spoke to Pharaoh and his two servants.*

*I pray You speak to me thorough Scriptures*
*And Your internal guidance so I'll do Your will.*

The chief cup bearer said, "This reminds me of something I should have done earlier. You were angry with me and the chief baker and put us in prison. One night we both had a dream, and each of our dreams had a different meaning. There was a Hebrew salve of Potiphar's in prison who interpreted our dream. We told him individually the dream and he interpreted each dream separately and both predictions came to pass. I was restored to my position and the baker was executed."

Then Potiphar called for Joseph to be brought out of the prison. He was shaved and dressed in appropriate clothes and ushered into Pharaoh's presence.

Pharaoh said to Joseph, "I had a dream and no one can interpret it, but I've been told you can interpret dreams."

Joseph answered, "I don't have the ability to do it, only God can interpret dreams. He will tell you what it means and set your mind at rest."

Pharaoh said to Joseph, "In my dream I stood by the Nile River and seven fat healthy cows come out of the river and they feed on the grass near the river. Next, seven skinny, miserable-looking cows come out of the river. I've never seen such ugly looking cows. They ate up the healthy cows. After they had eaten, I couldn't tell they had eaten anything because they were as skinny as before. At this point I woke up. Then I dreamed again that seven fully ripened ears of grain grew on a single stalk. Next, I dreamed of seven more ears of grain that were shriveled by a hot eastern wind. The shriveled ears of grain ate up the seven fully ripened ears. I told this dream to the magicians but none could interpret the dream."

Joseph said to Pharaoh, "Both dreams mean the same thing. God has told you what He is about to do. The seven fat healthy cows and the seven full ears of ripened grain are seven prosperous years that are coming. Likewise, the seven skinny, miserable-looking cows and the seven ears of grain shriveled by a hot eastern wind are seven years of famine that are coming. This is what God is about to do."

Joseph explained, "There will be seven years of abundance all throughout Egypt, and next there will be seven years of famine that will consume everything. Everyone will forget about the good years. The famine will be truly horrible."

Joseph explained why there were two dreams, "Because God has determined these things will happen soon." Then Joseph suggested, "Find the wisest men in Egypt and put him in charge of agriculture. Let him receive 20 percent of the produce in the seven years of abundance. He should receive the produce and store it to be used for food for the cities in the coming years. This stored food will feed the people in the coming seven years of famine so that the nation is not lost."

The suggestion was readily received by Pharaoh and his officials, and he said, "Can we find a supervisor like this who has the Spirit of God in him?"

Pharaoh said to Joseph, "Since God has revealed this dream to you, and there is no one wiser than you, you will be in charge of all agriculture and everyone must do what you say. Only I will be greater than you and what you say." Pharaoh said, "You are in charge of all the things grown in Egypt." Pharaoh took off his signet ring and gave it to Joseph's hand, and had him clothed in fine white linen with a gold chain around his neck. Joseph rode in the second chariot and they yelled before him, "Bow down!"

*Lord, You sent Joseph through a valley of suffering*
*To prepare him for a life of service.*

*Help me understand Your purpose for my suffering*
*And prepare me for a life of service.*

Pharaoh passed a law that no one could lift a hand to work without Joseph's approval. Pharaoh named him Zaphenath-paaneah (revealer of secrets) and gave him a wife—Asenath—the daughter of Potiphera, priest of Heliopolis. So Joseph began managing the entire agriculture of Egypt. He was 30 years old when he was appointed by Pharaoh. He immediately began an inspection tour throughout the land.

During the first seven years, the land produced abundantly. Joseph collected grain and stored it in the cities. The grain collected around a city was stored in that city. Joseph collected so much grain—like the sand on a beach—that they couldn't keep count of its abundance.

Two sons were born to Joseph and his wife Asenath before the years of famine came. Joseph named the first Manassah (to forget), "Because God has caused me to forget all the pain I suffered from my family." The second Joseph named Ephraim (fruit), "Because God has made me fruitful in the land of pain."

The seven years of abundance ended just as Joseph predicted and the seven years of famine came on Egypt. Other nations suffered because of the famine but the Egyptians had food. When everyone began begging Pharaoh for food, he told them to go do what Joseph tells them to do. Since the famine spread everywhere, all countries came to Joseph to buy food and he opened the store houses to sell them food.

*Lord, some things about the future are predicted in Scripture;*
*Help me learn Your Word so I know what to expect,*
*Then give me strength to obey what You've taught in Your Word.*

Amen.

## Background Story of
## Joseph Interprets Pharaoh's Dream

### Genesis 41

Place: Egypt ⌒ Time: 1715 B.C.

Two years later, a midnight storm broke over Egypt, lightning flashed, and a Sahara windstorm came rushing over Pharaoh's palace from the east—Egyptians believed the eastern wind carried an evil intent. The following morning, the low clouds threatened rain, but the weather was not as threatening as Pharaoh's anger. He had gathered every wise man and magician into the Great Hall—the largest in the world—Pharaoh wanted them all to hear from his lips the dream that terrorized him. The Great Hall was as silent as the buried pyramids. Pharaoh told them the story of his dream.

"I was in my dream…" the magicians knew dreams were more predictive when the one dreaming stood in the events he dreamed. Pharaoh continued, "I stood by the River Nile to see seven beautiful fat cows come out from the river to feed in a lush green meadow. Then I saw seven cows— mangy and skinny—come up out of the river to the same meadow. But they didn't eat from the meadow, they ate up the beautiful fat cows. Then I awoke."

Pharaoh stopped to describe his fear, he told of perspiring with fever as the cold storm blew through the palace. In his heart Pharaoh knew the dream told of coming judgment and depression.

"What else?" a wise man asked.

"I slept to dream a second dream," Pharaoh told what he saw. "I dreamed of seven full ears of corn growing on one stalk. I knew that was good because most stalks have only four or five ears to the stalk. It was good sweet corn."

The silence of the Great Hall grew even more quiet because of its massive audience. The only sound that each heard was his own heartbeat. Pharaoh continued,

"Then seven skinny ears came out of the same stalk and ate the seven fat ears. Then I awoke," Pharaoh announced, "I awoke to terror. I knew these dreams tell of destruction. Tell me the interpretation!"

The wise men always had an answer for Pharaoh, sometimes they were right, sometimes they lied, but Pharaoh didn't know better. Sometimes the evil demonic spirit spoke to them, but demons don't know the future.

This time the wise men said nothing, for they had a greater fear of being wrong than their embarrassment with nothing to say.

"God interprets dreams," the scared voice of the chief butler filled the silent Great Hall. This was not the voice of a wise man or a magician. This voice came from the trusted chief butler. "I know a man who can interpret dreams, he can predict the future. I am afraid to keep silent," the butler told all.

He told of his miraculous deliverance from prison because of a prisoner who could interpret dreams with the help of God.

Pharaoh called for Joseph, but first they had to prepare the young Hebrew for Pharaoh's presence. They bathed Joseph, then shaved all the hair off Joseph's body, for the immaculately antiseptic Egyptians appeased their gods with cleanliness. Since body hair was dirty and sometimes afflicted with lice or vermin, Joseph had to appear spotlessly before Pharaoh, dressed in pure white linen clothes.

There in the silence of the Great Hall as Joseph, a lone figure, stood isolated before the most powerful man on earth; the ruler of the known civilized world. The symbols of Egypt's false gods were etched into the walls of the Great Hall—Ra, god of the sun; Osirus and Isis, mystery gods; Ptah, god of Memphis; Aton, the sun-disc.

Behind Pharaoh stood statues reflecting the dark side of Egypt's obsession with demonic powers. But Joseph knew only the one true God of Israel—the Creator of the universe—Joseph stood alone with the God of the Hebrews. The only God who could interpret dreams and predict the future.

Pharaoh was scared of those who could interpret dreams, for these people had power over his life. He carefully told the dream to Joseph, but this time added something he had not previously announced to his wise men and magicians. He wanted to be completely honest with this interpreter of dreams. He said the seven skinny cows did not get fat by eating seven fat cows, and the seven lean ears of corn did not get bigger when they ate the fat ones.

"The dream is one," Joseph announced to Pharaoh, "not two dreams." Then with boldness not usually seen in those who address Pharaoh, Joseph warned, "God is showing you what He is about to do! There shall be seven years of prosperity; the crops will be larger than ever before—bumper crops. Then seven years of famine will follow that will consume all the abundance of the seven full years. The famine will be so grievous that it will eat up all the fatness of the seven years of prosperity. The dream is one—but shown to you twice—to let you know God will quickly bring it to pass."

Joseph was not finished with his explanation. "Let Pharaoh appoint one man to prepare for the famine. Let this man organize officers throughout Egypt who will carry out the command of Pharaoh. Take 20 percent of all your workers to build warehouses to hold grain. Store 20 percent of all the grain in these storehouses. There will be so much harvest, no one will miss the 20 percent that is stored out of sight. Then there will be enough food in every city so that the people will not rebel in times of famine. This way Pharaoh's kingdom will be established."

The chief officer of the guard—Potiphar—smiled as he heard Joseph tell Pharaoh how to be a prosperous king. Potiphar remembered years ago when young Joseph explained to him the same way to organize his field. Potiphar remembered becoming wealthy because of Joseph. Potiphar intended to tell Pharaoh about Joseph's wisdom, but even before the captain of Pharaoh's body guards could act, Pharaoh exercised his awesome power, announcing,

"The interpretation is good," the massive audience gasped unexpectedly at Pharaoh's positive response. The ruler lifted his hands for silence. The audience fell mute, then Pharaoh spoke again, his voice echoing off the stone walls,

"My heart tells me the interpretation is true, Egypt will have seven years of prosperity; followed by seven years of famine that will ravish our nation."

"NO!" many in the audience cried out. The room buzzed with spreading fear of coming depression, Pharaoh again lifted his hands for silence; then spoke,

"There is none so wise in all my kingdom as this *revealer of secrets*. The Spirit of God is upon him. Can we find a better man to manage the coming predictions that God has shown to me? This man will be the Minister of Agriculture, all my people will obey him as we plan for the great famine."

Pharaoh left the Great Hall in his gold chariot, Joseph rode in the second chariot; the people understood they were to obey the new Minister of Agriculture, only Pharaoh was higher in authority than Joseph.

From that day Pharaoh called Joseph, Zaphnath-Paaneah, Revealer of Secrets, and gave him Asenath as his wife. During the seven bountiful years, Joseph had two sons born to him. The first he called Manasseh, which meant *God made me forget my past trouble;* the second he called Ephraim, which meant *God has caused me to be fruitful in the land of my affliction.*

## My Time to Pray

- Lord, thank You for honoring Joseph after all the pain and alienation he suffered. I know You will honor me, maybe in this life, maybe in the next: but I obey You because I trust You.

- Lord, thank You for the supernatural interpretation of dreams that led to saving the world.

- Lord, thank You for warning the world of a coming famine by predicting it through dreams. Thank You for warning the world of coming tribulation that You have predicted through Scripture. I will heed Your warnings.

- Lord, You have always prepared a servant of Yours to save humankind. Thank You for saving the world through Jesus Christ.

# Genesis 42

# JOSEPH'S BROTHERS COME TO BUY CORN

When Jacob heard there was corn available in Egypt, he said to his sons,
"Why are you sitting around staring at one another? There is corn
for sale in Egypt, go buy for us so that we will live and not starve
to death." So Joseph's brothers went down to Egypt, except
Benjamin, Joseph's younger brother. Jacob didn't send him
because he was afraid something might happen to him. The sons
of Israel came to buy corn along with others from Canaan because
the famine covered the entire area.

Joseph was governor over Egypt and was responsible for selling corn to
everyone. When Joseph's brothers arrived, they bowed before
Joseph on the ground.

Joseph recognized his brothers, but didn't reveal himself to them. Rather,
he spoke harshly to them asking, "Where are you from?" They
answered, "From the land of Canaan to buy corn." The brothers
didn't recognize him. Joseph charged them, "You are spies! You've
come to spy out our weaknesses." They answered, "Not so, we're
the sons of one man, we're honest men and we've come to buy
corn." Joseph repeated his charge, "No, you're spies." They
answered, "We are your servants, we are twelve sons of one man,
the youngest stayed with our father and the other is no longer."

Joseph continued his hard questioning, again saying, "You are spies.
Here's how you can prove to me you're not lying. As Pharaoh lives,
you will not leave Egypt, unless your younger brother comes here.
Send one to get your brother to prove to me you're telling the truth.
Until then, I will keep you in prison. Otherwise as Pharaoh lives, it

proves you are spies. Then Joseph put them all in prison for three days.

*Lord, You use circumstances to make us face our lies,*
*Just as You used Joseph to confront the ten sons of Jacob.*

*Help me always tell the truth so I won't have to be confronted;*
*Lord, I will live truthfully as a testimony to You.*

After three days Joseph had them brought before him. He said, "If you do what I say, you'll live, for I fear God. One of you will stay here in prison while the others carry corn back to your homes. But bring your youngest brother back to prove you're telling the truth, otherwise you won't see my face.

The ten brothers spoke among themselves, "We are guilty for what we did to Joseph. We saw the anguish on his face when he begged us not to sell him as a slave, but we wouldn't listen to him. This is why we are in trouble."

Reuben answered them, "Didn't I tell you not to hurt the boy, but you wouldn't listen to me; now we're paying the consequences for our sin."

The ten sons didn't realize Joseph understood everything they said because an interpreter had been translating their conversation up until then. So Joseph left the room to weep. When he returned, he ordered Simeon to be put in chains before their eyes and was then thrown into prison.

Joseph ordered their sacks filled and that their money be placed in the sacks and that they be given food for their journey home. Their donkeys were loaded and they left. That night as one of the brothers opened his sack to feed his donkey, he discovered his money, and he cried, "My money is here in my sack." The ten sons were terrified and they cried, "Why is God punishing us?"

The ten brothers returned to their father and told him everything that happened to them. "The man spoke angrily with us and accused us of being spies. We told him we were honest men, not spies. We told the man we were twelve sons of one father, the youngest is with our father and one is no longer. The man—the governor of all Egypt—told us he was keeping one of us in prison, and to take our grain and go. He told us we wouldn't see his face again unless we brought our youngest brother next time. The man said that was his way of knowing we were not spies, but honest men. The man said then he would return Simeon to us and we could do business in Egypt. But there is more to the story; each of us had our money returned in our sacks." When Jacob saw the money in the sacks, he was frightened.

Jacob said to them, "You have destroyed our family unity. Joseph is gone, Simeon is gone, and now you want to take Benjamin away. This will be the death of me."

Reuben said to his father, "Put Benjamin in my care. If I don't bring him back, take the lives of my two sons."

Jacob answered, "Benjamin will not go to Egypt with you. His brother Joseph is dead; Benjamin is all I have left. If anything happened to him, I would die with grief."

*Lord, evil actions always have consequences*
*And the ten sons had to face the lies they told and lived.*

*Thank You for covering all my sins by the blood of Christ,*
*Help me walk in the light.*

Amen.

# Genesis 43

## JOSEPH'S BROTHERS DECIDE TO RETURN TO EGYPT

The famine wouldn't let up in Canaan, so when Jacob's family ate all the corn they bought in Egypt, Jacob said to his sons, "Go and buy us some more corn." Judah said to his father, "The man in Egypt told us we couldn't see his face if we didn't bring our younger brother. We will go buy corn if you will send Benjamin with us, but if you refuse, it's useless for us to go there."

Israel answered, "Why did you cause this problem by telling him you had another brother?" They answered, "The man interrogated us thoroughly, he asked if our father were alive and if we had any other brothers. We just answered the questions he asked. How did we know he would demand we bring our younger brother to prove we were telling the truth?"

Judah said to his father, "Please send Benjamin with me so we can go get food, otherwise our family will die. I will personally guard him so he will be safe. I will personally guarantee his safety. If I don't bring him back to you, I will bear the blame, no one else. If we had not been arguing this matter, we would be there by now."

Jacob concluded, "If that's the way it's got to be, so be it. Take your sacks and go. But let's bribe the man with some of our delicacies. Take some healing resin, a little honey, sweet-smelling gum, opium, and some almonds and nuts. Take twice the money, enough money to pay for the corn you got last time, and money to pay for the corn we get this time. Take Benjamin also. Go see the man and may almighty God—El Shaddai—cause the man to like you and be gracious to you so that he will release Simeon and send back Benjamin to me. What else can I do, if I lose my children, I'll just lose them."

The brother prepared for the trip, taking twice as much money, the gift for the man, and Benjamin. Then they traveled down to Egypt and stood before Joseph.

When Joseph saw Benjamin with the ten brothers, he said to his manager, "Take these men to my home. Prepare a banquet, for I will sit with these men at noon."

The manager brought them into Joseph's house and the brothers became fearful saying among themselves, "This is because our money was in our sacks, now the man will say we stole the money. The man will take our donkeys and make us slaves." So they explained to the manager, "Please...we're telling you the truth, our money was in our sacks when we opened them. We have brought back that money to return it, and we brought more money for more corn. We don't know how our money got into our sacks." The manager answered them, "Don't be afraid, the God you serve, and the God of your fathers took care of you. As far as your money is concerned, I put it in the sacks."

Simeon was brought out to them. The manager took them into the house and gave them water to wash their feet. Then he fed their donkeys. The brothers got their gift ready to give to the man when he arrived at noon. When Joseph arrived, they gave him their gift and bowed themselves before Joseph on the ground. Joseph asked, "Is your father alive and well, the elderly man you told me about?" They answered, "Yes, your servant—our father—is well."

As the brothers bowed in respect, Joseph saw his younger brother, then he asked, "Is this your younger brother that you told me about?" Then Joseph said to Benjamin, "May God be with you, my son."

Then Joseph left the room hurriedly to go weep at his private quarters. When he composed himself, Joseph returned and commanded the meal be served.

They served Joseph separately, the Hebrew brothers by themselves, and the Egyptians that were present were also served separately. That's because the Egyptians don't eat with Hebrews, they consider it an abomination.

As they were seated facing Joseph, they were surprised that the first born was in the place of honor. Afterward, each was seated according to his birth. They were all served, but Benjamin was given five times as much as any of the others.

*Lord, You placed us in our family with fathers, mothers, sisters, and brothers,*
*Help me bless my family and bless me through them.*

*May I always show appropriate respect to them,*
*And may You work Your will in my family.*

Amen.

# Genesis 44

## Joseph's Cup Found in Benjamin's Sack

Joseph directed the manager, "Fill each man's sack as full of corn as they can carry and put each man's money in it. Put my silver cup in the sack of the youngest along with his money."

The brothers left at daybreak with their donkeys, but before they had gone very far, Joseph sent his manager after them and told him to say to the brothers, "Why have you given evil for good? You have stolen the cup my master drinks from, it's the cup he uses for divination."

The brothers said to the manager, "Why are you accusing us of evil? We would never do that. To prove what we say, didn't we bring back the money that was put in our sacks last time we were here? If you find money in any of our sacks, let that one be put to death and the rest of us will be your Lord's slaves."

The manager changed the penalty from death to slavery. He said, "The one who has the silver cup will be my Lord's slave, the rest of you will go free." They all put their sacks on the ground and the manager searched them from the eldest to the youngest, and the cup was found in Benjamin's sack. The brothers cried in grief, and tore their clothing. Then they loaded their donkeys and headed back to the city. When they arrived at Joseph's house, he was still there. Joseph said, "Did you think you could get away with this? Don't you know I have the power of divination?"

Judah spoke for the brothers, "I don't know what to say. There's no way we can prove we are innocent. God has shown us our guilt. We are your slaves, including the brother in whose sack the silver cup was found. Joseph answered, "I would not put all of you into slavery, only the one who has the cup. Now the rest of you go to your father in peace."

Judah approached Joseph and asked to speak to him privately. "You are like Pharaoh and can do anything to us you please. Don't be angry with us. You said to us, 'Do you have a father? Do you have a brother?' We told you we had a father and a younger brother that he loved dearly. You said we would not see your face again unless we bring our younger brother. We told you our father would die if anything happened to the boy, but you insisted. So we told our father what you said. Then when our corn ran out, our father told us to come buy more corn. We answered and said we can't go unless the younger brother goes with us because the man won't see our face unless we have the younger brother. My father said, 'My wife bore me two sons, the first went out and the wild beasts surely tore him to pieces, and if you take the second one to Egypt and something happens to him, I will die.'"

Judah further explained, "If I go to my father without the boy, he will see that his youngest son isn't with me and he will die, and I'll be responsible. I personally guaranteed the boy's safety to my father, so I beg you, take me as your slave instead of my brother. Let the boy go to his father with his brothers. If I don't have the boy with me when I return, my father will die and I couldn't live with the grief of causing my father's death."

*Lord, this is a wonderful picture of my redemption;*
*Jesus who came from the tribe of Judah*
*Took my punishment so I could go free,*
*Just as Judah was willing to take the punishment, so*
*Benjamin could go free.*

Amen.

# Genesis 45

# JOSEPH REVEALS HIMSELF
# TO HIS BROTHERS

Joseph couldn't control his emotions in front of his servants so he told them, "Leave immediately." When no one was with him, Joseph revealed himself to his brothers, saying, "I am Joseph, is it true that my father is still alive?" His brothers couldn't speak, they were filled with great fear for what he would do to them, yet they were truly glad that he was alive.

The servants in the house heard Joseph crying, so did the Egyptians who worked for Joseph.

*Lord, it's all right to weep when our hearts are deeply stirred;*
*May I always weep at the great things You do.*

*May my heart never become too hard to cry*
*Over sin in my life or over the good things You do.*

Joseph invited his brothers to come close, assuring them, "I am your brother Joseph whom you sold as a slave. Don't be afraid or angry with one another. God sent me ahead to preserve the life of our family and the whole world. There is a worldwide famine; we've had two years of drought, and five years remain. There will be no planting or harvest. God sent me before you to save our lives and to make sure our descendents will survive. You didn't send me into slavery, it was God who sent me here. God has made me a father to Pharaoh, governor of his household, and ruler over all the agriculture of Egypt."

*Lord, I believe You work behind the things that I can't see,*
  *I believe You govern this world through Your laws,*

*But You arrange circumstances to carry out Your purposes;*
  *Bringing circumstances into my life so I can do Your will.*

Joseph told his brothers, "Go quickly to my father and tell him I'm alive.
  Tell him God has made me Lord over the agriculture of Egypt,
  and I want him to come to Egypt immediately because there are
  five more years of famine coming. Tell him not to delay because
  he will live in the land of Goshen with his children, his grandchildren,
  flocks, herds, everything he possesses. Tell my father he will live
  near me in Egypt. He will become poor and starve to death if he
  stays in the land of Canaan. Benjamin, my brother, will tell my
  father these things are true. Tell my father about my honor and
  power in Egypt, I will take care of everyone."

*Lord, You see the future that is coming that I don't see;*
  *You arrange things that I should have.*

*I yield my life and future to Your plan;*
  *Guide me, protect me, and use me for Your glory.*

Joseph embraced his brother Benjamin and they wept together. Then
  Joseph kissed each of his brothers and they wept together.

Rumors in the palace reached Pharaoh that Joseph's brothers were there.
  Pharaoh and the servants were pleased. Pharaoh said to Joseph,
  "This is what they must do, 'Load up their donkeys and go to the
  land of Canaan and get your father and your families and come
  live here in Egypt.'" Then Pharaoh gave a command, "Take our
  wagons to bring your children, wives, and your father to me. I
  will give property to all of you. Don't worry about bringing your
  stuff, you shall have everything new in Egypt."

The sons of Israel did what Pharaoh commanded and Joseph gave them wagons. Pharaoh gave them provisions for the journey. To each, Pharaoh gave a set of new clothes, but to Benjamin he gave five sets of clothes, and seven and a half pounds of gold. To Jacob, Pharaoh sent ten donkeys loaded with the finest things of Egypt, ten female donkeys loaded with grain, and food for him to eat on the return journey. The brothers were sent back to Canaan. Joseph told them, "Don't quarrel among yourselves on the way back home."

*Lord, why is it that brothers quarrel and families fight?*
*A family should have natural love for one another.*

*Lord, thank You that I'm a member of Your family*
*Where I have supernatural love for others.*

When the brothers got back to the land of Canaan, they told Jacob, "Your son Joseph is still alive. He is governor of the agriculture of all Egypt." They reported to him everything Joseph had said. But Jacob was stunned, he couldn't make himself believe. It wasn't until he saw the wagons that Joseph sent that his faith was revived. Israel said, "This is it, my son Joseph is alive, I must go see him before I die."

*Lord, sometimes it's hard to believe You move mountains,*
*I have a deceitful heart and I'm spiritually blind.*

*Rule my heart, so I can fully accept what You promise,*
*Give me spiritual sight so I can see what You can do.*

*Give me faith to believe Your promises because without faith*
*It's impossible to please You.*

Amen.

# Genesis 46

# JACOB AND FAMILY GO TO EGYPT

Jacob took everything he owned in his journey to Egypt. When he got to Beer-sheba, he offered sacrifices to the God of his father Isaac. That night God came to him in a vision saying, "Jacob, Jacob!" He answered, "I am here." God said, "I am the God of your father. Go boldly to Egypt and don't be afraid because it's in Egypt that I will make a great nation out of you. I will go to Egypt with you and I will bring your descendents back after Joseph buries you."

The sons of Israel brought Jacob from Beer-sheba to Pharaoh in wagons including his sons and grandsons, daughters and granddaughters, and all his descendents. These are the names of Jacob's sons whom he brought to Egypt: the sons of Reuben; Hanoch and Pallu and Hezron and Carmi. The sons of Simeon: Jemuel and Jamin and Ohad and Jachin and Zohar and Shaul the son of a Canaanite woman. The sons of Levi: Gershon, Kohath, and Merari. The sons of Judah: Er and Onan and Shelah and Perez and Zerah (but Er and Onan died in the land of Canaan). And the sons of Perez were Hezron and Hamul. The sons of Issachar: Tola and Puvvah and Job and Shimron. The sons of Zebulun: Sered and Elon and Jahleel. These are the sons of Leah, whom she bore to Jacob in Paddan-aram, with his daughter Dinah; all his sons and his daughters numbered 33. The sons of Gad: Ziphion and Haggi, Shuni and Ezbon, Eri and Arodi and Areli. The sons of Asher: Imnah and Ishvah and Ishvi and Beriah and their sister Serah and the sons of Beriah: Heber and Malchiel. These are the sons of Zilpah, whom Laban gave to his daughter Leah; and she bore to Jacob these 16 persons. The sons of Jacob's wife Rachel: Joseph

and Benjamin. Now to Joseph in the land of Egypt were born
Manasseh and Ephraim, whom Asenath, the daughter of Potiphera,
priest of On, bore to him. The sons of Benjamin: Bela and
Becher and Ashbel, Gera and Naaman, Ehi and Rosh, Muppim
and Huppim and Ard. These are the sons of Rachel, who were
born to Jacob; there were fourteen persons in all. The sons of
Dan: Hushim. The sons of Naphtali: Jahzeel and Guni and Jezer
and Shillem. These are the sons of Bilhah, whom Laban gave
to his daughter Rachel, and she bore these to Jacob; there were
seven persons in all. All the persons belonging to Jacob, who came
to Egypt, his direct descendants, not including the wives of Jacob's
sons, were 66 persons in all, and the sons of Joseph, who were
born to him in Egypt were two; all the persons of the house of
Jacob, who came to Egypt, were 70 (Gen. 46:8-27 NASB).

*Lord, the lineage of the Jews are important to me,*
*Because it demonstrates that Jesus came from the*
*Right family, just as You predicted.*

*Also, lineage is important, and Jesus never sinned;*
*That qualified Jesus to be my sinless Savior,*
*I praise Him for dying for me.*

Jacob sent Judah ahead to make sure they found the right way to Goshen.
They finally arrived in Goshen. Then Joseph prepared his chariot and
went to Goshen to meet his father. He presented himself to Jacob
and embraced him and they wept together.

Israel said, "Now I can die because I have seen you one more time and I
know you are alive." Joseph told his father and brothers, "I will go
tell Pharaoh that my father and brothers have come from the land
of Canaan and are here with me. They are shepherds and keepers
of livestock. They have brought their flocks, herds, and all their
possessions. When you appear before Pharaoh and he asks, 'What
is your occupation?' tell him you're servants and keepers of

livestock from your youth, both now and your ancestors. This will guarantee you will live in the land of Goshen because shepherds are abominable to Egyptians."

*Lord, help me be sensitive to others as Joseph instructed his brothers*
*To tell Pharaoh they tended livestock*
*Because shepherds were an abomination to Egyptians.*

*Help me always tell the truth to others*
*As the brothers told Pharaoh they were shepherds*

*Because that's what they were.*

Amen.

## Background Story of
## The Ten Brothers Confronted by Joseph

### Genesis 42-46

Place: Mount Gilead ᴧ Time: 1706 B.C.

Seven boney fingers of famine reached out from Egypt to snatch life from the rest of the civilized world. There was no rain from Heaven. The land of Canaan that God promised would flow with milk and honey was covered with a thin veneer of sand. Nothing grew!

The ten brothers of Joseph searched everywhere for green pastures for their herds, but found little. Nothing they planted grew. When old animals died, few were born to take their place. Old Jacob stood in his tent door to announce,

"I have heard corn is plentiful in Egypt." Jacob symbolically pointed south with his famed walking stick. He told his ten sons, "Go buy corn that we may live and die not."

The ten brothers took money and donkeys down to Egypt where they were required to appear before the Minister of Agriculture—Joseph—for every sale was approved by him. Joseph sat upon his throne—second highest in Egypt—looking down the line of foreigners waiting to see him; then he saw them, his brothers were waiting in line.

"Bad Eyes," he instinctively whispered a name he hadn't used in years.

The grungy ten brothers stood out in obvious contrast to the immaculately clean hall where Joseph received emissaries. Joseph's white linen robes, and the spotless robes of his staff made the shepherd's dirty leather garments appear even grubbier. When it was their time, the scared ten brothers ran forward to prostrate themselves before Joseph.

At first they angered Joseph because he knew their hypocrisy, they would do anything to get what they wanted. But his anger turned to a smile when Joseph remembered his dream as a boy that his brothers would bow before him. His smile was reassurance from God that his dreams did predict the future.

"WHAT DO YOU WANT?" Joseph spoke harshly to them through an interpreter. He didn't use Hebrew, his mother's tongue. "WHY HAVE YOU COME SO DIRTY BEFORE ME?"

The ten brothers explained they were shepherds from Canaan who desperately needed corn.

"YOU'RE SPIES," Joseph accused them of an ulterior motive.

"NO," their fear made them babble before the mighty ruler who controlled enough corn to feed the world. "We are the sons of one man, our father has twelve sons, and we are not a nation that seeks war with Egypt. We are a family that struggles to survive this terrible famine."

"IF YOU ARE TWELVE SONS," Joseph continued to speak harshly to his brothers, "WHERE ARE THE OTHER TWO BROTHERS?"

"The youngest brother is home with our father," they explained the youngest—Benjamin—never leaves home because their father would die if anything happened to their youngest brother. Then in reference to Joseph, they explained, "His other brother is no more."

"YOU ARE LYING," Joseph raised his voice higher. "YOU ARE SPIES."

Joseph threw them into prison and left them there for three days—three the number of completion—for Joseph wanted them to experience the feeling of fear and alienation in a foreign dungeon that he had experienced in the pit. When they fully drank of his prison, Joseph had his brothers brought back to his court, saying to them,

"Because I fear God, I will give you a chance to live. I will keep one of you in prison, the rest of you may take corn back to your family. But you must bring the youngest brother to me so I will know that you are not lying...otherwise you will not see my face again."

The brothers were horrified when they heard the decision of the Minister of Agriculture. They looked among themselves saying in Hebrew,

"This is God's judgment because of the way we treated our brother Joseph. We heard the anguish of his soul when he begged us not to sell him as a slave."

Joseph understood their Hebrew speech but they didn't know he was their brother. He had to leave the room to weep in private for that experience made him relive the bitterness of the pit in Dothan. But Joseph also wept because it was the first sign of repentance he had seen in "Bad Eyes."

When Joseph returned to them, he had Simeon locked in shackles in front of the other brothers. He wanted to make sure they understood the seriousness of his words. His final words of warning to them,

"You will not see my face unless you bring the youngest brother with you!"

Joseph privately instructed his manager to return their money in their sacks of corn. The ten brothers were surprised they were allowed to leave for home with their corn and donkeys. They had great relief to be leaving

Egypt, even though they were without Simeon. Then when they found their money in corn sacks, their hearts froze again in fear. They said to one another,

"God has punished us a second time!"

When the brothers got home, they explained reluctantly to Jacob what happened in Egypt. The old man had been grieving over the loss of Joseph for over 20 years, now his problems were compounded. He suffered in the tent door all day, repeating his grief,

"Joseph is not...Simeon is not...they want to take away Benjamin." Old Jacob punished himself saying, "The evil deeds of my youth have destroyed any joy of old age."

The famine deepened, constant blowing sand in their camp reminded them of their deteriorating conditions. The corn in the sacks was gone, the seeds they planted died and everyone was hungry. Judah, the fourth-born son—the only son left who seemed to fear God—approached Jacob as he dozed in the hot sandy wind,

"We must do something," Judah's desperation was reflected in his voice. "We'll die if we don't go to Egypt to buy corn. We have money, but we can't eat gold coins!"

"All right..." Jacob relented. "Go buy corn in Egypt."

Judah explained, "We must carry Benjamin with us because the man said we couldn't see his face if we didn't bring our youngest brother with us. The man said we were liars and that he would not believe us unless we bring our younger brother."

"I'll die." Jacob's wet tears left streaks on his dirty face from the blowing sand. The moaning wind reflected their feelings.

Judah explained that he would protect Benjamin with his life. The older brother said,

"I'll be a hostage for Benjamin. If I do not return the lad to you, I'll bear responsibility forever. You can blot my name from the family heritage."

Jacob believed the pledge of Judah, so he agreed in his heart to let Benjamin travel to Egypt. But the sly old Jacob knew he had to do something to touch the heart of the man in Egypt. He suggested,

"Take the Egyptian ruler a present...some of our best honey...some of our sweetest fruit...some of our tasty nuts; take him a gift that will sweeten his disposition." Finally Jacob prayed, "God Almighty, give them mercy before the man."

The brothers took double money with them—new money for new corn and the old money that was returned in their sacks—and with Benjamin they headed for Egypt. As they stood in line to see the man, Joseph saw them and for the first time in years, he saw his brother the other son born to his mother. He saw Benjamin. Turning to his manager, Joseph commented,

"Take them to my private home for a banquet at noon," Joseph commanded his manager to kill the fattest animal for the feast. The brothers were afraid when soldiers accompanied them to Joseph's private home, they expected more punishment from God. When they arrived at Joseph's home, they explained quickly that the money they paid for corn on their first trip had reappeared in the mouth of their sacks of corn. The manager knew what happened because he had returned their money, but he misled them,

"Your God put treasure in your sacks, I have the money you paid for corn."

The brother that had been shackled in their sight—Simeon—was returned unbound. Their feet were washed by servants, a custom of hospitality given only honored guests. They clung tightly to their present for the man hoping it would sweeten his disposition toward them. When Joseph arrived home for the meal, his first question was,

"Is your father alive?" Joseph yearned to know about Jacob. He asked, "Is he in good health?"

"Jacob is alive and well," the boys answered, bowing in reverence to Joseph their brother, the one they still didn't recognize.

Joseph turned to study the face of Benjamin—the brother that looked like him—for they both had their mother's beautiful eyes. When Joseph saw himself in his brother's face, he remembered all the joy they experienced growing up together. He couldn't control himself. Joseph quickly exited to his private chamber to cry—he couldn't let "Bad Eyes" see his "Red Eyes."

Because Egyptians consider it an abomination to eat with Hebrews, the 11 brothers were seated at another place by themselves, not with Joseph. As the servants directed them to their seats, the 11 brothers were startled to find themselves seated in birth order—from Reuben the first born to Benjamin the last born.

"Who told them?" each seemed to ask.

"Not me," each seemed to answer.

Joseph chose food from the elegantly spread at the head table for each of the brothers; but he sent five times as much food for Benjamin as for the others. For the first time, the brothers known as "Bad Eyes" felt comfortable in the presence of the man. When the banquet was over, the brothers were ready to leave. But they would not be completely happy until their sacks were filled with corn, and they were leading their donkeys out of the city toward home. They didn't know Joseph had again returned their money to their sacks; and to precipitate a crisis, Joseph had his personal cup put in Benjamin's sack.

They were gone, but not far. Before their food could digest and before the dust of travel could dirty their forehead, Joseph sent soldiers to overtake them and return them to him. Their momentary joy evaporated as panic seized each of them, for they again feared the man. When they were returned to Joseph's house, they were asked,

"Why have you rewarded evil to the man who gave you food? Why have you stolen his personal cup from which he drinks?"

The brothers stammered with fear. "We returned the money...we didn't steal his cup." They were sure of their actions. They swore by their God that none of them stole the prized cup. Then to prove their honesty, they boasted, "If you find the cup in one of our sacks—let that brother die—then we'll be your slaves forever." Hearing this stern affirmation, Joseph said,

"That will be the punishment," Joseph was used to making firm judgments. But this decision was easy, for Joseph knew the results before the sacks were searched. For all the evil ways they had hurt Joseph, now the whip was turned on "Bad Eyes." Quickly the sacks were searched.

The cup was found in Benjamin's sack.

The brothers fell to the ground in disbelief and horror, as though they were dead. They cried out and wept, wishing to die. Their worst imagination had come.

"DIDN'T YOU KNOW I COULD PREDICT THINGS?" Joseph again spoke roughly to them. "TAKE YOUR CORN AND GO," Joseph commanded, "THE LAD WILL BE MY SLAVE...ACCORDING TO YOUR WORDS."

Judah asked to come near to the man, he explained their anguish and again explained why they were innocent. Judah reminded the man they were a family, he told the man that if Benjamin did not come back with them,

"Our father will die because his life is bound up in the life of Benjamin."

Judah explained that he promised to be a hostage for Benjamin and if anything happened to the lad, their father Jacob could blot his name from the family heritage. Then Judah pleaded,

"Let me be your slave instead of Benjamin," now Judah was the one crying. "I'll be your bond slave forever."

Joseph could constrain his tears no longer, he cried. In the background were heard the moans and soft weeping of the other brothers.

"LEAVE ME," Joseph commanded his servants. Even in the other room, they could hear their master Joseph openly weeping. When he could stand it no longer, speaking to them in Hebrew, Joseph said,

"I am Joseph, your brother." Then to make sure they understood the situation, he added, "I am Joseph whom you sold as a slave into Egypt."

The fear that "Bad Eyes" had just experienced after being accused of stealing the cup was now compounded, for now they were afraid of Joseph's retribution. He could do whatever he will, only Pharaoh was over him. Even before "Bad Eyes" could beg for mercy, Joseph embraced his brothers, telling them,

"God sent me to Egypt to preserve your lives."

Joseph explained they had suffered only two years of famine. He told them five more years of suffering lay ahead of them. Joseph sent his brothers back to tell Jacob all that God had accomplished in Egypt through him. Joseph invited his family—father, brothers, their families and servants—to move to Egypt because of the famine. This was God's plan to protect the sons of Abraham and to expand them into a great nation—in Egypt.

Back in Canaan, Jacob sat listening to his sons tell him about Joseph. The boys had once lied to him, telling Jacob the coat with colored sleeves was bloodied when a wild animal killed Joseph. It was a lie then, why should he believe them now. They had lied to him so often, what could he believe? The moaning wind continued to blow sand in his face. Jacob's spirit was still crushed, he still had his grief. *What can I believe?*

Then they all heard it at the same time, it was the unmistakable squeak of wagons—big wagons—coming over the sand-blown horizon. Joseph had sent wagons for the whole family, all 70 of them. When Jacob saw the wagons, his spirit revived; he believed what his sons told him. His grief left. Old Jacob had a son, Joseph, who was father to them all. Joseph would take care of them in Egypt.

## My Time to Pray

- Lord, I'm amazed how some members of a family will hurt other members; help me always be kind to everyone.

- Lord, help me always be kind to others for I never know when I'll need them to be kind to me.

- Lord, help me be kind to those who have hurt me, just as Joseph was kind to his brothers because I'll never know that You are working through the circumstances of life.

- Lord, when I lose faith and don't trust in You, send some outward things—"the wagons"—to restore my faith in Your work in my life.

# Genesis 47

# Pharaoh Welcomes Jacob

Joseph went and told Pharaoh, "My father and brothers are here from Canaan with their flocks, livestock, and all their possessions, living in the land of Goshen. Joseph presented five of his brothers to Pharaoh who asked them, "What is your occupation?" They answered, "We are shepherds, both now and our ancestors." Then the brothers added, "We have come to live in Goshen because there remains no longer pasture for our flocks in Canaan because of the famine. Please let us—your servants—live in the land of Goshen."

Pharaoh said to Joseph, "The land of Egypt is before your father and brothers. Let them live in the best location, let them live in Goshen. Further, if some of them are especially competent, let them look after some of my livestock."

Joseph brought his father Jacob in to see Pharaoh. Jacob blessed Pharaoh, then Pharaoh asked, "How old are you?" Jacob answered, "I have lived on this earth 130 years. My years are few and difficult. They are fewer than my fathers lived." Then Jacob blessed Pharaoh and left. Joseph got land for his father and brothers and gave it to them in the best location in the land of Rameses as Pharaoh directed. Joseph provided corn for his fathers and brothers, taking care of them.

*Lord, help me always respect those in authority over me,*
*Even as Jacob properly respected Pharaoh.*

*When I can't respect the character of the one in office,*
*At least I can respect the office they fill.*

Because the draught was so severe, there was no food anywhere. As Egypt
and Canaan hungered, Joseph collected money in exchange for corn
from both Egypt and Canaan depositing the money in Pharaoh's
treasury. When there was no money left in Egypt and Canaan, the
people begged, "We are going to die, give us something to eat."
Joseph answered, "Give me your livestock if you have no money
and I will give you corn." So Joseph gave them corn for their
livestock—horses, cattle, donkeys—all in exchange for corn. Then
the people came to Joseph again and said, "We are penniless, you
have all our money and livestock. We have nothing left but our land
and ourselves. Give us food and we will give you our land and be
your slaves." Joseph acquired all the land of Egypt for Pharaoh as
one by one the landowners gave their land to Joseph and sold
themselves as slaves. Only the land of the priests did Joseph not take
from them because the priests received provisions from Pharaoh.

Then Joseph announced, "I have acquired your land for Pharaoh. I will give
you seed to plant on the land. When you harvest your crops, you
will give 20 percent to Pharaoh. Eighty percent will be yours for
food and seed for the following year to plant again." The people
agreed, "You saved our lives, we will be Pharaoh's slaves." So Joseph
made a law that 20 percent of everything was a tax for Pharaoh.
Only the land belonging to the priests did Pharaoh not take.

This enabled Egypt to become the most powerful nation in the world and
Pharaoh became its dictator. Then Pharaoh did much good and
much evil and Egypt became a factor in the world's politics.

*Lord, if You had not raised up Joseph to power,*
    *The course of history would have been different.*

*Help me see Your hand in today's politics*
    *And follow Your leading for my life.*

Amen.

# Genesis 48

## JACOB BLESSES EPHRAIM AND MANASSEH

Joseph heard his father Jacob was ill. He went to visit Jacob, taking his two sons Manasseh and Ephraim with him.

Jacob heard his son Joseph was coming to see him, so Jacob used all his strength to sit up in bed. Then he said to Joseph, "God—El Shaddai—appeared to me and blessed me at Bethel in the land of Canaan. God said to me, "I will make you a multitude of families, you will be fruitful and numerous. I will give this land to you so your people can possess it forever.

*Lord, it's good to remember what You've done for me,*
*I will guide my future based on Your past works.*

Jacob claimed the two sons born to Joseph in Egypt were his—he was legally adopting them—the two boys of Joseph would be his as much as were Reuben and Simeon. For the purpose of inheritance, Manasseh and Ephraim would be counted with Jacob's other sons.

Jacob told how Rachel died when he was traveling through the land of Canaan, and that he buried her on the road to Bethlehem.

When Jacob—Israel—saw the two boys, he asked, "Are these the two boys of yours?" Joseph answered, they were his two sons. Jacob said, "Bring them to me so I can bless them."

Israel couldn't see well because of his eyes. Then Joseph guided his sons to his father, Jacob kissed them and hugged them. Then Israel said to Joseph, "I never expected to see you again, but God has allowed me to see you and your children."

Joseph guided the two boys to stand before their grandfather. Joseph
guided Ephraim toward Jacob's left hand and Manasseh, his first
born, toward Jacob's right hand. Then Joseph bowed on the ground
in prayer.

*Lord, there are moments when You work evidentially on earth,*
*Teach me to recognize those moments and look for Your plan.*

Israel put his right hand on the younger Ephraim and his left hand on the
older brother Manasseh—he intentionally changed the order of
inheritance—even though Manasseh was the older.

The old Jacob blessed them, "May You Lord bless these boys, as I have lived
all my life in Your presence, as You blessed Abraham and Isaac. You
have been a shepherd to me all my days as a shepherd. May You
who has guided me bless these boys. May they remember their
grandfather—who I am and what I stand for—and may they have
an abundance of peoples as an inheritance.

When Joseph saw his father put his right hand on Ephraim's head, he
disagreed and lifted his father's right hand to put it on Manasseh's
head. Joseph said to his father, "You've done it backward. Put your
left hand on Manasseh's head, he's my first born."

Jacob refused to do what Joseph asked saying, "The younger will be greater
than his older brother, and his descendents will become great
nations." Then Jacob added for Joseph's sake, "Manasseh also will
become a great people and have many nations come from him."

That day Jacob blessed his grandsons with this blessing, "The people of
Israel will use your two names in their unique blessing saying "May
God bless you like Ephraim and Manasseh." In this way, Jacob put
the younger—Ephraim—before the elder—Manasseh.

Jacob told Joseph, "I am dying, but God will be with you and your people
will be brought back to the land of our ancestors. But I am giving

you the double blessing—two sons will be tribes—beyond the
blessing I give to ten other tribes."

*Lord, I want a double portion of Your blessing in my life,*
    *You already have given me the presence of the Holy Spirit.*

*I yield to Him to receive the good things You have for me;*
    *May the Holy Spirit anoint me to serve You.*

Amen.

## Background Story of
## Jacob Blesses Ephraim and Manasseh

### Genesis 48

Place: Egypt ⌒ Time: 1700 B.C.

*"Then Israel stretched out his right hand and laid it on Ephraim's
head, who was the younger, and his left hand on Manasseh's head,
guiding his hands knowingly, for Manasseh was the firstborn, he
prayed, "The Angel who has redeemed me from all evil, Bless the
lads; Let my name be named upon them, the name of my fathers
Abraham and Isaac; And let them grow into a multitude in the
midst of the earth"* (Genesis 48:14,16).

His laughter echoed off the white-marbled walls of the palace; young
Ephraim was running through the halls to his brother's bedroom.
Ephraim's black flashing eyes reflected his father Joseph, a Hebrew; his
dark skin reflected his mother, an Egyptian. Because of his father—second
to Pharaoh—servants were stationed everywhere throughout his palace
and both boys had a private attendant.

"Manasseh," the younger boy yelled out the name of his older and larger brother, "Guess where we're going today?" His exciting yell turned the servants' heads. Ephraim burst into his brother's bedroom to announce,

"We're going to see Grandpa Jacob today."

Ephraim and Manasseh huddled with excitement to leave the hot city and travel to Grandpa Jacob's farm country in the Nile Delta where everything was green and lush. Sheep and cows were everywhere. In the city where the boys lived, white stone buildings rose from the white surrounding sand. Everything was dry, hot, arid.

Grandpa Jacob always told stories of traveling to the far nation of Mesopotamia and being a shepherd and sleeping on the ground, under the stars. Jacob's tales of killing wild predators thrilled the boys.

The boys' other grandfather, Potipherah, priest of On, worshiped the Egyptian god Re. When their mother Asenaph took them to visit her father, Grandpa Potipherah tried to teach the boys the Egyptian name of the different stars and how to worship the stars.

But the boys believed in Grandpa Jacob's God named Jehovah, not in Grandpa Potipherah's god.

As the chariot rumbled through the burning sands of the Egyptian desert, they saw camels—the desert travelers. As they got closer to Grandpa Jacob's home, the landscape slowly changed to the green pastures of the Nile Delta where they saw sheep and cattle grazing in green fields.

A rank of soldiers headed the procession; they went everywhere with Joseph, not so much for protection, but as a statement of prestige. Behind the boys came servants and other Egyptian dignitaries.

Grandpa Jacob knew the boys were coming, so he had forced himself to get dressed, slipping into his comfortable shepherd's tunic faded with age, rumpled and worn. Like most old people, Jacob didn't pay attention to his clothes for he didn't don't see well, and style didn't matter when you're ready to die. The coat had the smell of sheep and perspiration, but old people don't smell as well as when they were younger; Jacob was dressed comfortably.

Joseph greeted his father warmly, as he had always done. Egyptian scribes were along to record the events, for the last words of great men were important for posterity, and they wanted to record what Jacob would say.

Joseph had brought the best doctors who knew the latest cures, and could mix many herbs and potions. But old Jacob shook his head no to the doctors; he relied on the techniques he had learned in the field, shepherding his sheep.

Jacob took control of the meeting, telling everyone, "When I was a young man running away from home, God Almighty appeared to me in a mountain named Bethel—which means the House of God—and I needed reassurance from the Lord. My brother, Esau, wanted to kill me. That night God appeared to me in a dream saying,

*"Behold, I the Lord will prosper you in all that you do, I will give you many children, and you will become a great nation. I the Lord promise this land to you—a promised land—that you shall inherit this land for an everlasting possession."*

Then Jacob told the part of the story that hurt. He told how his ten sons hated Joseph and tried to kill Joseph, but sold him into slavery. In slavery, God protected Joseph and elevated him to rule over all the agriculture of Egypt.

Then Grandfather Jacob abruptly asked, "Are these your two sons— Ephraim and Manasseh—who were born to you in the land of Egypt before I came here?"

Then Jacob made the pronouncement that the two grandsons would be adopted by him. Even though Ephraim and Manasseh were half Egyptian, old Jacob wanted everyone to know that these two boys would have a Hebrew inheritance so he announced before all, "These boys are mine." Then he turned to the scribes noting,

"Write it down, just as I said."

To make sure that they all understood, Jacob continued, "These two boys are mine, just as much as Reuben and Simeon are mine."

Again, Jacob turned to the scribes noting, "These shall be placed in order after their brethren in my inheritance."

Even though Joseph was one of the richest men in Egypt, and Joseph could give his sons more wealth than Jacob ever conceived, it was important for the old man to give the boys something. Jacob's inheritance was important because every one of his sheep and cattle were given by God. When a few things are all that the man has, these few things are important to him and to his grandsons. And in giving to his grandsons what he had, Jacob was giving them his identity, his character, and his life.

"Bring your sons to me," Jacob said, pointing to Ephraim and Manasseh. The situation that followed was filled with tension, for Joseph knew what should be done, but wily old Jacob knew what he would do.

Joseph brought the boys to his father, according to their birth order. Jacob's left hand was to be on the head of younger Ephraim, his second born. Jacob's right hand—the hand of authority—was to be on the head of Manasseh, his first born. Then Joseph bowed in reverence. As the boys approached, Jacob crossed his arms, placing his right hand on the head of Ephraim who was the younger and his left hand to Manasseh, the older. The old grandfather blessed his grandsons;

"Lord, You redeemed me from the evil one; now Lord, protect these young boys from evil. Let my name be on them, and let my inheritance, be their inheritance. May the name of Abraham, Isaac, and Jacob be upon these boys and may they grow into a multitude on the earth."

When Joseph looked up, he saw that Jacob's right hand was on Ephraim, the younger son. He objected saying, "Not so, Father, you have your hand of blessing on Ephraim, but he is the second born."

Jacob didn't respond, but smiled inwardly, knowing he was doing God's will. He told Joseph, "Remember God's principle of choice. When I was born second, the Lord told my mother that the *older child shall serve the younger,* meaning the second born will rule the first born." That day Jacob gave Ephraim the spiritual birthright, which included the spiritual leadership of the family clan, as well as the right to pray for all the family.

Jacob could not have known what would happen to Ephraim, but God knew. One day the entire nation of Israel would be called by the name *Ephraim,* and one day the tribe of Ephraim would have more people than any other tribe, and more soldiers than any of the other 12 tribes of Israel. The prosperity of the tribe of Ephraim would flow into all of the other 11 tribes, making each of them wealthy and rich.

But not to leave the other son Manasseh out, Jacob explained to Joseph, "Manasseh will be a great people, he will become a great nation, but his young brother Ephraim will be a greater people and the children of Ephraim shall lead the children of Manasseh."

"Write what I have said," Jacob again turned to the scribes and said, and they did.

"Behold, I die!" Grandpa Jacob told everyone in the room.

When Jacob used the word *death,* no one knew whether he meant minutes...hours...days...or even years. But somehow in their hearts, they knew death was imminent. Jacob added a final blessing for all his family,

"God will be with you, and bring the nation out of Egypt back in to the Promised Land; because God promised, He will take you back to the land of our fathers."

## My Time to Pray

- Lord, everyone must die, even me. Help me to embrace the inevitable for when I pass through the valley of death, I'll meet You.

- Lord, keep my faith strong right to the end of my life, just as You kept Jacob's faith strong to the end.

- Lord, I pray for my children and grandchildren, may they stand upon my shoulders and reach for greater spiritual things.

- Lord, may I add spiritual value to my children and grandchildren, may I bless them with what You have given me.

- Lord, help me pass my faith on to my children and grandchildren. May they all love and serve You.

- Lord, I did foolish things in my youth, just as Jacob; I pray for You to forgive me the consequences of all my sins and use me when I get older, just as You forgave and used Jacob in his old age.

# Genesis 49

# JACOB BLESSES HIS TWELVE SONS

Jacob called his sons together and told them, "Listen, sons of Jacob, I will tell you what will happen in the future; pay attention to Israel your father."

By faith, Jacob leaned on his walking stick where the signet of each son was carved. Each son saw his place in the family lineage (Heb. 11:21).

Jacob blessed Reuben saying, "You are my first born, my strength, the fruit of my power. Although you are superior in determination and courage, you are as unstable as water, so your integrity won't last because you defiled my bed; you had sex with my concubine."

Jacob didn't bless Simeon and Levi saying, "You are brothers of violence, for in their anger they killed men and destroyed a city. I will not be a part of their thinking, nor bestow my honor on them. I curse their anger, for it is fierce and they have been cruel. I will send them throughout Israel."

Jacob blessed Judah saying, "Judah, your brothers will acknowledge you and your hand will be on the neck of your enemies. My other sons will bow before you. Judah as a young lion, you will crouch like a lion and stand victorious over your prey. No one will provoke you. The scepter will not depart from Judah and the lawgivers will come from him until He (Shiloh) comes who will govern His people. He will hitch his donkey to a vine and his donkey's colt to the tender vine. His eyes will be fiery red in indignation against sin.

He will wash his clothes in the blood red wine of judgment, yet his teeth will be white as righteousness."

Jacob blessed Zebulon predicting, "He will live near the sea, ships will anchor along his coast, all thy way to Sidon."

Jacob blessed Issachar saying, "He will be strong as a beast of burden, who will be as gentle as a sheep. He will see his resting place and he will live in that pleasant countryside. He will bend his back to the burden of work and will be a servant of many."

Jacob said, "Dan will judge one of the tribes of Israel. He will be like a viper lying beside the road who strikes a horse's foot so that the rider falls off backward." Then Jacob prayed, "Lord, I wait for Your deliverance."

Jacob didn't immediately bless Gad, but said, "Gad's name means troop, so a troop will trample him." Then Jacob blessed him, "But in the end, Gad will 'troop' over them."

Jacob said of Asher, "Your food is rich and will be served to a king." Then to Naphtali Jacob said, "You are a doe that is free, you will have many fawns."

Jacob blessed Joseph saying, "Joseph is a fruitful plant growing by the water and his fruitful branches spread out to all. Archers have attacked him and wounded him, but his hands remain strong and he is encouraged by the God of Jacob, the Shepherd, the Rock of Israel will help him; El Shaddai (God Almighty) will bless him with Heaven's blessings, so he'll have many children, and enjoy the good things from above and beneath. The blessings of my Father will be on him and his blessings are more powerful than any thing. May all these be on Joseph, a prince among his brothers."

Jacob blessed Benjamin saying, "He is a hungry wolf in the morning, he will devour his prey; in the evening he will divide its spoil."

Jacob declared, "These are the twelve tribes of Israel, and these are my blessings on them. I've given to each his appropriate blessing that is their destiny."

Then Jacob charged them, "I am going to join my fathers. Bury me in the land of Canaan in the cave at Machpelah in the field of Ephron the Hittite which Abraham bought from him. That's the place where Abraham and Sarah his wife are buried, as well as Isaac and his wife Rebekah, and there I buried Leah."

When Jacob finished charging his sons, he pulled his legs up into his bed, and breathed his last and was gathered unto his people.

Amen.

## Background Story of
## Jacob Blesses His Twelve Sons

### Genesis 49

Place: In Goshen, Egypt ↶ Time: 1689 B.C.

J acob heard the yell out in the front yard, "Your grandsons are coming!" He knew immediately it was Joseph's sons, Ephraim and Manasseh. He struggled to get to his feet. *Can't let my grandsons see me as an invalid,* Jacob thought to himself.

*Got to pull myself up before they come through the door.* He reached for his walking stick just as he had done thousands of times when sleeping on the ground. He used the trusty rod to pull himself up to a standing position. But he was weak, he couldn't walk far; so Jacob leaned on his staff, just as he had done throughout his adult life. He was standing on the pallet where he slept as his grandsons entered the room. (Don't think of a bed with springs and mattress.) Remember what the writer of Hebrews said, "By faith Jacob, when he was dying, blessed each of the sons of Joseph, and worshiped, *leaning* on the top of his staff" (Heb. 11:21).

Was the staff something convenient to steady Jacob? No! Did he use the staff out of habit? No!

Jacob probably told the boys he got the staff from his father, Isaac, and it was Abraham's walking stick that came from Mesopotamia. Was Jacob just referring to family heritage? No! that staff reminded each son of the promises God Almighty made to Abraham that He would bless His seed and they would become a great nation.

Jacob probably fingered each signet of his fathers as he stood on his pallet. The moment was sacred and Jacob wanted God there to touch the heart of each boy as the blessings were pronounced.[21]

## My Time to Pray

- Lord, when Jacob blessed his sons, he was "adding value" of God's benevolence to each son. Help me to "add spiritual value" to my children and grandchildren.

- Lord, when elders raise the "bar" for my life, help me to attain their aspirations and reach higher.

- Lord, this chapter tells me how important the family is. Help me to invest in my children and grandchildren so they may follow my faith, yet reach higher.

# Genesis 50

## Joseph's Death

When Jacob died, Joseph fell on him, kissed him, and cried. Then Joseph commanded the physicians to embalm his father and they did so. They spent 40 days embalming the body according to the tradition of the Egyptians. They mourned for him 70 days.

When the period of mourning was over, Joseph asked the house of Pharaoh, "I would like to carry my father to the land of Canaan to bury him." Joseph continued, "My father made me swear that I would take him to the place of family burial. Let me go and I will return back here."

Pharaoh said, "Go bury your father as he made you swear." Joseph went to bury his father along with Jewish servants and Jewish leaders of Pharaoh's household and Jewish leaders of Egypt. But they left their children, flocks, and cattle in the land of Goshen. Egyptian chariots and horsemen also went with Joseph. They came to the threshing floor in Atod, and there they raised loud lamentations for Joseph's father seven days. When the Canaanites saw the mourning, they said, "How deeply the Egyptians are mourning, therefore the place was called, "mourning of Egypt."

Jacob's sons did as he commanded them, they buried him in the cave Machpelah which Abraham bought from Ephron the Hittite as a burying place. And Joseph, his brothers, and all the Jewish people who went with him returned to Egypt after they buried Jacob.

After Jacob's funeral, the brothers were afraid that Joseph would hate them and punish them for selling him into slavery. They sent a message to Joseph saying, "Your father gave us a command before he died that we should tell you, 'Forgive the sin of your ten brothers because they are servants of the God of your father.'" Then the ten brothers prostrated themselves before Joseph and said, "We are your slaves."

Joseph wept when the ten brothers spoke to him.

*Lord, the ten brothers tried to cover up their sin against Joseph by*
*Telling a lie about what their father said.*

*Lying is the original sin of Jacob the Deceiver*
*Lived out in the deception of his ten sons.*

*Help me always be honest in speech and thought,*
*And may I forgive others before they forgive me.*

Joseph told them, "Don't be afraid, am I in the place of God? You planned evil against me, but God meant it for good so that many people could be saved. I will take care of you and your children." Joseph reassured them of their safety.

Joseph and his father's families continued living in Egypt, Joseph living 110 years, then he died. Joseph lived to see Ephraim's great grandchildren and Machir, the son of Manasseh; all were brought up by Joseph.

When Joseph was dying, he said, "I am dying but God will remember our family and bring us out of Egypt into Canaan the land God swore to give to Abraham, Isaac, and Jacob. Then Joseph made them promise, "God will visit you and take you to the Promise Land. Take my bones with you and bury me there." So Joseph died when he was 110 years old; they embalmed him and put him in a coffin in Egypt.

Amen.

## Background Story of
## Joseph in a Coffin

### Genesis 50

Place: Egypt ↶ Time: 1625 B.C.

H E'S DEAD!" the cry filled the palace. Quickly news spread from one set of servants to another; from cooks, to the cleaning staff, to stable hands. Tears swelled up in many eyes, and finally an attendant told Pharaoh as he was walking by the Nile River, "Joseph is dead."

The most powerful man in the world stopped abruptly. His countenance fell for Pharaoh knew that the Hebrew slave he encountered in prison that interpreted his dreams and predicted the future had saved the world and made him the most powerful man in the world. Thutmose III wondered, "Did Joseph predict the day of his death?"

Pharaoh realized he had given Joseph power over all the agriculture of Egypt, but in return Joseph had given him power over all the known world. Before Joseph arrived on the scene, Egypt was one people nationally and ethnically; but politically, Egypt was ruled by thousands of powerful property owners, each one a fiefdom itself, each only gave lip service to Pharaoh. But Joseph stored corn and then the seven-year famine swept over Egypt and the world. These fiefdom landowners had to buy corn from Joseph. When their money gave out, they traded their land to Pharaoh for corn, and when the "grim reaper" of starvation visited each, they sold themselves into slavery to Joseph and Pharaoh for corn.

Yes, everyone would miss Joseph for he had fed the world. Pharaoh decreed all Egypt show appropriate respect. "Everyone must mourn for Joseph 70 days." Then Pharaoh thought privately, *Could Joseph who kept the world alive, not keep himself alive?*

A group of shepherds gathered in the courtyard, asking for Joseph's body. They wanted to bury Joseph Hebrew style.

"No…absolutely not," shrieked Reziff, Joseph's executive administrator. Reziff (Re means my god) ran through Joseph's throne room barking orders. Then in a symbolic grab for power, Reziff sat on Joseph's throne, something he'd never done, nor had anyone else. *This feels good,* he smiled to himself.

"No, we shall not give Joseph's body to those dirty shepherds." Reziff told a servant to send them away. "Joseph may have had Hebrew blood running through his veins, but not for long." Reziff gave the executive order and with the seal of Joseph, made the order official, "Embalm the body." An attendant ran to tell the physicians.

To embalm a corpse, the left arm is raised and a long incision is made down the rib cage—long enough for a hand to reach in and pull out the main artery. The vein is sliced and all the body's blood is sucked out. Then embalming fluid is pumped into the waiting vein to fill the body.

The Hebrews won't embalm a body, for they believe the life is in the blood and when the blood is sucked from the body, the soul is lost for the soul lives in the blood. The Hebrews bury quickly for the known consequences of congealed blood. As long as a person is alive, the plasmatic nature of blood holds apart the life-giving particles from the death-decaying maggots. It was abhorrent to the Hebrews to see—almost immediately—the presence of maggot worms in the blood.

"Joseph will no longer be Hebrew when all his blood is gone," Reziff told Joseph's staff. Then Reziff with possessive passion told them, "Joseph is Egyptian…he dresses Egyptian…he thinks Egyptian…he lives like an Egyptian." Reziff reminded them when Joseph's family—the dirty shepherds—came to Goshen, Joseph didn't go live with them nor did he dress like a shepherd.

"Joseph lived Egyptian…Joseph died Egyptian…and Joseph will be buried Egyptian." Reziff sent off official papers for Pharaoh to sign so Joseph's coffin would be placed in a burial vault in the pyramid built for Thutmoses III, Pharaoh himself.

Pharaoh signed it and Reziff thought he won a battle.

But God used the racism of Reziff to complete His plan. For God had spoken through Joseph that his bones were to be carried back into the Promised Land and buried there.[22] So God allowed Reziff to perpetuate the corpse of Joseph so he could be carried back to Canaan. Joseph's coffin would wait patiently in Pharaoh's tomb until the exodus led by Moses.

Reziff may have hated the shepherd ancestry of Joseph, but he loved Joseph. His tears were real for Joseph, the savior of Egypt, had saved Reziff's wife and children from starvation.

Reziff took Joseph's staff from next to Joseph's throne. Joseph's staff only had one signet carved into the top. It was Joseph's seal written in Hebrew. When the master woodworker wanted to carve the signet of Joseph's two sons—Ephraim and Manasseh—into the family lineage, Joseph said, "No...not now, not until after my death."

Joseph remembered his father Jacob had legally adopted Ephraim and Manasseh. The boys' signets would be carved on Jacob's walking stick to perpetuate the Hebrew line. There would be 12 sons of Israel, not 13 sons. Joseph would not be a tribe of Israel—he was Egyptian.

The scepter of Joseph, with only one signet—because the family ceased—was placed in the casket on top of Joseph's body. Before closing the lid, Reziff stroked the beard of Joseph, a divine Osird form of the beard, which was a long, narrow beard of several strands plaited like a pigtail with the end jutting forward. Only Pharaoh and those who sat on one of the thrones of Pharaoh had the official chin whiskers. To Reziff, the Osird beard showed Joseph was Egyptian.

Reziff had won, Joseph the savior of Egypt, the one who rode in the second chariot, was buried Egyptian. But isn't God always victorious in the details? When humans can't see what God is doing, God is "working all things for good" (Rom. 8:28).

The Book of Genesis begins with a glorious creation, "In the beginning, God created the heavens and the earth" (Gen. 1:1). What better introduction to a book than Adam and Eve living in Paradise. God had glorious hopes for His creation. What a bleak ending to a book that began so gloriously, *Genesis* ends with the word "coffin."

What irony, the Book of Genesis ends with God's man outside the Promised Land and God's man is a corpse in a coffin. "So Joseph died when he was 110 years old, and the Egyptians embalmed him and put him in a coffin" (Gen. 50:26 ELT).

## My Time to Pray

- Lord, You sit in Heaven and laugh when humans try to work their will contrary to what they think You want. Thank You for preparing the body of Joseph to be buried in the Holy Land.

- Lord, Joseph's bones are somewhere waiting a new body in the resurrection and I know I too shall be raised in the resurrection morning.

- Lord, You fulfilled Your promise of sending the Hebrews to Egypt to become a mighty nation, and You fulfilled Your promise to bring them back into the Promised Land.

- Lord, when I read Genesis, I see lies, murders, demon-worship, hatred, and deception. Deliver me from all of that.

- Your man—Joseph—ended up a corpse in a coffin, but we can look forward to a resurrection body and eternal life with You.

- Lord, thank You for this wonderful Book of Genesis that tells me how everything began.

# ENDNOTES

1. The Bible declares Moses could read and write, "Moses was learned in all the wisdom of the Egyptians, and was mighty in word and deed" (Acts 7:22).

2. The Phoenicians were from what is called Lebanon today. When children learn to write and spell by sounding a word, it's called Phonics, a method Moses learned from the Phoenicians.

3. Some question whether Moses could write, or if he were the author of the first five books of the Old Testament. The authority of the New Testament and Jesus Himself is on the line because they credit the authorship of the first five books of the Bible to Moses: Matt. 8:4, 19:7, 22:24; Mark 1:44, 7:10, 10:3, 12:19; Luke 2:22, 5:14, 20:28, 24:27, 44; John 1:17, 45, 7:19, 7:23, 8:5, 9:29; Acts 3:22, 13:39, 15:5, 26:22, 28:23; Rom. 10:19, 1 Cor. 9:9; 2 Cor. 3:15; Heb. 9:19.

4. The Old Testament Jewish Rabbis had many traditions about the source of the rod of Moses. While these have no biblical verification, and their stories were probably not true, yet they were accurate in describing that family lineage was carved into the rod or staff. There are some unbelievable stories such as Adam broke a branch off the Tree of Knowledge of Good and Evil and it became his walking stick. Also, this was the stick used by Cain to kill Abel. They also suggest Jacob's walking stick was inherited by Joseph and the sons who became the 12 tribes of Israel began their own family lineage with their own family walking stick. The legend suggests that somehow Moses got it (thus the story I made up that an escaped slave brought it into the Sinai Desert). See Löw, *Aramäische Pflanzennamen*, (The History of Moses' Rod), 81ff; http://www.sacred-texts.com/chr/bb/bb30.htm; accessed July 25, 2007.

5. Enoch's sermon is a transliteration of Romans 1:18-31. This is the basis by which God will judge all heathen who have not heard the good news of salvation, the Gospel.

6. For many years the Jews wrongly assumed there were only 70 ethnic groups in the world outside the Jewish race because of this chapter. However, since seven and its multiples is God's favorite number, then perhaps Moses under the inspiration of the Holy Spirit chose to include only 70 nations in this list

because these were the nations that would have some future influence on Israel and God's plan for His people.

7. Shem's sons settled the Near East and the Eastern nations beyond. Ham's sons settled Africa. Japheth's sons settled Europe.

8. Gomer settled the Crimea, or Southeastern Europe.

9. Magog settled Southern Russia and the descendents were the Tartars.

10. Madai settled Southern Russia and the Bible calls them Medes from the word *midway* between the seas, the Black Sea and the Caspian Sea.

11. Javan settled in Greece.

12. Tubal spread north and east, probably the tribal name Tobolsk of those who settled Spain.

13. Mentioned with Tubal and Magog, and other nations directly north of the Euphrates Valley, Russia.

14. Progenitor of Thracians, people who inhabited the eastern, central and southern part of the Balkan Peninsula, as well as the adjacent parts of eastern Europe.

15. Cush settled Ethiopia.

16. Mizrain settled Egypt.

17. Put settled Libya.

18. Canaan settled the land of modern day Israel that Christians call the Holy Land.

19. Elam settled the area today known as Iraq or the Tigris Euphrates Valley.

20. Arphaxad settled southern Iraq and Abraham, the father of the Jews, come from their family.

21. Which son got the walking stick when Jacob died? No one knows, but maybe Joseph got it because of his position in Egypt. Maybe the other sons of Jacob insisted Joseph get the prized walking stick because of his position in Egypt. Maybe Joseph used the staff as his scepter, after all Pharaoh had a long scepter. Was the walking stick/scepter buried with Joseph when he died? We have no idea. Many Old Testament rabbis believed this walking stick ended up in Moses' hand. This was the rod of God that he used to do miracles.

22. Genesis 49:29ff.

# ABOUT THE AUTHOR

D R. ELMER TOWNS is an author of popular and scholarly works, a seminar lecturer, and dedicated Bible teacher. He has written over 125 books, including several best sellers. In 1995 he won the coveted Gold Medallion Book Award for *The Names of the Holy Spirit*.

Dr. Towns co-founded Liberty University with Jerry Falwell in 1971 and now serves as Dean of the B.R. Lakin School of Religion and as professor of Theology and New Testament.

Liberty University was founded in 1971 and is the fastest growing Christian university in America. Located in Lynchburg, Virginia, Liberty University is a private, coeducational, undergraduate and graduate institution offering 38 undergraduate and 15 graduate programs serving over 40,000 resident and external students (11,000 on campus). Individuals from all 50 states and more than 70 nations comprise the diverse student body. While the faculty and students vary greatly, the common denominator and driving force of Liberty University since its conception is love for Jesus Christ and the desire to make Him known to the entire world.

**For more information about Liberty University, contact:**

**Liberty University**
**1971 University Boulevard**
**Lynchburg, VA 24502**
**Telephone: 434-582-2000**
**E-mail: www.Liberty.edu**

# ALSO FROM ELMER TOWNS

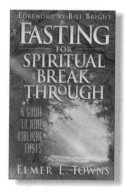

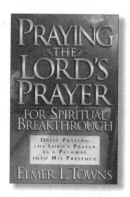
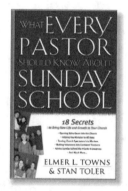
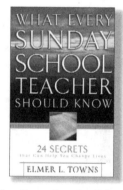

Additional copies of this book and other book titles from DESTINY IMAGE are available at your local bookstore.

Call toll-free: 1-800-722-6774.

Send a request for a catalog to:

**Destiny Image® Publishers, Inc.**
P.O. Box 310
Shippensburg, PA 17257-0310

*"Speaking to the Purposes of God for This Generation and for the Generations to Come."*

**For a complete list of our titles, visit us at www.destinyimage.com.**